I0810433

IMAGES
of America

JEWISH PITTSBURGH

On the Cover: The cover picture is of Upper Fifth Avenue in Pittsburgh in 1928. At that time, this area in the so-called "Hill" district of the city was a thriving wholesale and retail corridor, which attracted customers from far and wide. The street housed wall-to-wall Jewish businesses. In this picture, there is a kosher butcher, a Jewish delicatessen (Richest), a music shop, a dentist, and an Army/Navy store. Fifth Avenue was the center of a Jewish wholesaling district and the hub of Jewish commercial life for decades in the early 1900s. (Rauh Jewish Archives at the Heinz History Center.)

IMAGES
of America

JEWISH PITTSBURGH

Barbara Burstin, PhD

ARCADIA
PUBLISHING

Copyright © 2015 by Barbara Burstin, PhD
ISBN 978-1-4671-2295-5

Published by Arcadia Publishing
Charleston, South Carolina

Printed in the United States of America

Library of Congress Control Number: 2014947147

For all general information, please contact Arcadia Publishing:
Telephone 843-853-2070
Fax 843-853-0044
E-mail sales@arcadiapublishing.com
For customer service and orders:
Toll-Free 1-888-313-2665

Visit us on the Internet at www.arcadiapublishing.com

This book is dedicated to all those who teach history,
write history, read history, and make history.

Contents

ACKNOWLEDGMENTS

To put a book like this together is no easy task. Fortunately, we have in Pittsburgh the Rauh Jewish Archives at the Heinz History Center, which has been the repository for many donated papers and photographs. Unless otherwise noted, all photographs appear courtesy of the Rauh. There are also important archival collections at the University of Pittsburgh Archives Service Center, Carnegie Library, and Rodef Shalom Congregation. Recognition must be given to several historians who did groundbreaking research and writing. They include Jacob Feldman, Ida Cohen Selavan, Corinne Krause, and Carol Bleier. Eileen Lane and Lois Michaels should be noted for initiating the Jewish Women's Writing Project to document the lives of important Jewish women in Pittsburgh. This project drew on the research that this author did for two books: *Steel City Jews: 1840–1915* and *Steel City Jews in Prosperity, Depression & War: 1915–1950*. (See pittsburghjewishhistory.com for more information.)

In telling the Pittsburgh Jewish story, Eric Lidji was indispensable in tracking down many of the photographs needed to do that. This book simply would not have happened without his knowledge of the photograph archives. He also handled technical aspects, making sure that the pictures acquired were up to the proper standards for reproduction. His commitment and dedication to this project were much appreciated. Eric's efforts notwithstanding, however, the hunt was still on for other images to include. Phone calls were made, emails were exchanged, and pictures were dropped off. The Jewish Federation of Greater Pittsburgh and the Jewish Healthcare Foundation of Pittsburgh have to be recognized for their support and encouragement in this undertaking. Pittsburgh is fortunate to have these two major organizations committed to preserving the past as well as to planning for the future in their respective ways. Finally, the Pittsburgh Jewish community itself should be acknowledged for its vitality and contribution to the greater good for more than 150 years. The problem was not that there was a dearth of material to include; rather, there was an abundance, and cuts had to be made given publishing guidelines and restrictions. On balance, it was a good problem to have.

INTRODUCTION

The story of the Jews depicted here is a story of personal achievements and communal responsibility. It is a story of individuals who lived their Jewish identities in a variety of ways—from religious observance and Jewish study to civic engagement and philanthropic efforts. The Jews on these pages sought to contribute to the Jewish and general community. They, like other immigrant groups, tried to blend into the fabric of life in Pittsburgh and take advantage of opportunities that were afforded them. They arrived in America determined to put the hardships, despair, and persecution of the past behind them as they sought to make new lives for themselves in the New World. Education was considered the way out of the ghetto, the key to upward mobility, independence, and a better life. As one historian has noted, Jews have always had "a mania for education." Jews faced economic challenges in this country like all immigrants; in some generations, they faced discrimination and prejudice. The journey for most in the immigrant generation was not easy, but their children and grandchildren were often able to overcome and move on, making a living and contributing to the vitality of their adopted city.

While there had been a small community of Jews in Pittsburgh before the Civil War, it was not until the period after 1880 that the Jewish population in the city and in America increased dramatically. More than 2.5 million Eastern European Jews fleeing pogroms and poverty came to the United States between 1880 and 1920. They came from the Russian Empire, the Austro-Hungarian Empire, and Romania. Thousands came to Pittsburgh, and when they did, they did not go into the mines and mills that were making this city an economic powerhouse. Instead, unlike the other European immigrants of that generation, the Jews sought to eke out a living in light industry, often in stogie factories or as peddlers or petty shopkeepers. They lived on "the Hill," an area of the city adjacent to downtown, which in the early 1900s had become a poor neighborhood, dilapidated, overcrowded, and dirty. In 1905, there were 12,000 Jews in Pittsburgh; by 1912, the figure had jumped to 35,000, and by 1927, Jewish numbers peaked at about 53,000—fully eight percent of the Pittsburgh population at the time (632,000).

The 1920s were a time of prosperity for many, and—with a sense of confidence in the future and a feeling of unlimited possibilities characteristic of the Roaring Twenties—Jews built new institutions or enlarged existing ones: a new hospital, a new Young Men & Women's Hebrew Association (YM&WHA or Y), new synagogues in different city neighborhoods, and an expanded neighborhood settlement house on the Hill. However, when the stock market crashed in 1929 and the Great Depression ensued, it wreaked havoc not only on individual Jews and non-Jews, but it also threatened the financial viability of an overextended Jewish community. The Depression also sparked unprecedented levels of anti-Semitism in America as Jews became scapegoats for America's economic woes. Beyond domestic concerns, Jews in Pittsburgh were distraught over what was happening overseas in Europe to their coreligionists with the rise of Hitler in 1933. Some Pittsburgh Jews would be directly involved in efforts to combat Nazism and rescue its victims. Others sought to respond with renewed vigor to realize the Zionist dream of a Jewish homeland in Palestine. The murder of six million Jews in Europe during the Holocaust would profoundly affect Jews everywhere. The 1940s, a decade that began with World War II, ended with the war against the invading Arab nations as Jews fought to establish the state of Israel. In the postwar era, Israel continued to be a vital concern, but there was also a determination and commitment to better intergroup relations in America, to confront anti-Semitism, to combat discrimination against African Americans, to fight for civil rights, and to teach tolerance and understanding in Pittsburgh schools.

While this book generally does not deal with more recent decades, it is important to point out that today the Jewish community numbers some 42,000 people who live in and around the Pittsburgh. New and improved facilities have been established, like the Hillel-Jewish University Center, the Jewish Residential Services, the Friendship Circle, and Chabad Houses, to respond to communal needs and promote Jewish identity. These and other major institutions, including the Jewish Association on Aging, Riverview Towers, the Jewish Community Center, the Jewish Family and Children's Service, the three day schools (Yeshiva, Hillel Academy, and Community Day), and multiple synagogues, are primarily located in Squirrel Hill or Oakland. The fact that so many Jews still live within the city in several neighborhoods is unique to Pittsburgh since in other cities in the country, Jews have generally moved to the suburbs. This concentration notwithstanding, the Jewish population of the South Hills has grown so that this area now has its own Jewish Community Center and synagogues. There are also Jewish communities north and east of the city with their own synagogues as well.

Throughout the years, the Jewish Federation of Greater Pittsburgh has galvanized fundraising efforts to support the institutions that have sustained Jewish life in the city. Millions of dollars have been collected to help support Jewish agencies that minister not just to Jews, but sometimes to non-Jews as well. The Jewish community has established an elaborate network of cultural, social, and educational institutions, agencies, and organizations that reflect a vibrant Jewish life today in Pittsburgh. Yet despite this extensive Jewish network, Jews have seen themselves not just as members of a particular ethnic or religious community; they also identify themselves as members of the larger community. Thus, there have been numerous examples of individuals who have given their time and/or their dollars to causes beyond the Jewish community and who have made significant contributions to the political, economic, cultural, professional, or civic life of the city of Pittsburgh. Their impact has been profound and has helped make Pittsburgh the vital city that it is today and will continue to be in the future. It is a fascinating story that needs to be told. The pictures in this book help to do just that.

One

Who Are the Jews?

This simple question has a complicated answer. To be a Jew means different things to the people who classify themselves as Jews. For many today, as in the past, their lives revolve around synagogue worship and strict adherence to laws and traditions of the Jewish religion. For others, there is more flexibility in their religious life, with less observance of Jewish rituals or prayer. Yet, notwithstanding the diversity of religious belief and practice, there is often a sense of family, of shared traditions and cultures, a feeling of connectedness with Jews and Jewish concerns both near and far.

There is a particular calendar of events observed by Jews. Some of the holidays depicted here commemorate pivotal events in the history of the Jewish people. Jews have a commitment to *zachor*, to remember the past. With the Holocaust and the founding of the state of Israel, new holidays have been added to the Jewish calendar. Various life-cycle events and particular practices characterize Jewish life, and some of those observances and practices are depicted in these pages. The understanding of Jewish peoplehood, a connection and responsibility to Jews both locally and afar, has been expressed in various ways over the generations. Thus, included in this section are several pictures that relate to the Jewish commitment to the Zionist cause and the establishment of the state of Israel. Annual campaigns by the Jewish Federation to provide funds for local needs as well as for Jews overseas have been ongoing in the Jewish community. Remembering the past has been the driving rationale of the Oral History Program of the Pittsburgh chapter of the National Council of Jewish Women. The final picture in this section of the Jewish Community Center is symbolic in that it represents a place where all Jews, of whatever belief or observance, can and do come together as a community. The challenge in this chapter was to offer some sense of the broad scope and meaning of Jewish life given a limited number of pictures.

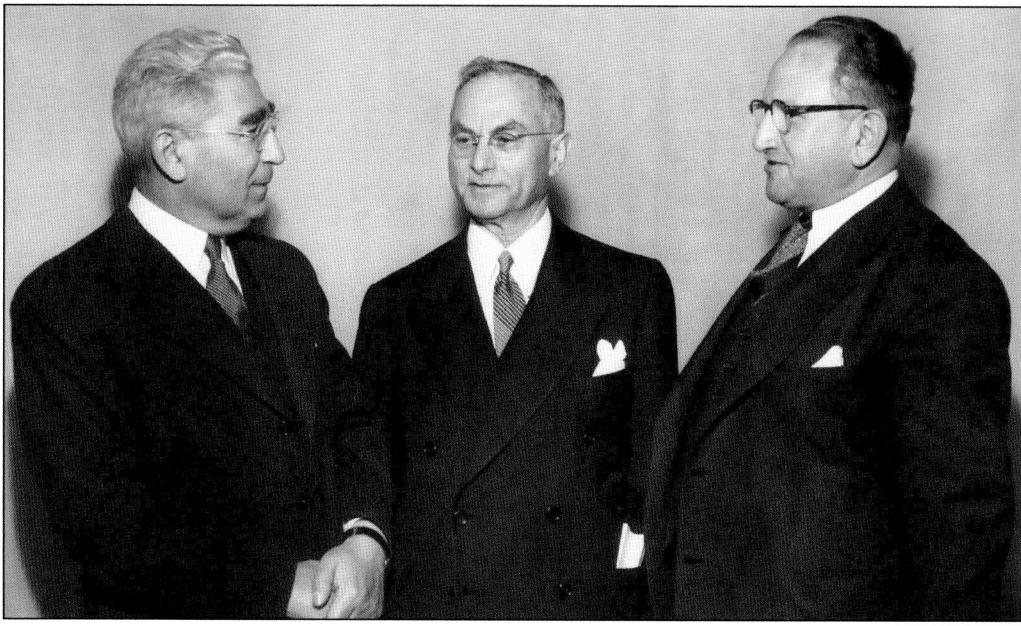

Pittsburgh has, over the years, had very important rabbinic leadership. This picture from about the 1950s is of Rabbi Freehof (left) of Rodef Shalom Congregation, Rabbi Lichter (center) of the B'nai Israel Synagogue, and Rabbi Herman Hailperin (right) of the Tree of Life Congregation. Dr. Freehof was a leading authority on the interpretation of religious laws in the Reform movement. Rabbis Lichter and Hailperin were both highly respected Conservative rabbis.

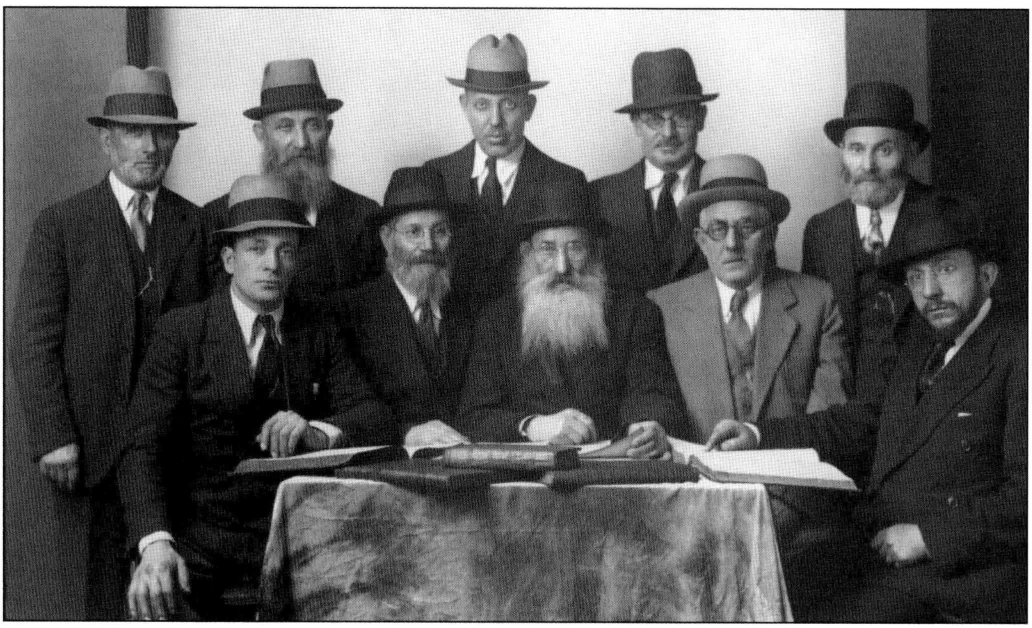

These men are studying Jewish texts in 1935 at Kether Torah, a small Orthodox synagogue on the Hill. Originally, the members were all from the Russian province of Volhynia, but in 1914, the decision was made to expand the membership. In 1920, a synagogue building was dedicated at the corner of Webster Avenue and Erin Street. The building is still standing, but it is no longer a synagogue.

Miriam Schoenfeld was born in 1887, and from 1907 until her death in 1934, she was the beloved supervisor of the Religious School Committee for the Pittsburgh Chapter of the National Council of Jewish Women, overseeing religious school classes in 30 to 35 schools in small Jewish communities throughout southwestern Pennsylvania.

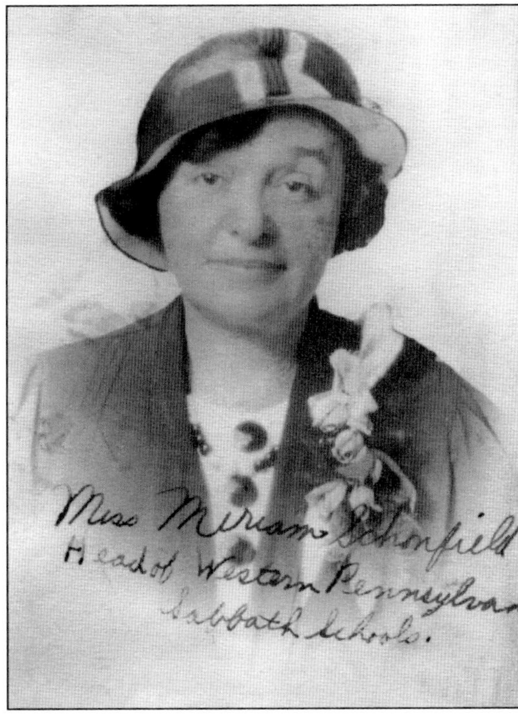

This is the bimah, or pulpit, in the Adath Jeshurun Synagogue, an Orthodox synagogue in the East End. In 1916, a group split from the B'nai Israel Congregation, but they did not formally open this new synagogue until 1924. The building had more than 1,000 seats. Rabbi Morris Levin led the congregation from 1924 until 1947, when a severe heart condition forced his retirement. Rabbi Morris Landes succeeded him.

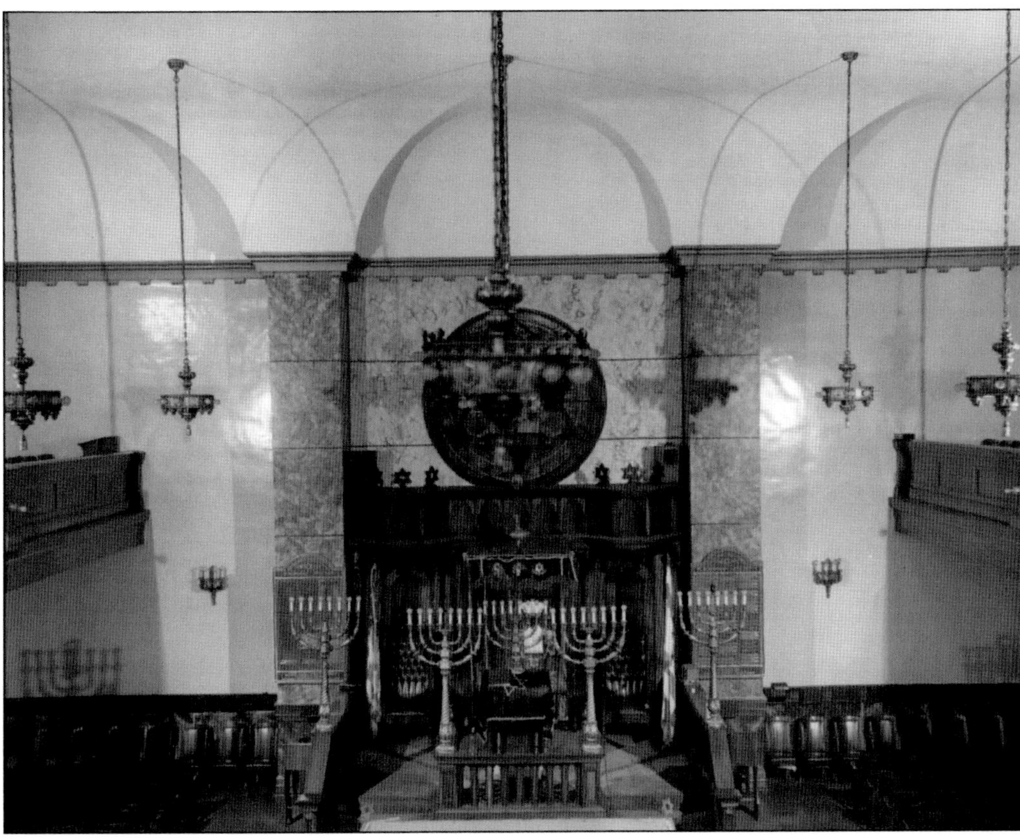

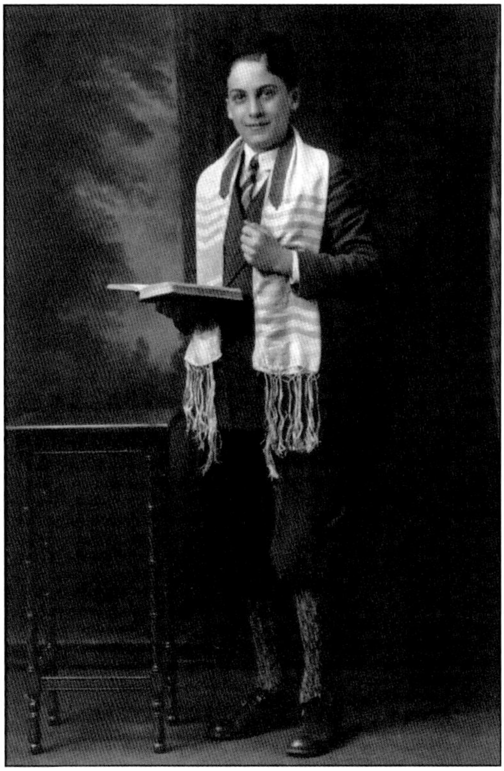

Louis Zeiden was born on the Hill in Pittsburgh to immigrant parents. In 1927, at the age of 13, he became a Bar Mitzvah at Shaare Zedeck Synagogue. The Bar/Bat Mitzvah is a ceremony that signifies passage into Jewish adulthood for Jewish boys and girls.

Rabbi Bernard Poupko of Shaare Torah Congregation in Squirrel Hill in 1951 is seen inspecting a Heinz soup facility to make sure that the soup is prepared according to kosher laws. *Kosher* is a Hebrew word that means "suitable" or "pure." To keep kosher is an obligation for observant Jews. (H.J. Heinz Company.)

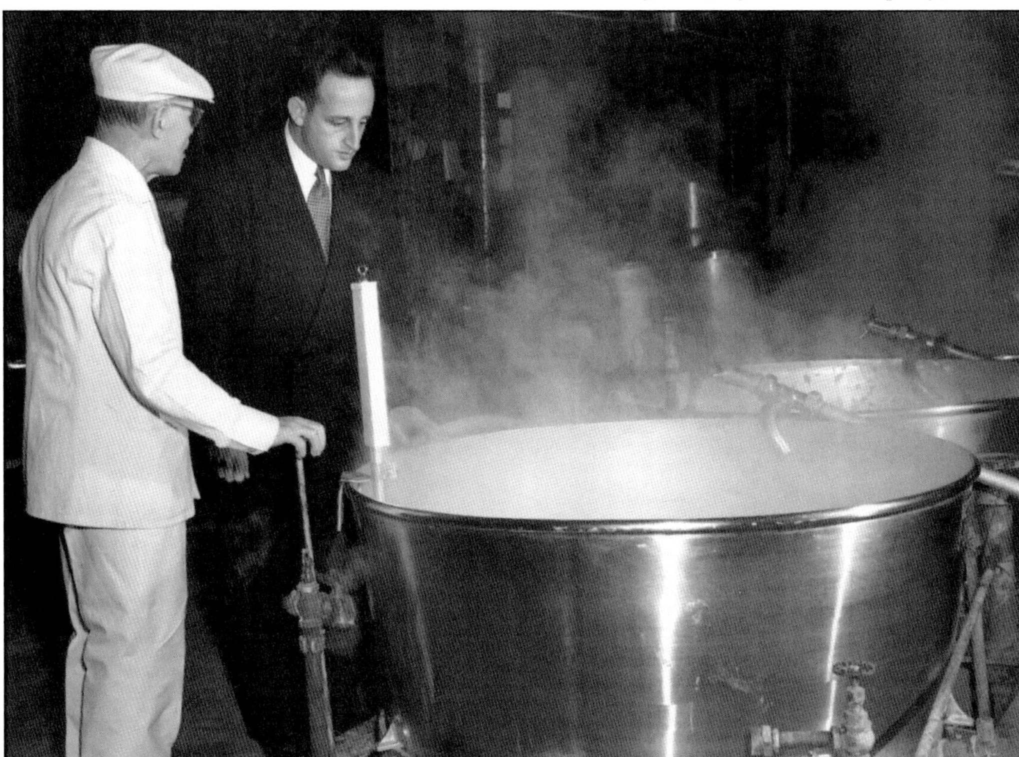

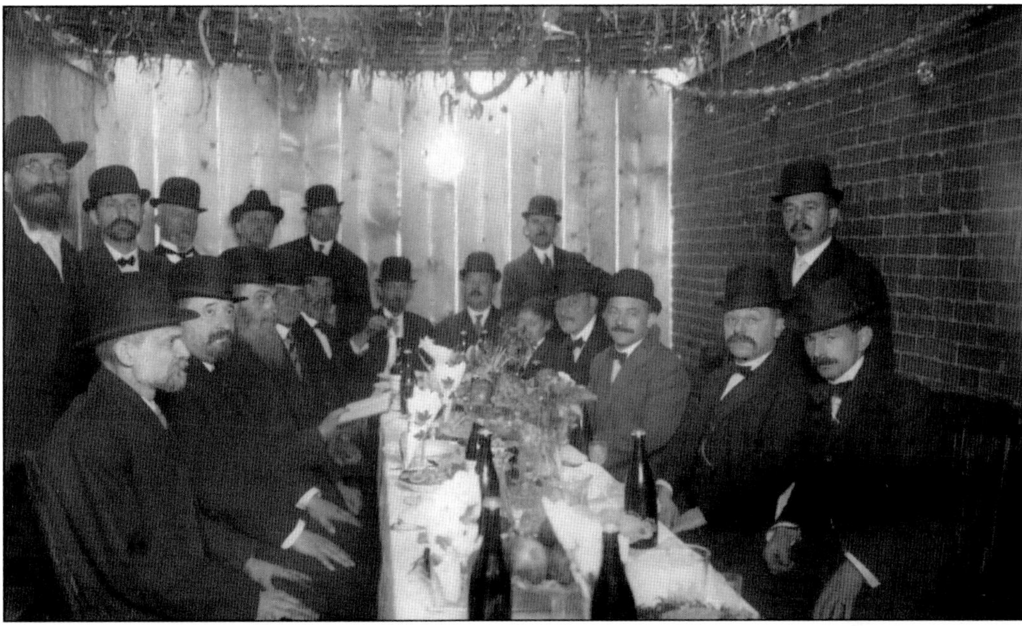

This is the sukkah (booth) of B'nai Israel Congregation in 1915. It is part of the observance of the Festival of Sukkot, a holiday of cheerfulness in contrast to the solemnity of Yom Kippur, the Day of Atonement, five days before. The sukkah is a temporary dwelling constructed every year to commemorate the wandering of the Jews in the desert. Sukkot is also a harvest festival, which in America is often compared to Thanksgiving.

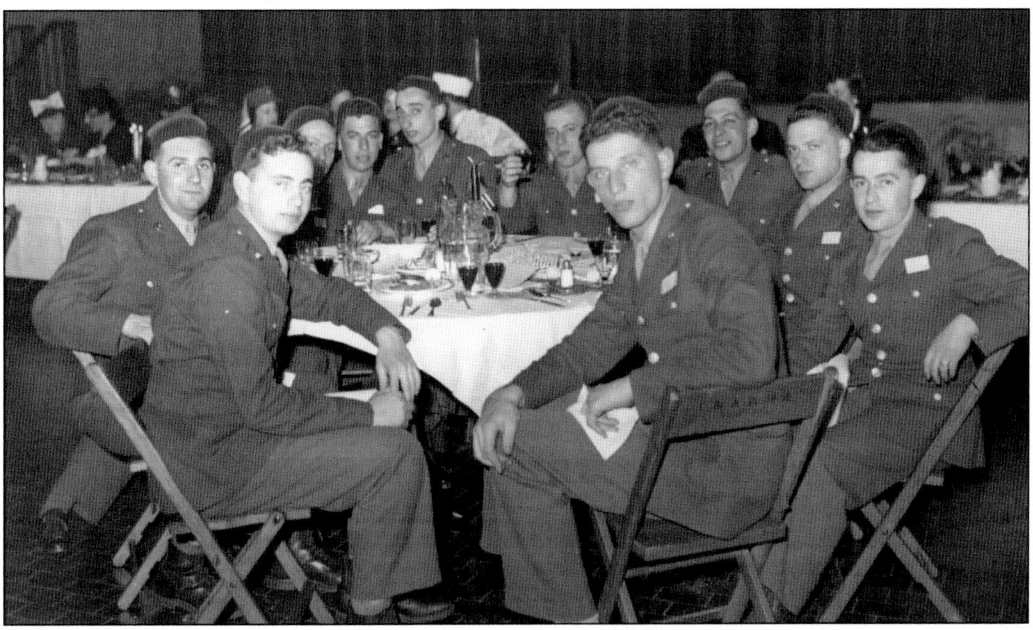

Jewish soldiers celebrate Passover at the Y Canteen during World War II. The holiday commemorates the Biblical story in the book of Exodus when the Israelites, led by Moses, escaped from Egyptian slavery. Every year, Jews gather for a Passover meal or seder. On the seder plate is *maror* (bitter herbs), representing the bitterness of slavery. The holiday's theme of freedom from bondage is a universal one.

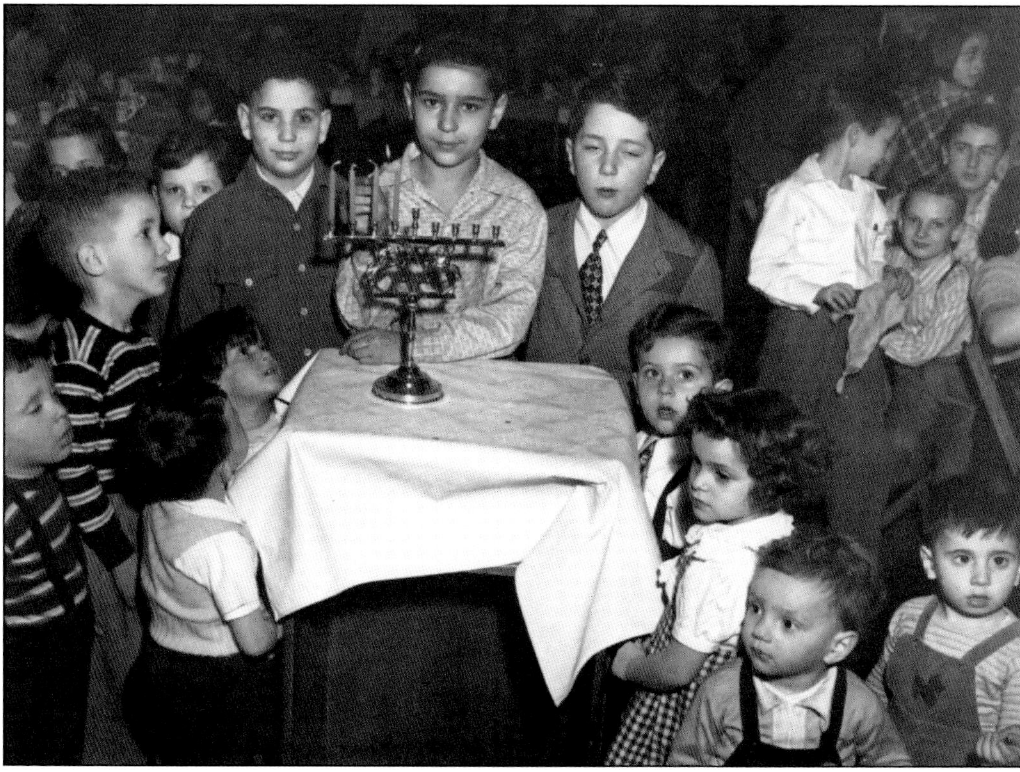

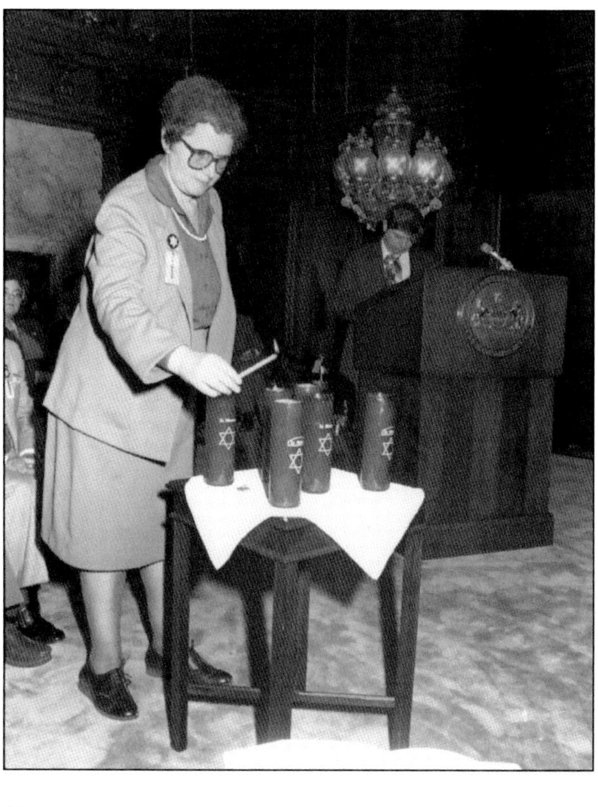

In this 1950 image, the children of the Friendship Club, a group made up of German refugees, are celebrating Hanukkah by lighting the menorah. Hanukkah, the story of the victory of the Maccabees over the Syrian Greeks, typically falls in December. The menorah, or Hanukkah candelabra, is lit for eight days, and in America, children customarily receive gifts at this time.

Shulamit Bastacky, a Holocaust survivor from Poland, is lighting the candles commemorating the Holocaust at the community observance of Yom Hashoah in April 1987 at the state capitol building in Harrisburg, Pennsylvania. Bastacky at the time was president of the Holocaust Survivors Organization of Pittsburgh. Born in Vilna in 1941, she was a baby when a Roman Catholic nun hid her in a cellar for years, thereby saving her life.

This is a *tsedakah* donation tin from the Jewish National Fund, established in 1904 to plant trees in what would become the state of Israel. *Tsedakah* is a Hebrew word meaning "justice" or "righteousness." To give is an obligation of Jews to make the world a better place.

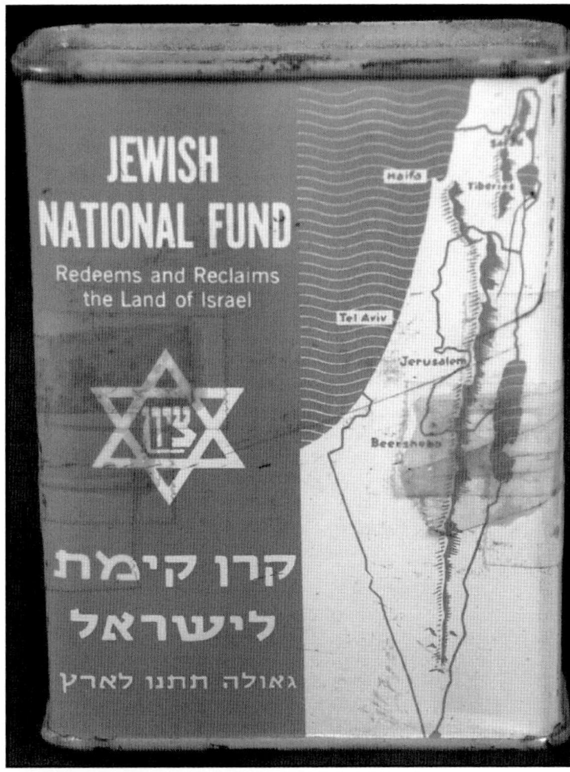

The Pioneer Women (now Na'amat), founded in Pittsburgh in 1925 under Chana Osheroff, was devoted to the cause of Labor Zionism in Palestine. Golda Meir (second row, fifth from left), a future prime minister of Israel, was a guest of the group in 1934. The first women's Zionist organization in Pittsburgh was the Pittsburgh chapter of Hadassah, organized in 1916 with Rachel Vixman as founder and first president.

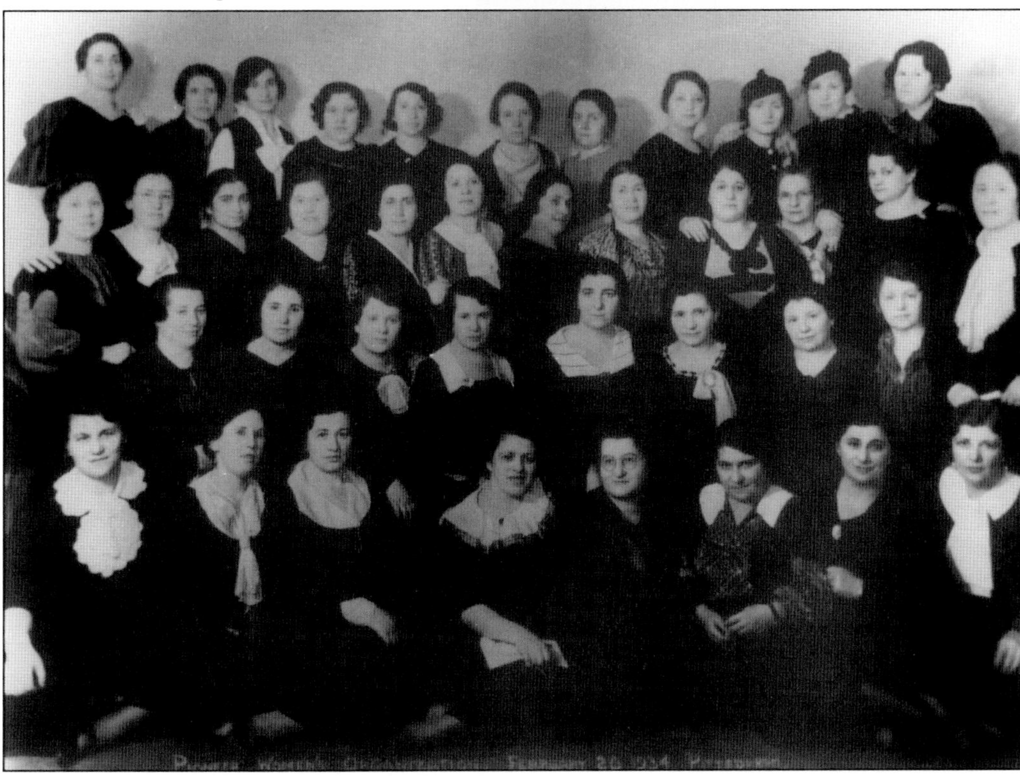

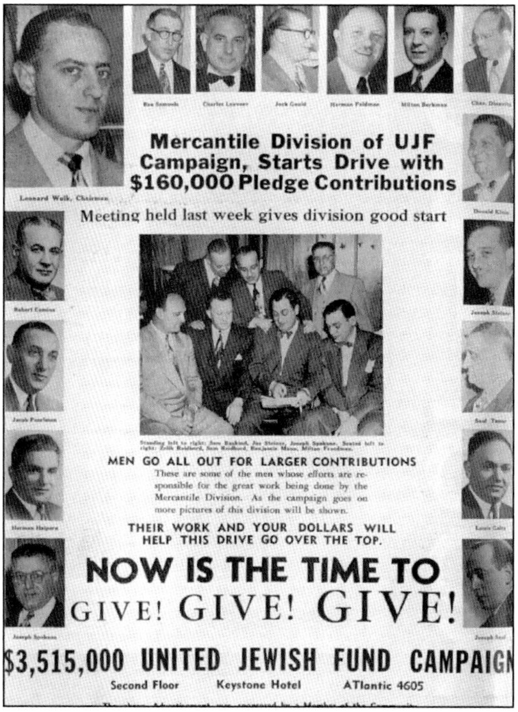

Mercantile Division of UJF Campaign, Starts Drive with $160,000 Pledge Contributions

Meeting held last week gives division good start

MEN GO ALL OUT FOR LARGER CONTRIBUTIONS

These are some of the men whose efforts are responsible for the great work being done by the Mercantile Division. As the campaign goes on more pictures of this division will be shown.

THEIR WORK AND YOUR DOLLARS WILL HELP THIS DRIVE GO OVER THE TOP.

NOW IS THE TIME TO GIVE! GIVE! GIVE!

$3,515,000 UNITED JEWISH FUND CAMPAIGN

Second Floor Keystone Hotel ATlantic 4605

Fundraising campaigns to help Jews in need both at home and abroad have been annual happenings in the Jewish community. The picture at left, from 1935, was for a drive to respond to growing needs overseas in Europe and in Palestine, as well as to assist in the resettlement of refugees coming to Pittsburgh. The one below is from a campaign in 1966 for local and international needs. The pictures reflect the careful organization of these fundraising efforts, which crisscrossed the community and drew upon the efforts of multiple volunteers to do the soliciting. The *Jewish Criterion*, which was the primary local Jewish newspaper, made the campaigns front-page stories and covered their progress, noting individual donations and campaign results.

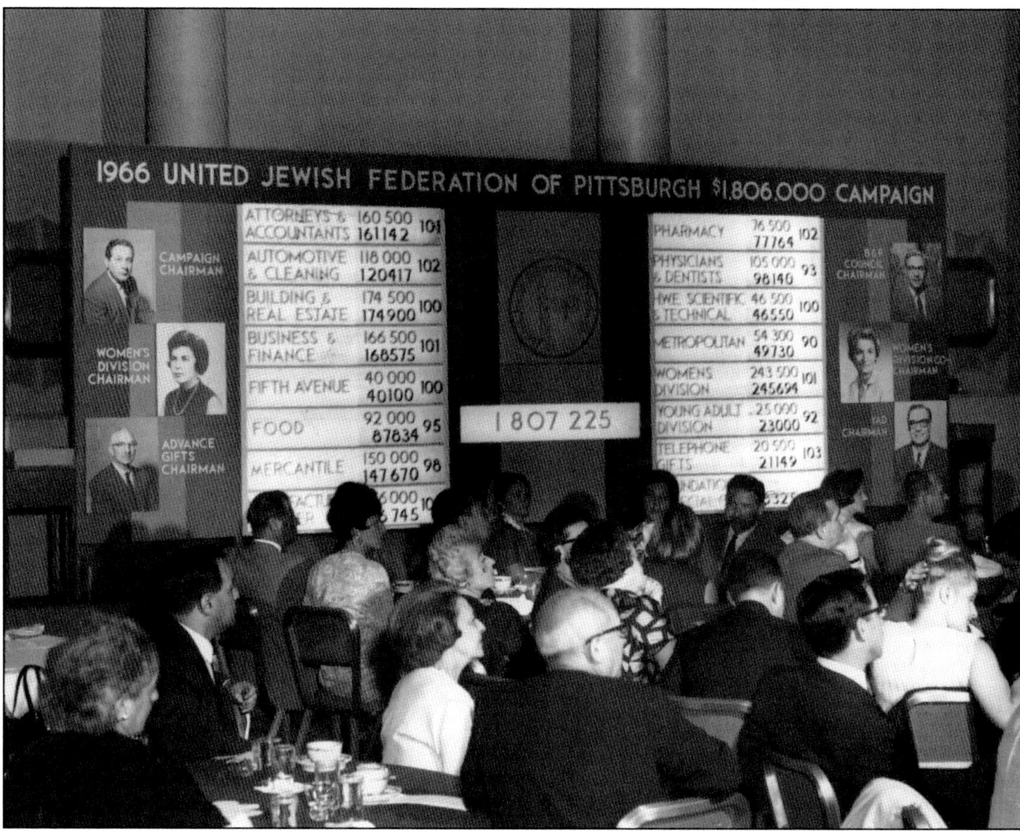

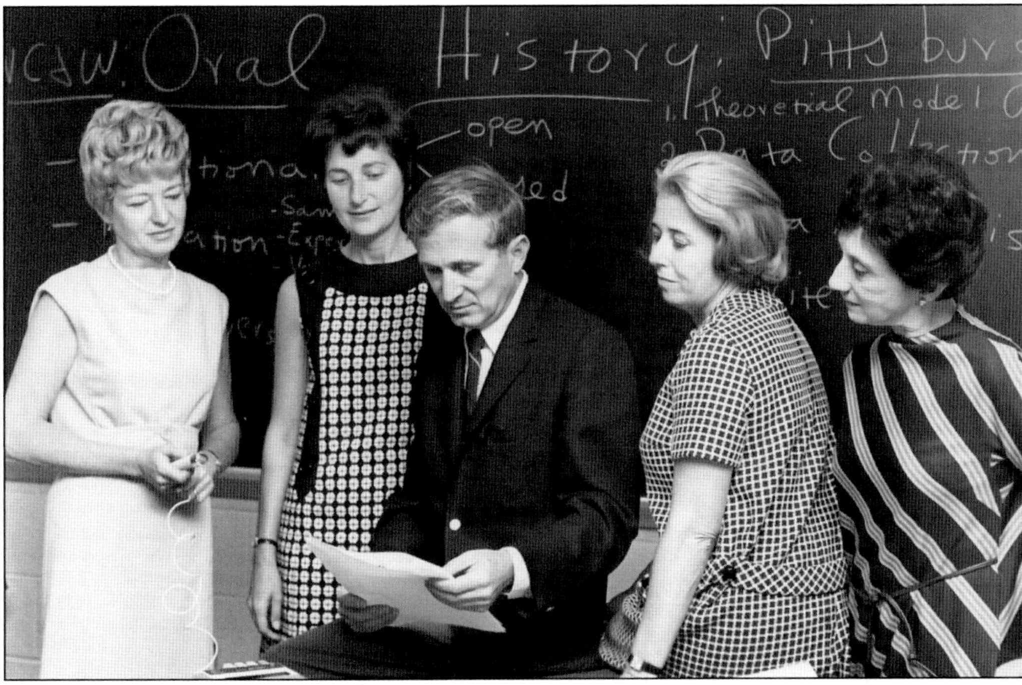

The Oral History Program of the Pittsburgh chapter of the National Council of Jewish Women was begun in 1968. Councilwomen interviewed hundreds of Jewish Pittsburghers, from the prominent to the not so prominent, to record their life experiences. The archive is accessible now online. (Archives Service Center, University of Pittsburgh.)

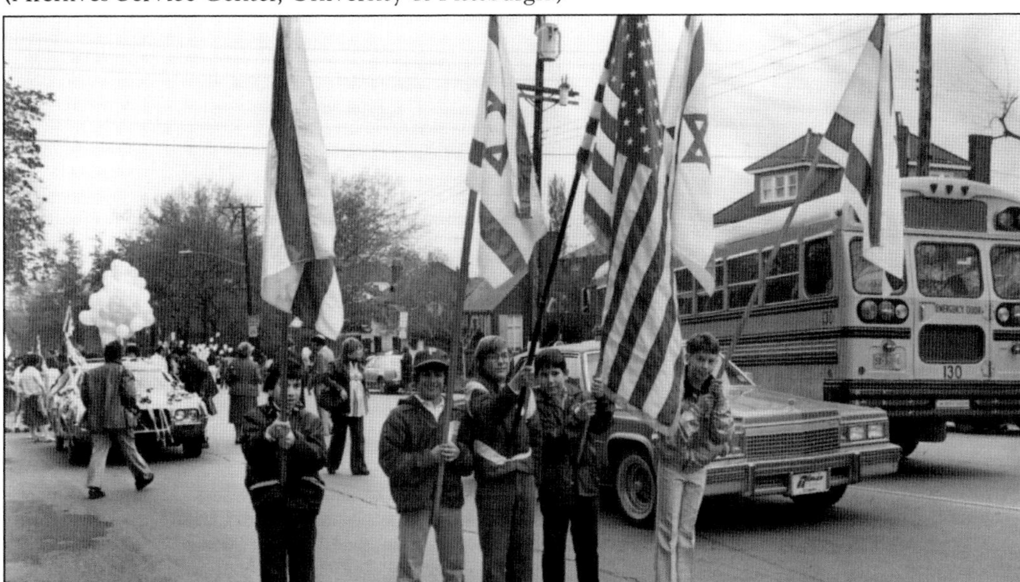

This Israel Day celebration (c. 1970s) commemorated the founding of the state of Israel on May 14, 1948. Every year, the Jewish community celebrates this holiday of Yom Ha'atzmaut with activities for children and adults. This is one of the more recent holidays in the Jewish calendar, along with Yom Hazikaron, which honors the memory of those Jews who have fallen in terrorist attacks or in battle.

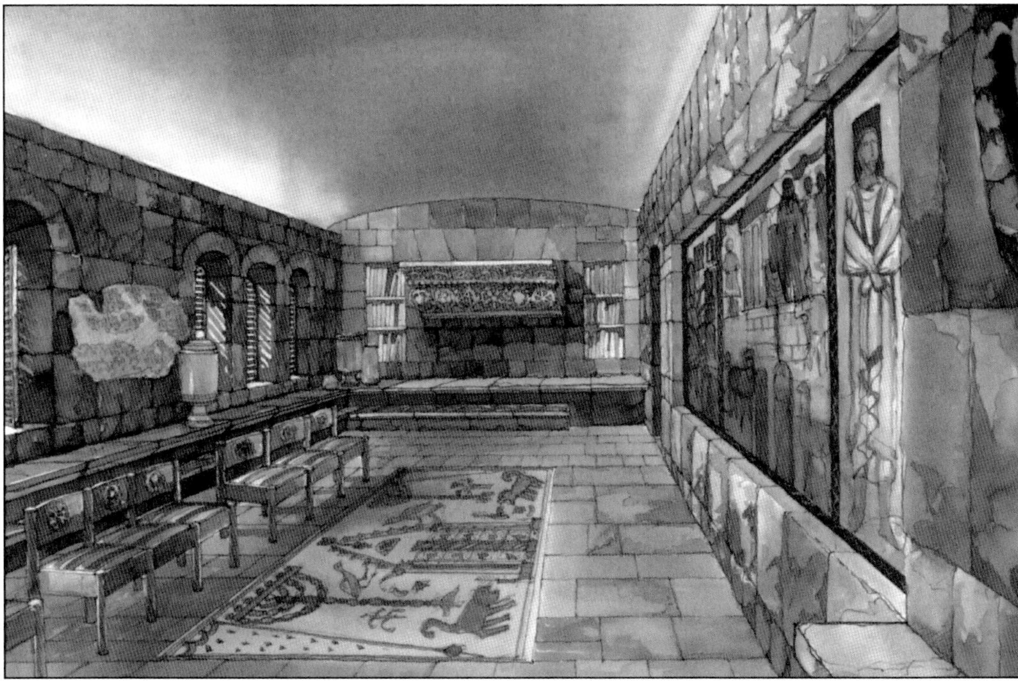

This is a mock-up of the Israel Heritage Room, which was established in 1987 as one of the Nationality Rooms in the Cathedral of Learning at the University of Pittsburgh. It is an active classroom as well as a tourist attraction. (Archives Service Center, University of Pittsburgh.)

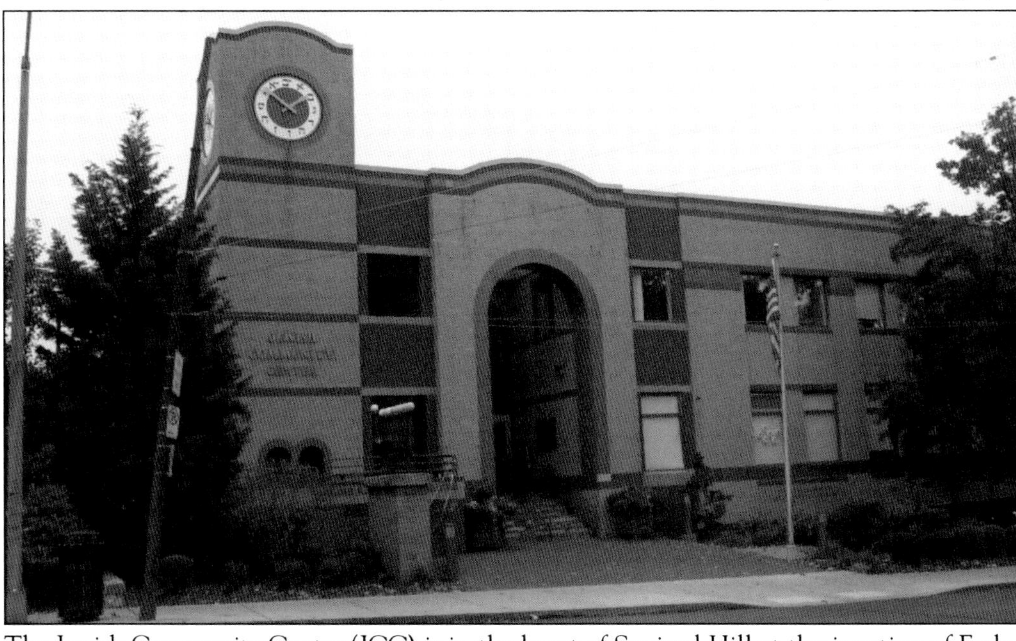

The Jewish Community Center (JCC) is in the heart of Squirrel Hill at the junction of Forbes and Murray Avenues. It is the hub for all kinds of cultural, recreational, educational, and social activities, and its doors are open to Jews as well as non-Jews. Today, under the JCC umbrella, there is a JCC building in the South Hills, the James and Rachel Levinson Camp in Monroeville, and the Emma Kaufmann Camp in West Virginia.

Two

Destination Pittsburgh

America is a nation of immigrants who came to take advantage of this country's promise. Sometimes the distinction between immigrant and refugee was blurred as newcomers fled oppressive conditions in Europe. They came to Pittsburgh despite the city's reputation as "Hell with the lid on" and "Hell with the lid off." Immigrant Jews began arriving in Pittsburgh in the 1840s, leaving the discrimination and hardship of southern German lands. They established Rodef Shalom and the first Jewish Benevolent Association. They were soon joined by Jewish families from more northern and eastern regions of Europe, who organized the Tree of Life Congregation. They lived first downtown but then moved into more desirable neighborhoods on the north shore, then known as Allegheny City. Meanwhile, by the latter decades of the 19th century, much larger numbers of Jews from Eastern Europe fled to America, attracted by the prospect of a better life. Those who came to Pittsburgh began populating the area known as "the Hill." The German Jews who had arrived earlier, as well as the Eastern Europeans themselves, soon established important institutions and organizations like the Irene Kaufmann Settlement (IKS), the House of Shelter, the Jewish Home for the Aged, the Hebrew Institute, and numerous synagogues on the Hill that helped support the immigrants and ease their adjustment into American life.

With the rise of Hitler, Europe was about to be plunged into darkness, with the Jews singled out for destruction. Several prominent Pittsburgh Jews were engaged in important efforts of protest and attempted rescue. The Jewish community received desperate refugees before the outbreak of war who were lucky to have family or friends assist them in the frantic quest to get any of the limited visas to America. In the years immediately after the war, Pittsburgh became the destination for several hundred Holocaust survivors who came under the Truman Directive or Displaced Persons Act or who were drawn to the city somewhat later. Beginning in the 1970s, a wave of Soviet Jewish refugees came to Pittsburgh. Whether immigrant or refugee, all the newcomers enriched the city they would soon call home.

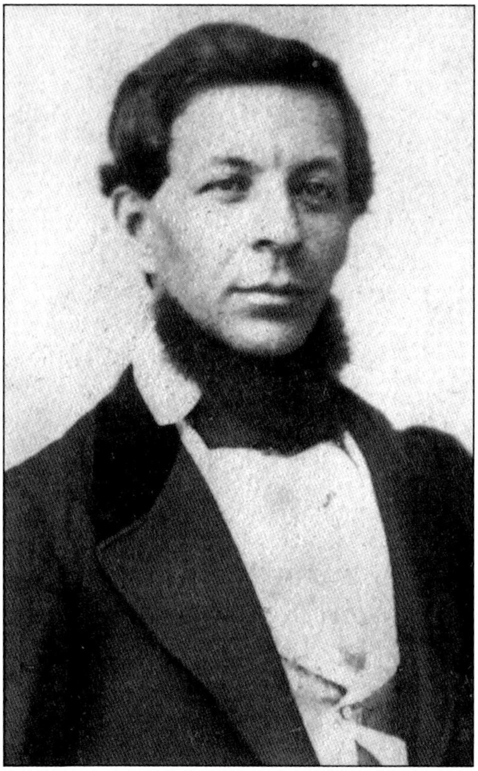

William Frank was one of the founding fathers of the Pittsburgh Jewish community. He and David Strasburger, both Bavarian immigrants, had a store together in eastern Ohio, but the partnership broke up, and each moved to Pittsburgh in 1846. Frank established a dry goods store and later went into the glass manufacturing business.

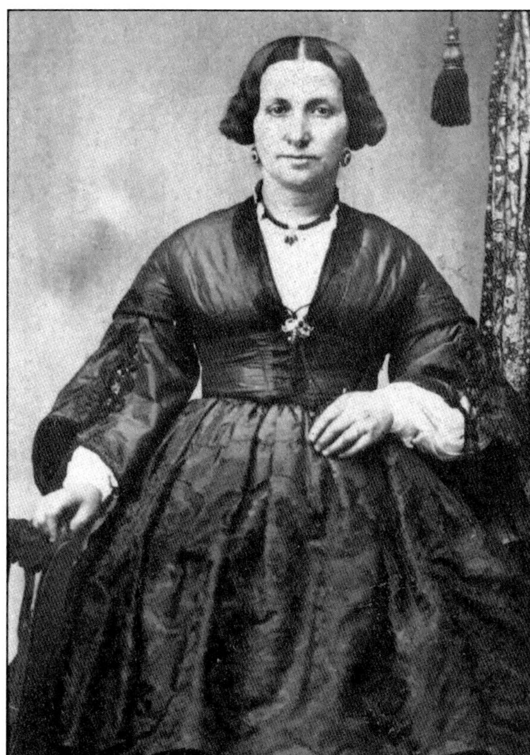

Pauline Wormser Frank was William Frank's wife. She was the founder and president of the Hebrew Ladies Aid Society during the Civil War. She witnessed the growth of the Jewish community over her 64 years in the city until her death in 1910.

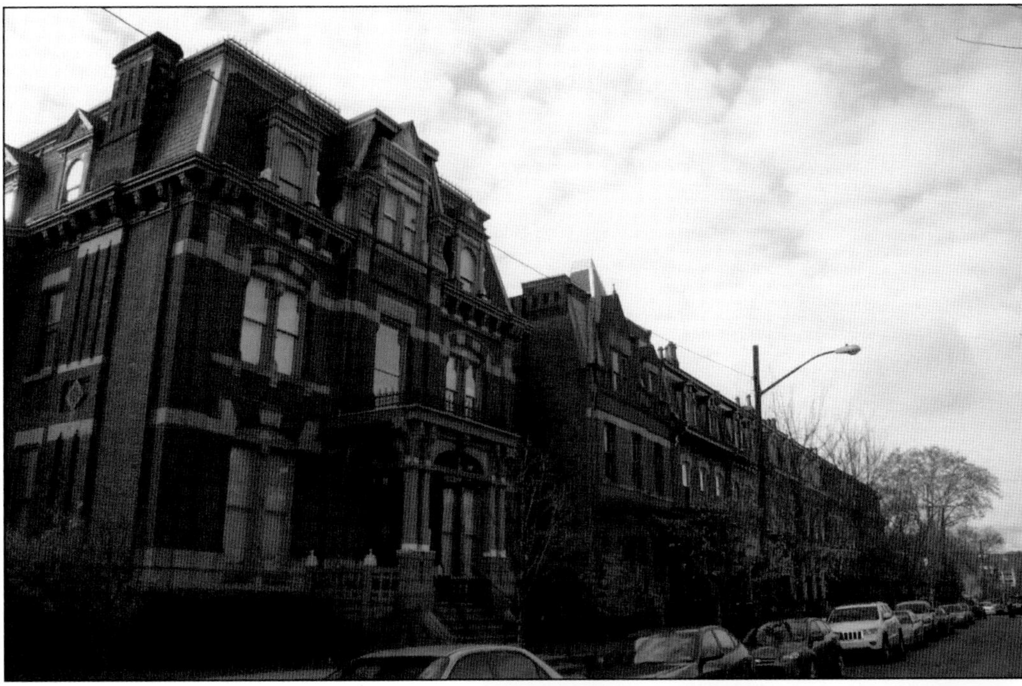

By the late 1850s, Jews were beginning to move across the river to Allegheny City (now the north shore), which was a quieter, less industrialized area. Liverpool Street, originally Locust Street, was heavily populated by German Jews who had succeeded enough in business to make the move. The area around Liverpool Street, because of its Jewish character, was called "Little Jerusalem."

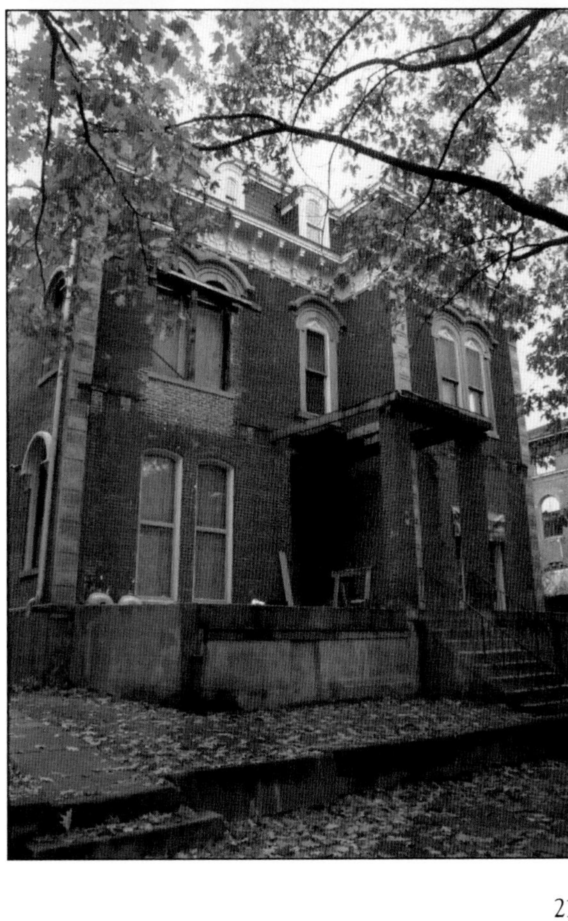

This restored house on the north shore is the home of the Morganstern family. Louis and Joseph Morganstern, early immigrants from Bavaria, were in the wholesale clothing business and made uniforms for the Union army during the Civil War. Both men were presidents of Rodef Shalom.

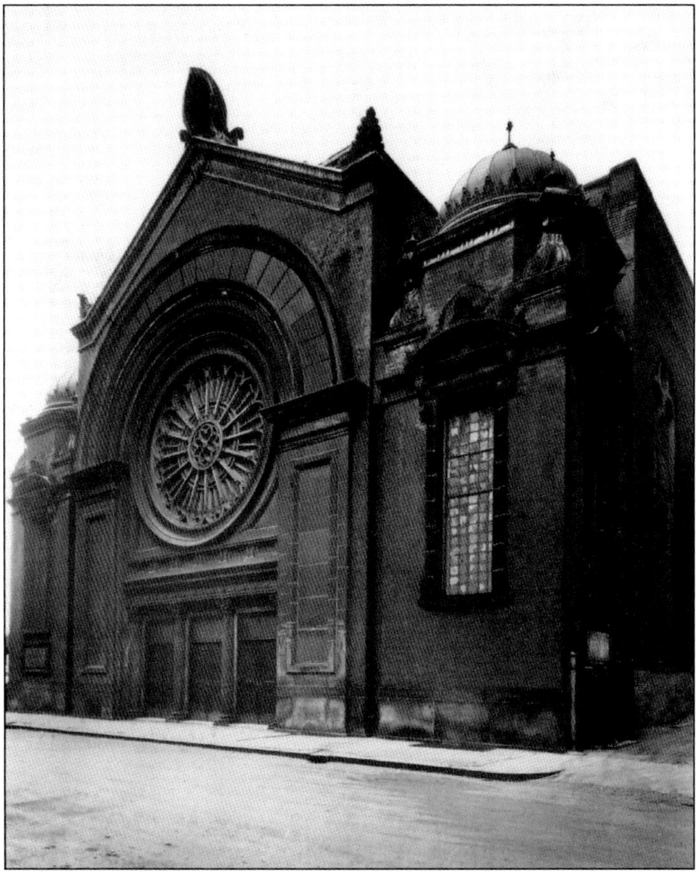

Rodef Shalom Congregation on Hancock Street downtown (later renamed Eighth Street) was dedicated in 1862. At that time, there were 350–400 Jews in Pittsburgh. This was the first structure built by the local Jewish community. In 1901, it was remodeled, but by 1907, with many of its members moving to the East End of the city, Rodef Shalom moved to its present location on Morewood Avenue in Shadyside.

The cemetery on Troy Hill was the original burial location for the early Rodef Shalom members. Its purchase in 1847 came none too soon because six months later, the infant son of William and Pauline Frank was laid to rest there.

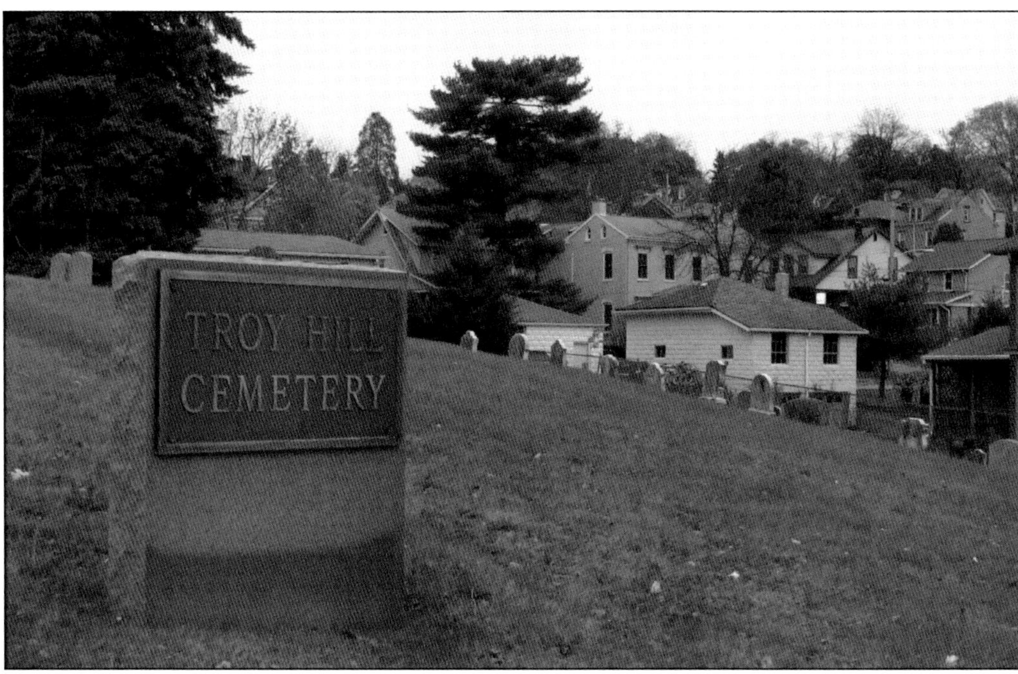

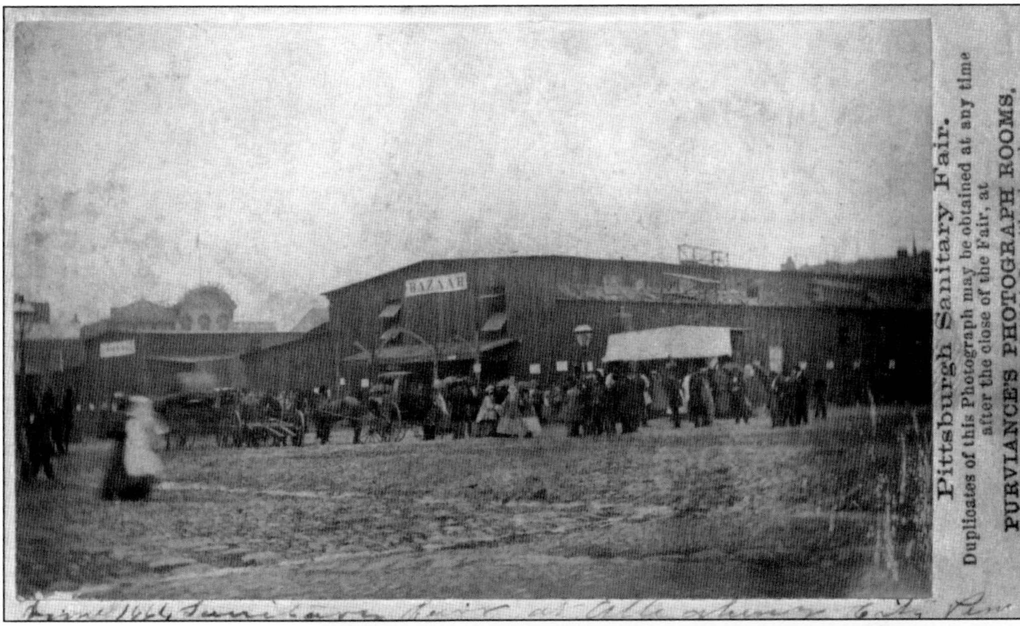

The US Sanitary Commission performed nursing services during the Civil War for the Union soldiers. The Hebrew Ladies Aid Society helped raise money for the commission and hosted a banquet that raised an astonishing $700 for the cause. (Heinz History Center.)

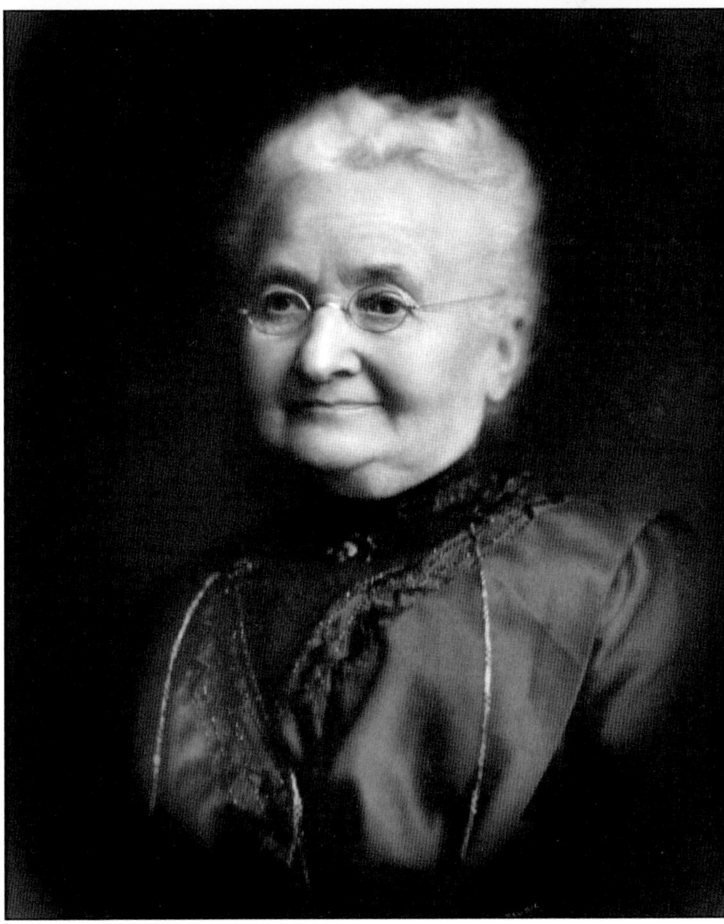

Rosalia Rauh, like Pauline Frank, was a grande dame of the Jewish philanthropic world. She served as president of the Hebrew Ladies Aid Society and then as vice president of the United Hebrew Relief Fund from 1880 until her death in 1915. She was the mother of Enoch and Marcus Rauh.

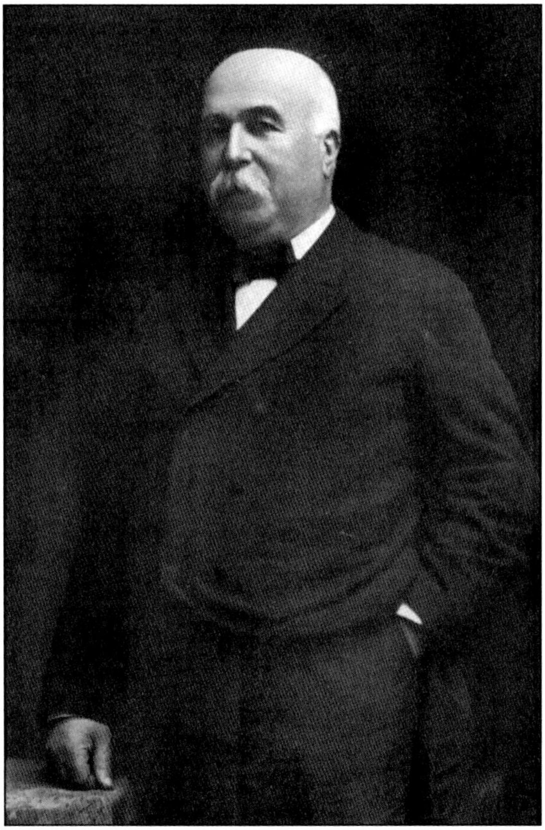

Abraham Lippman, the brother of Rosalia Rauh, was a key player at Rodef Shalom, serving as its president for many years, and at the United Hebrew Relief Fund. He had come from Bavaria and had started out in the dry goods business. He died in 1910, a wealthy bachelor.

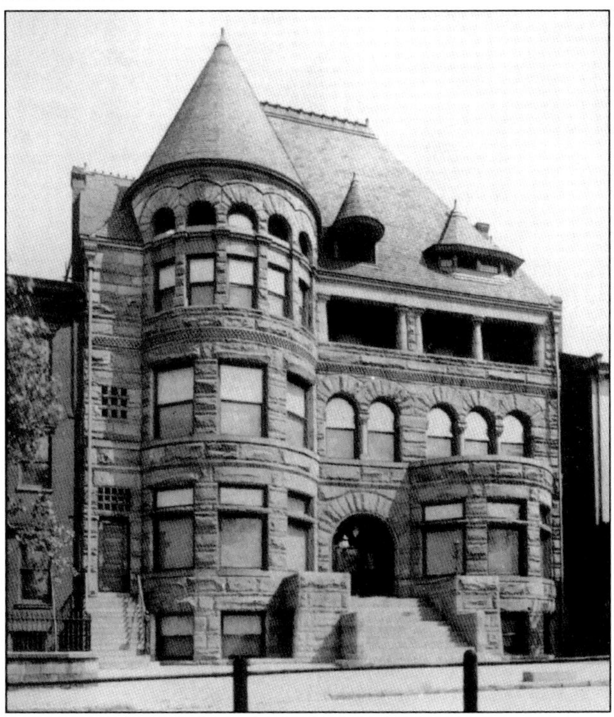

The Concordia Club, established in 1874 on Stockton Street in Allegheny City (pictured here), moved in 1913 to a location on O'Hara Street in Oakland (now the University of Pittsburgh Faculty Club). It was a social club for the German Jews who knew they would never be welcomed in the exclusive Duquesne Club downtown.

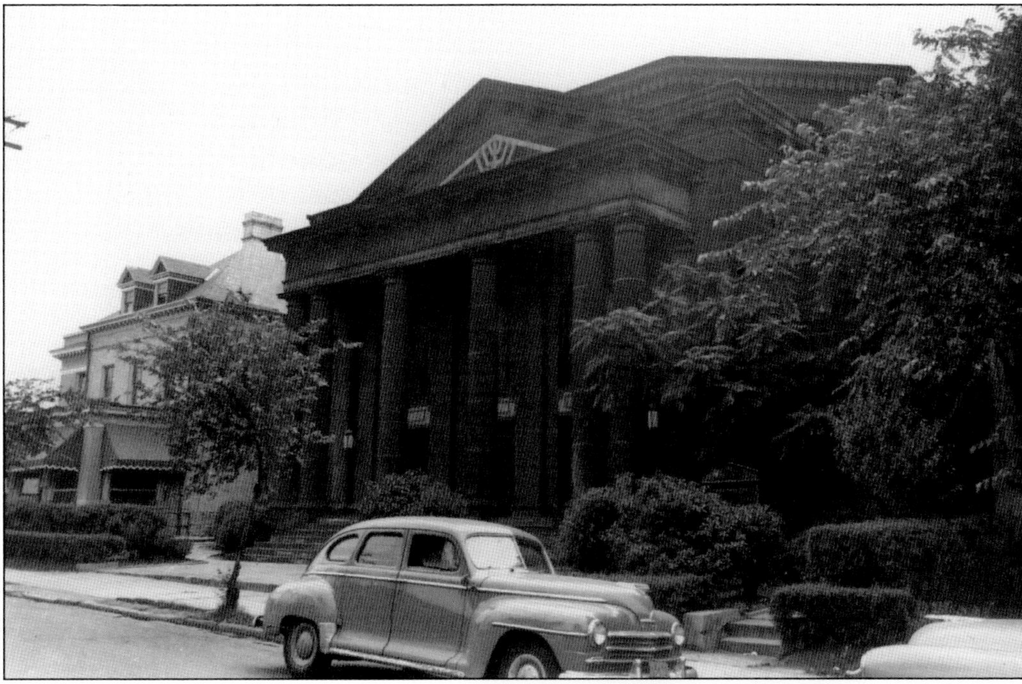

In 1864, a group of more traditional Jews, largely from Eastern German and Polish provinces, broke off from Rodef Shalom to establish their own congregation, the Tree of Life (Etz Hayim). They worshiped in rented spaces until they bought their first building in 1882 on Ross Street, but they moved in 1907 to a building on Craft Avenue (pictured above), which later became the Pittsburgh Playhouse. Today, Tree of Life is at the corner of Wilkins and Shady Avenues in Squirrel Hill. Gustav Grafner (pictured at right with his family) led the breakaway group from Rodef Shalom and was the first president of Tree of Life. It is interesting to note that, unlike most Conservative congregations that broke away from Orthodox congregations, this group left because the parent congregation was moving toward Reform Judaism.

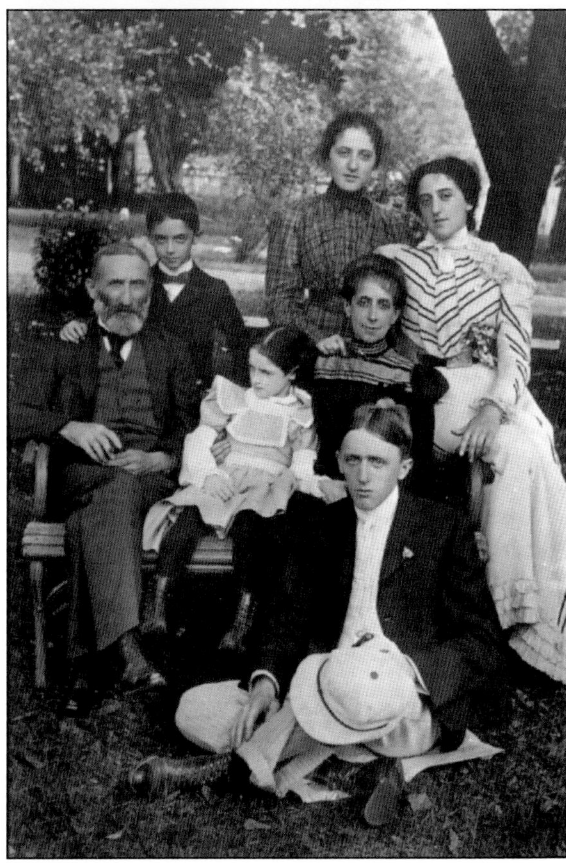

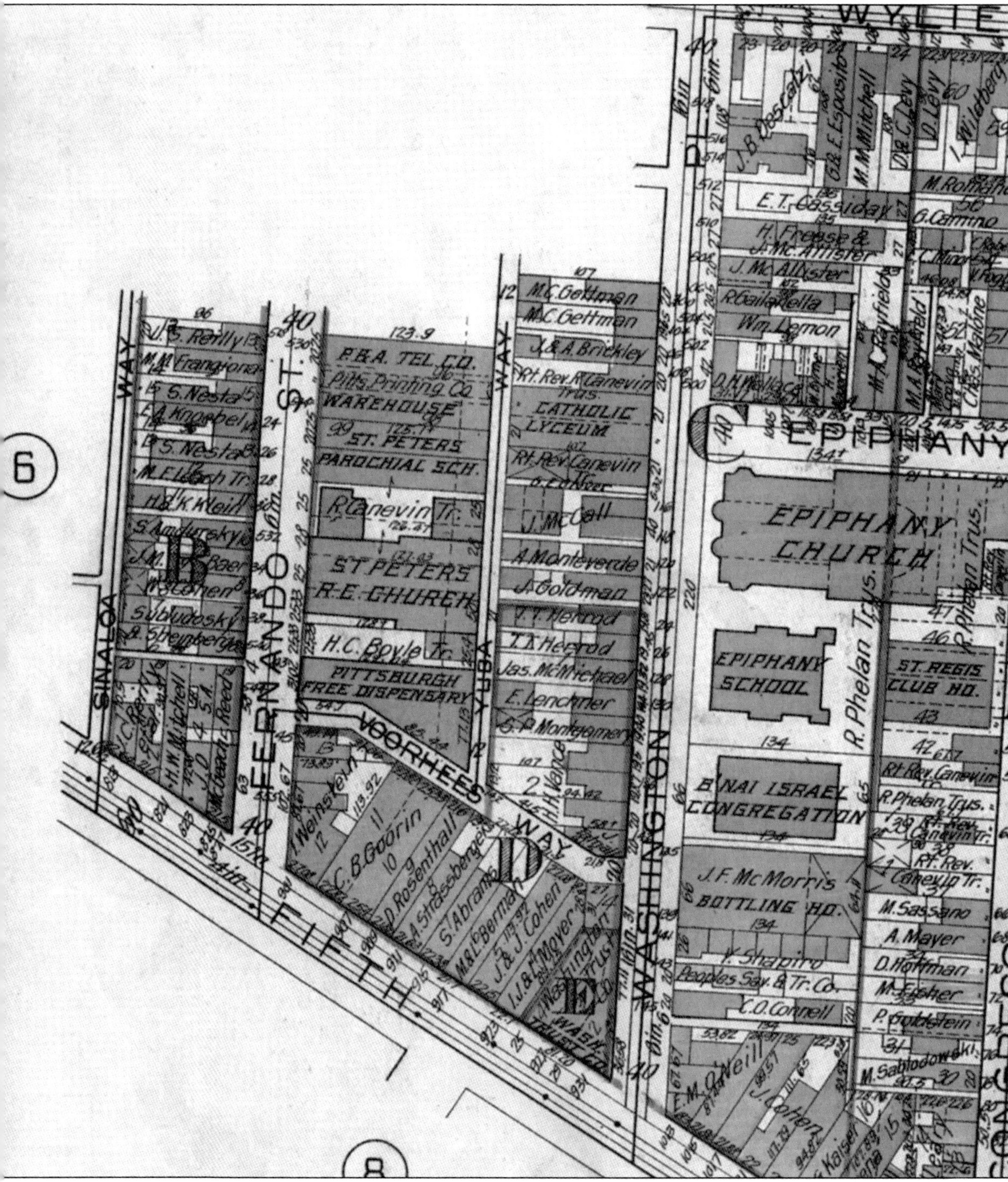

The Hill District is the area adjacent to downtown and to the former Pennsylvania Railroad Station that was the destination for the immigrant Eastern European Jews. This map shows the area dotted with synagogues representing the many Orthodox congregations whose members came from various parts of Eastern Europe. It also shows the concentration of Jewish institutions, including the Irene Kaufmann Settlement, the Zionist Institute, and the Labor Lyceum, that were

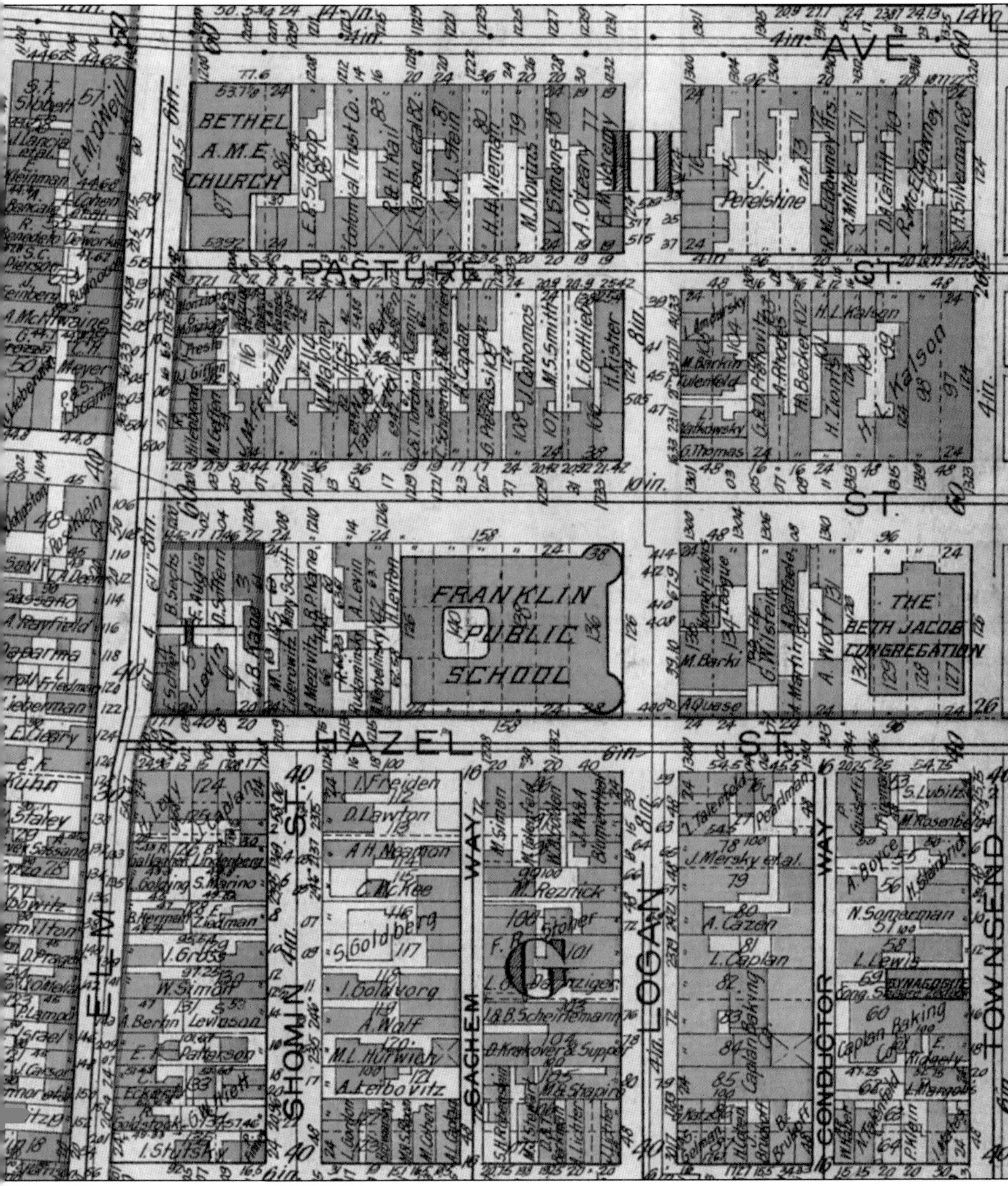

built by the Jewish community. While some Jews continued to live on the Hill in the 1940s, the exodus from the area began by the 1910s and continued in full force into the 1920s as Jews moved to Oakland and parts of the city farther east. At this same time, the Hill became the destination for poor African Americans migrating to Pittsburgh from the South.

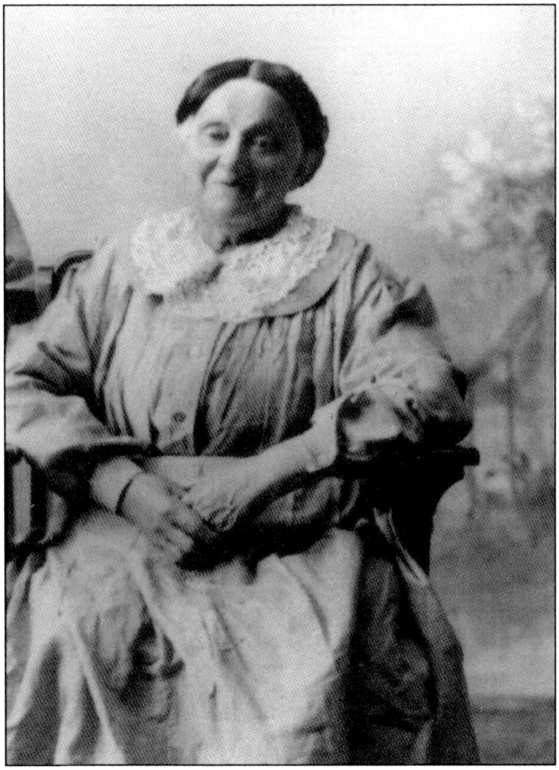

Hannah "Bobba" Sandusky was a trained midwife who emigrated from Kovno, a Lithuanian province, in 1861. Over the course of her career until her death in 1913, she delivered more than 3,500 registered births and many unregistered births on the Hill. One of her five daughters married Ralph Raphael, who was a prominent early Zionist in Pittsburgh.

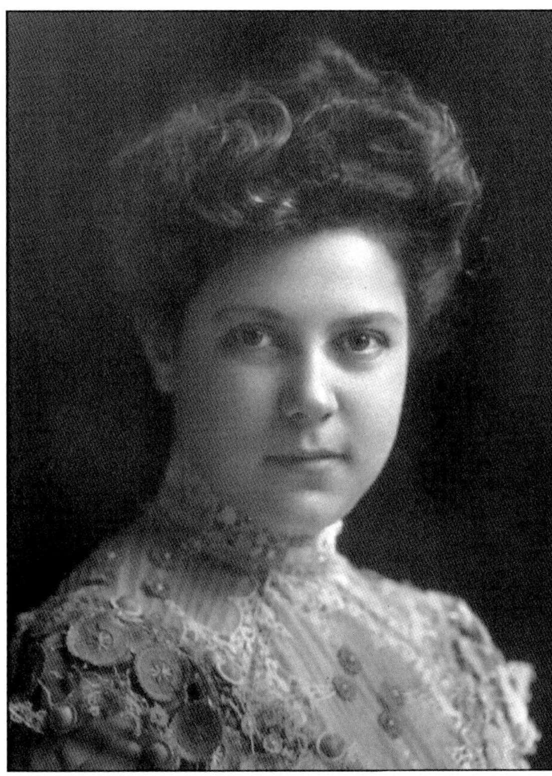

Inspired by the Jewish Women's Congress of the Chicago World's Fair in 1893, Pauline Hanauer Rosenberg was determined to organize a Pittsburgh chapter of the new National Council of Jewish Women. She became the founding president in 1894 of what in Pittsburgh was known as the Columbian Council, which established the Columbian Council School and Settlement, later to be renamed the Irene Kaufmann Settlement.

The Columbian Council building (right) on the Hill on Townsend Street housed the school and settlement, which was established by the mostly German, middle-class women of the Columbian Council to address the problems facing the Eastern European immigrants. Below is the Irene Kaufmann building on Center Avenue before the new auditorium was added in 1929. The auditorium, donated by Edgar Kaufmann in memory of his mother, Theresa Kaufmann, is all that is still standing and is now owned by the Hill House Association. The councilwomen were pioneers in assuming a public role at a time when women were expected to be seen and not heard. This effort was part of the larger settlement movement to provide services in poor immigrant neighborhoods. The settlements were crucial in the lives of families and true "spearheads of reform."

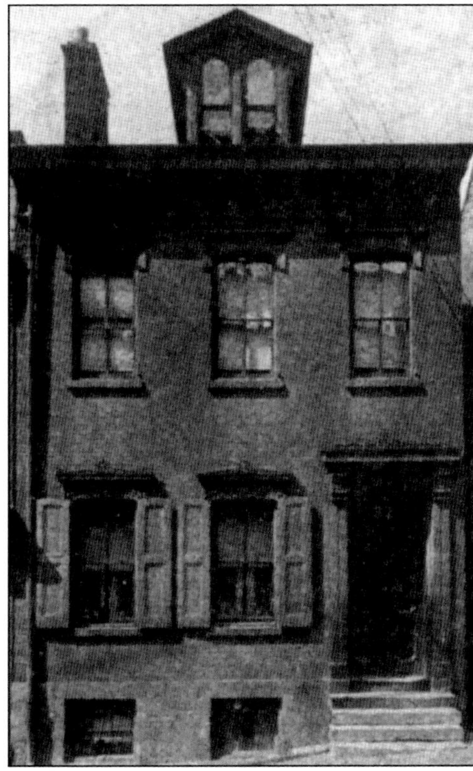

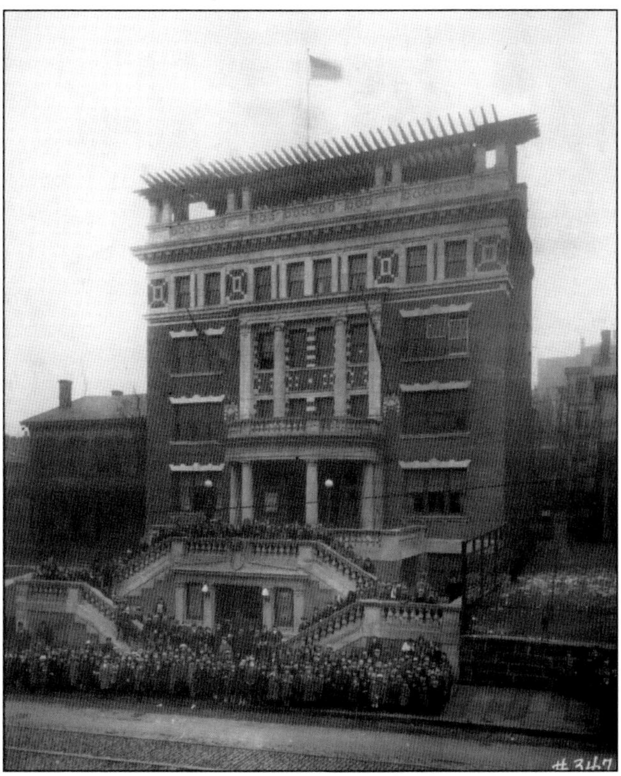

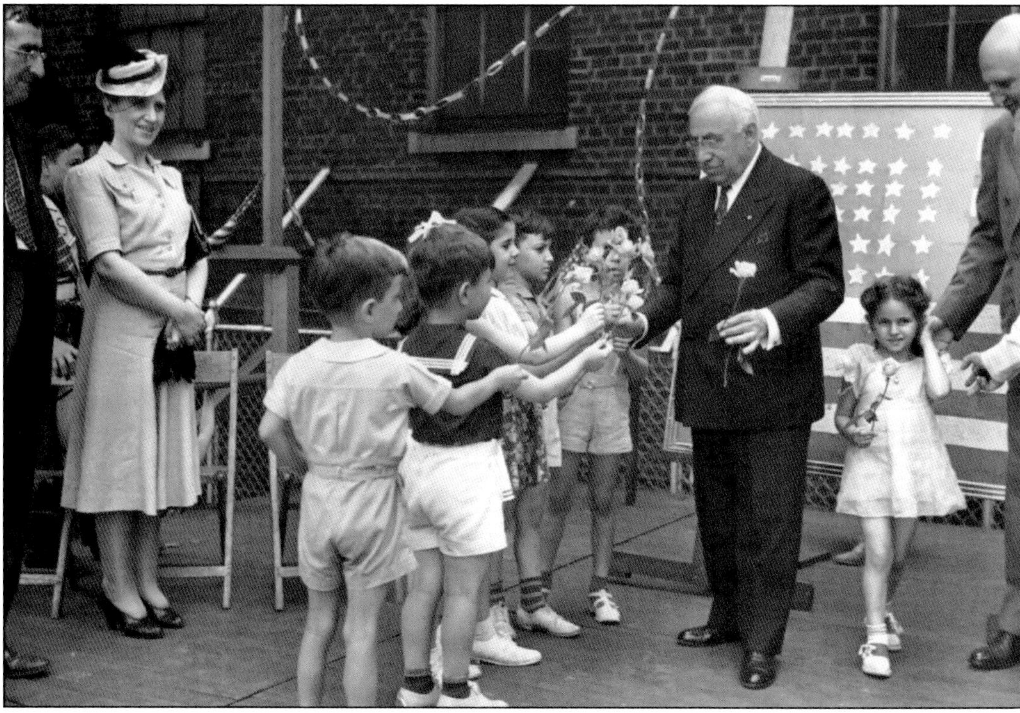

Henry Kaufmann was a major benefactor of the Irene Kaufmann Settlement. His gift in 1909 provided the funding for the Columbian Council to expand its activities. The settlement was named in memory of his daughter Irene. It is estimated that, over the course of his life, he gave as much as $2 million to the settlement. He was honored by the City of Pittsburgh for his philanthropy.

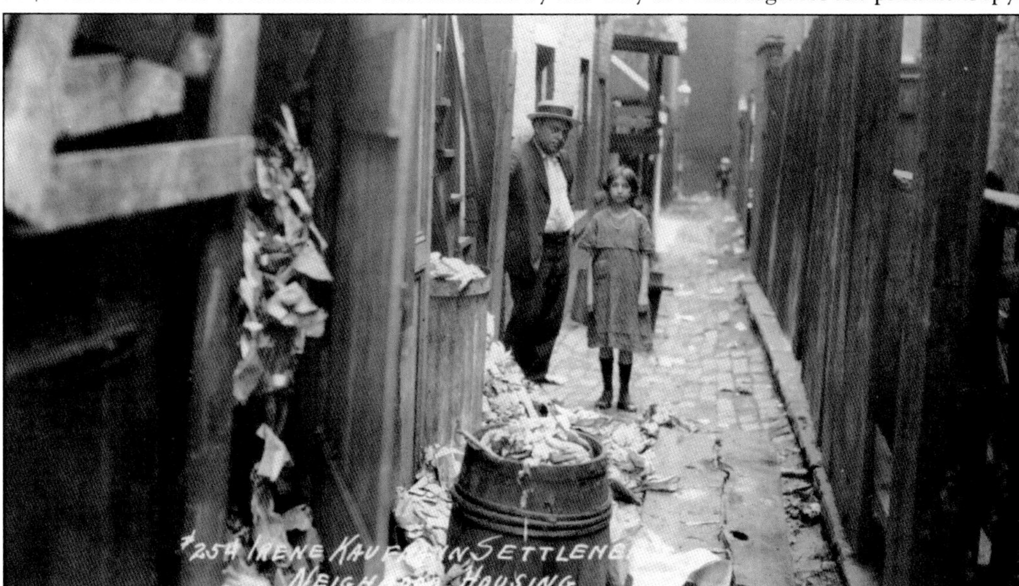

This 1923 picture of Sidney Teller, director of the Irene Kaufmann Settlement, in a neighborhood alley on the Hill illustrates the crowded, dilapidated housing that characterized much of the area. While some look back on the Hill with nostalgia, it clearly was an area with very challenging living conditions.

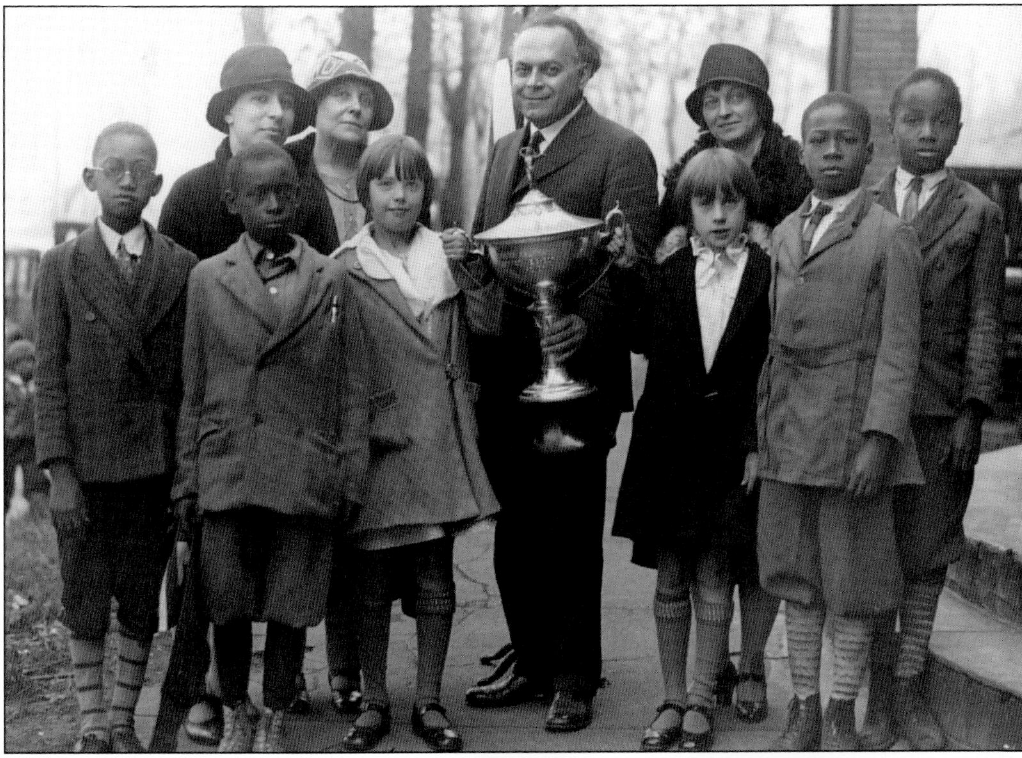

Here, Sydney Teller is presenting the Honor Cup to students at the Minersville School on the Hill as part of the "Better Neighborhood Contest" in 1928. Efforts were continually made by the Irene Kaufmann Settlement (IKS) to improve the area. This picture illustrates the mixed neighborhood of the Hill. Jews and blacks lived in close proximity to one another and, from all accounts, got along very well.

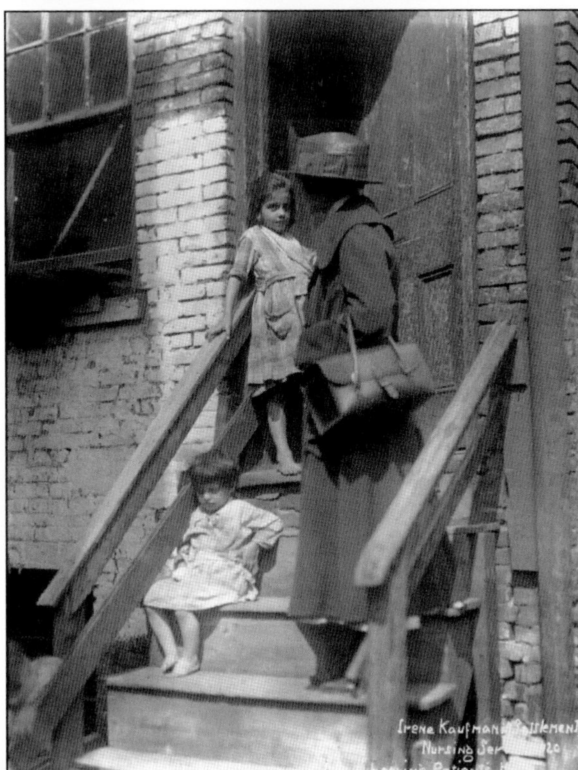

Providing nursing visits to immigrant families was a very important part of the services offered by the IKS. From its inception in 1900 until 1916, for example, some 100,138 nursing visits were made. A reporter for the *Pittsburgh Courier*, an African American newspaper, believed that without the nursing service of the settlement, the black community on the Hill would have been wiped out in a tuberculosis epidemic.

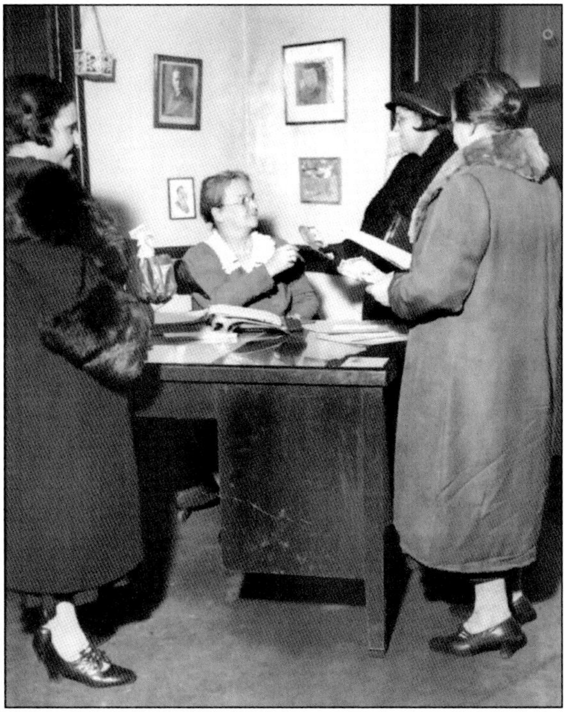

Known as the "Florence Nightingale of the Hill," Anna B. Heldman served as chief nurse of the IKS from 1902 until her death in 1940. She was not Jewish, but since she spoke Yiddish and lived at the settlement, most people assumed she was. Today, a street on the Hill is named in her memory.

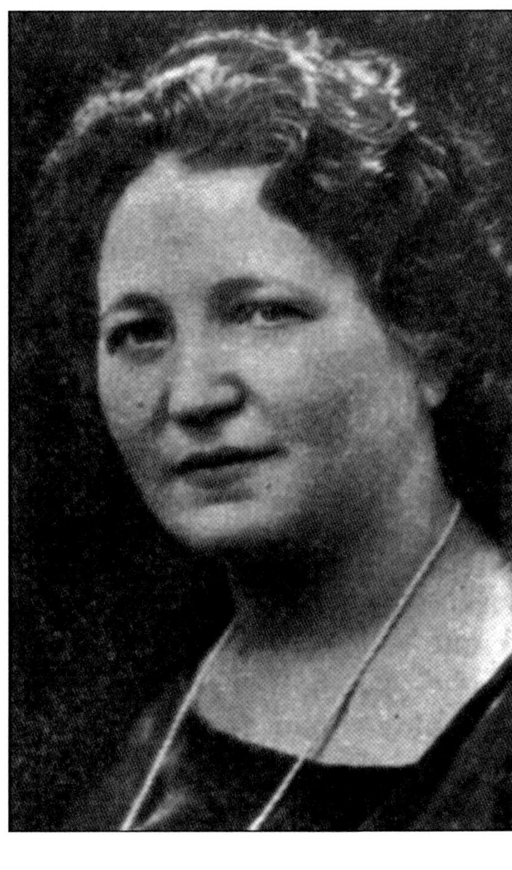

Dr. Luba Goldsmith, a Ukrainian immigrant, became the first woman and the first Jewish female graduate of the University of Pittsburgh School of Medicine. She was not only a practicing physician, but was also a public health pioneer. Soon after her untimely death at age 52 in 1931, an award was established to recognize the student with the highest grade average at the University of Pittsburgh Medical School.

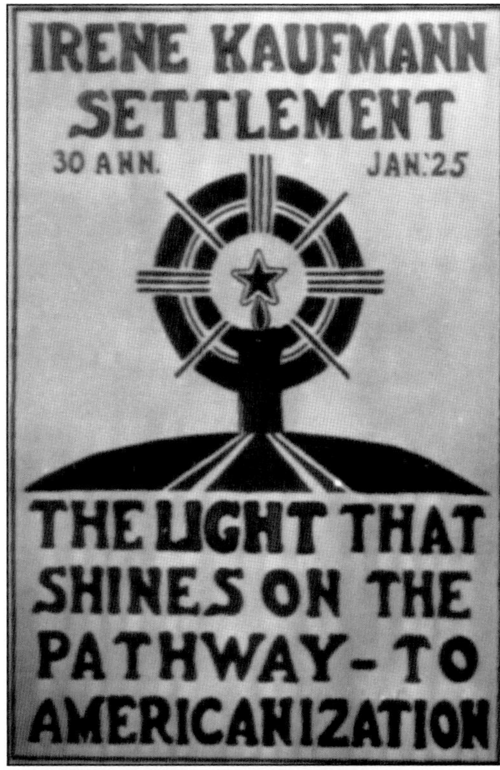

The Irene Kaufmann Settlement was determined to help immigrants adjust to American life. This mission is reflected by the Americanization sign and the Americanization home class of 1927 pictured. Their attempt to Americanize immigrants as quickly as possible was an important step in helping immigrants successfully get out of the ghetto, often in one generation. However, the emphasis on becoming an American, whatever that meant, sometimes ran afoul of Orthodox Jews and many Zionists who saw that effort by the IKS as inimical to preserving Jewish observance, traditions, and pride.

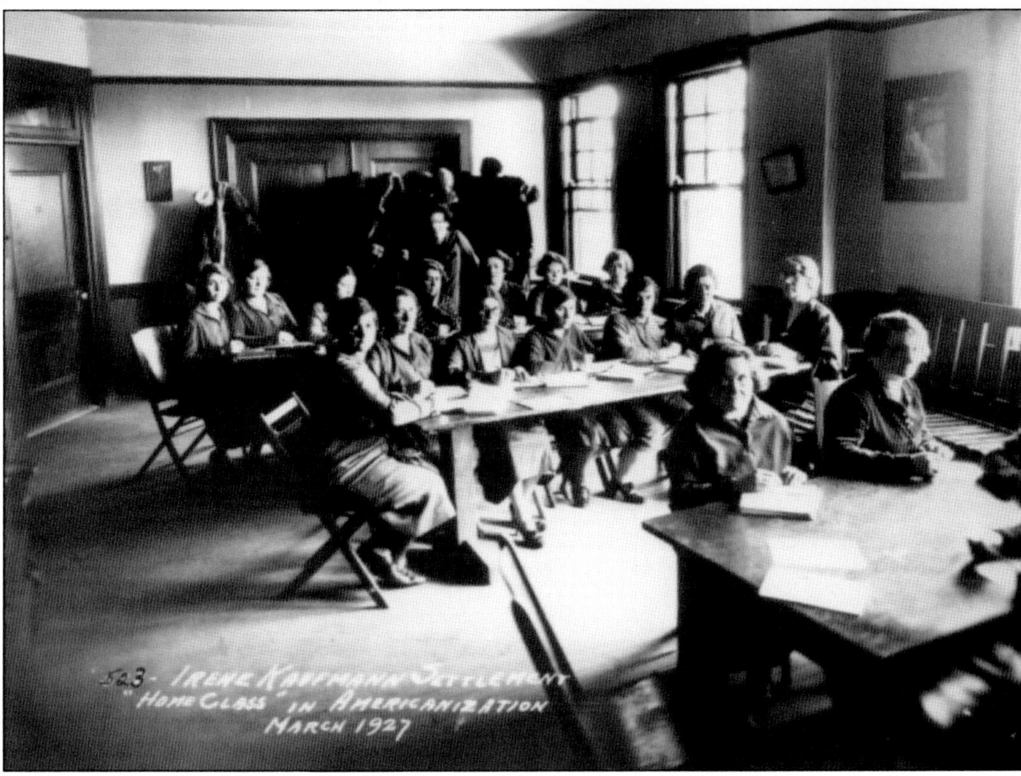

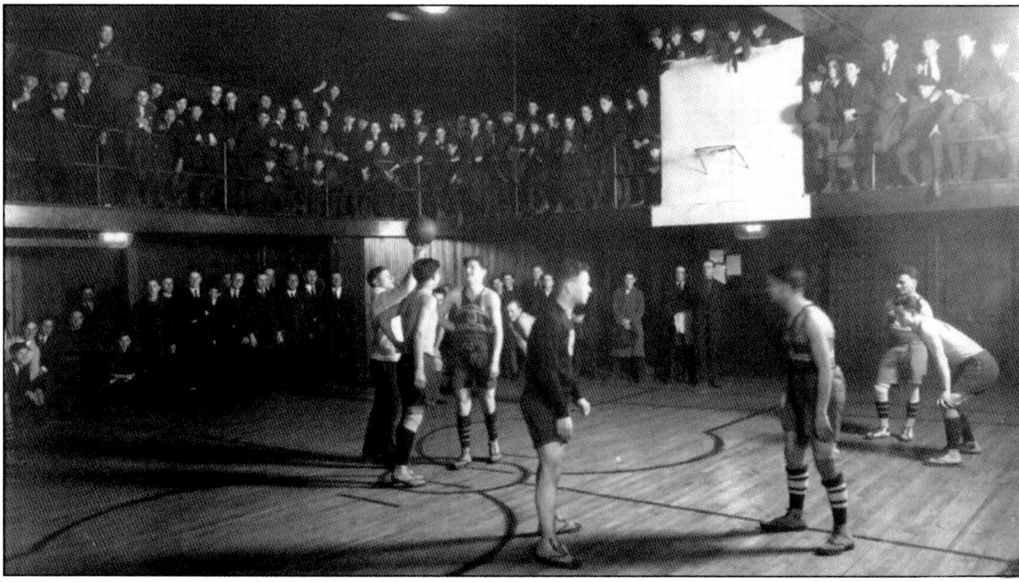

Pictured is a basketball game at the IKS. Basketball was an American sport that the young immigrant boys were eager to play. The IKS offered a variety of sporting activities to young boys and girls on the Hill. Sports were important for health and fitness, but they were also seen as a way of acculturating young immigrant Jews and possibly as a pathway to a college scholarship.

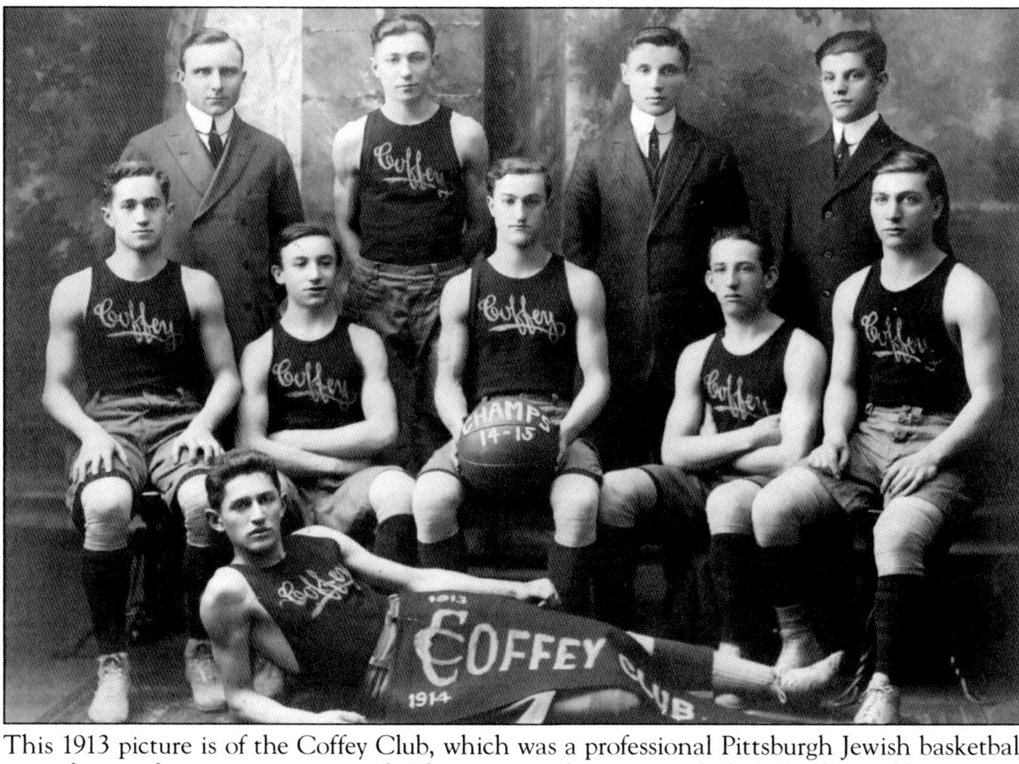

This 1913 picture is of the Coffey Club, which was a professional Pittsburgh Jewish basketball team famous for its winning record. The stars on the team included "Buck" Gefsky, "Kutsy" Levine, Dave Mervis, Sol Adler, and "Buckets" Sandomire. The team got to play the New York Celtics in 1923.

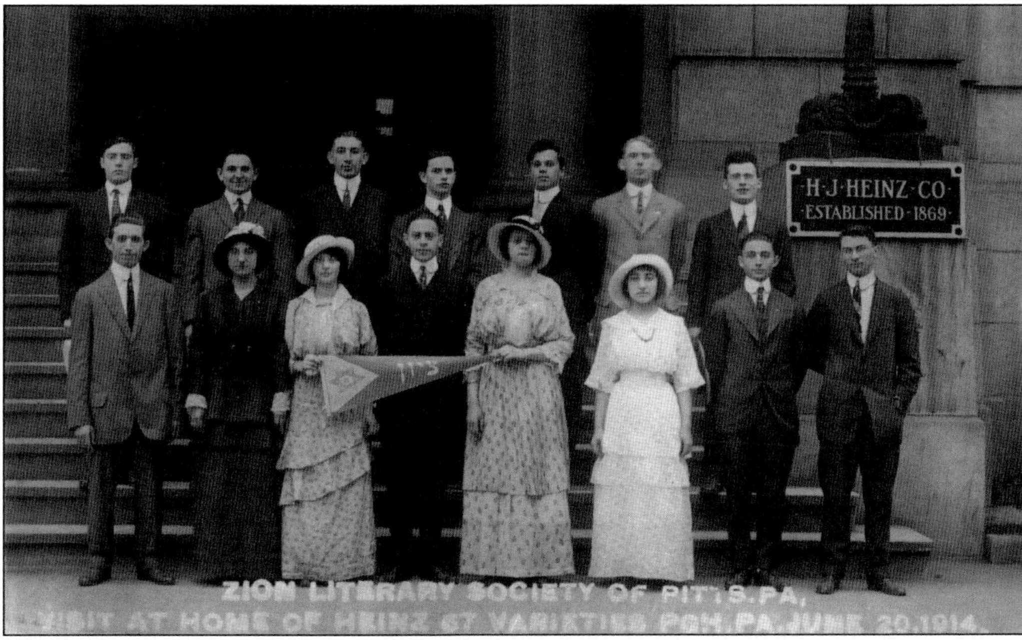

These are pictures of activities of young Zionists. Above is the Zionist Literary Society visiting the Heinz Company plant in 1914, and below is a Young People's Zionist League picnic in 1917. Zionism appealed to young people with its ideological goal and its social activities. The Young People's Zionist League was founded in Pittsburgh in 1916. It was a very active group, organizing weekly meetings, lectures, and social events. However, Zionist ardor was to cool in the 1920s with splits in the movement and a change in organizational structure.

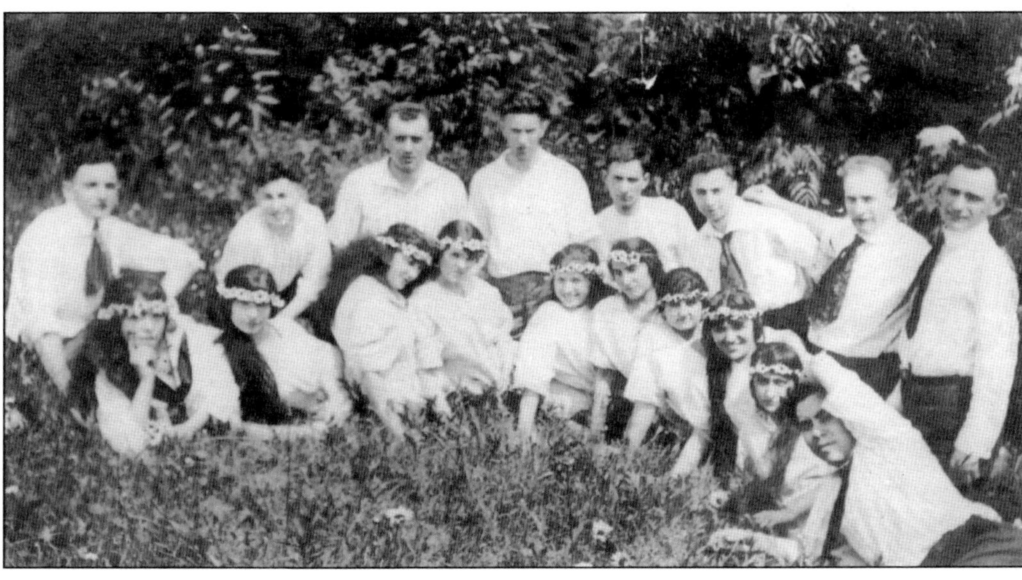

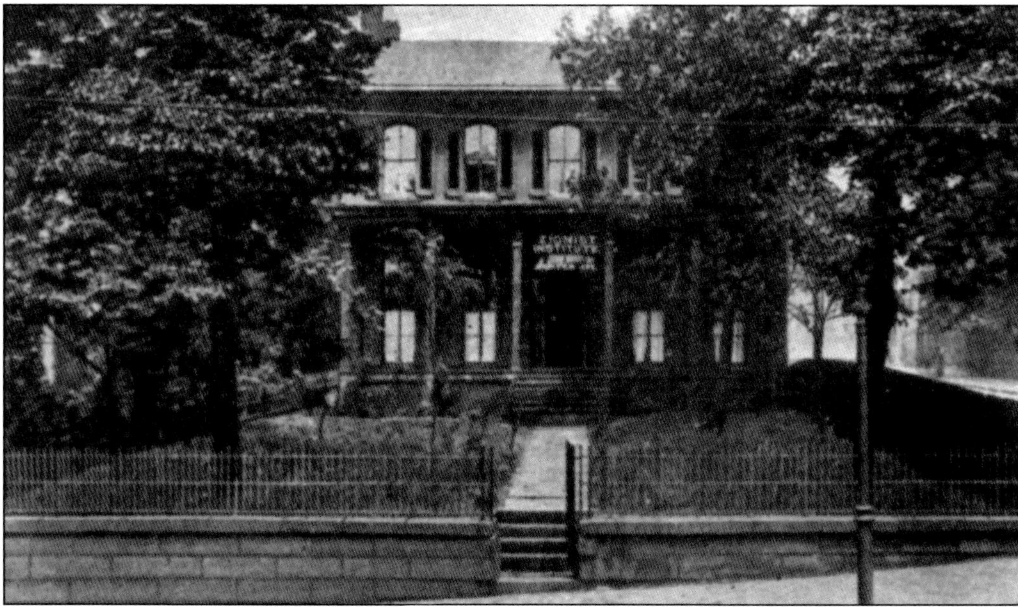

The Zionist Institute was established in 1906 just two doors down from the Irene Kaufmann Settlement. The two establishments were in competition with one another for the attention of the immigrant Jews on the Hill. The Zionist Institute emphasized Jewish nationalism and history. Given declining interest, the Zionist Institute was sold in 1926, with the $30,000 from the sale going to support settlement in Palestine.

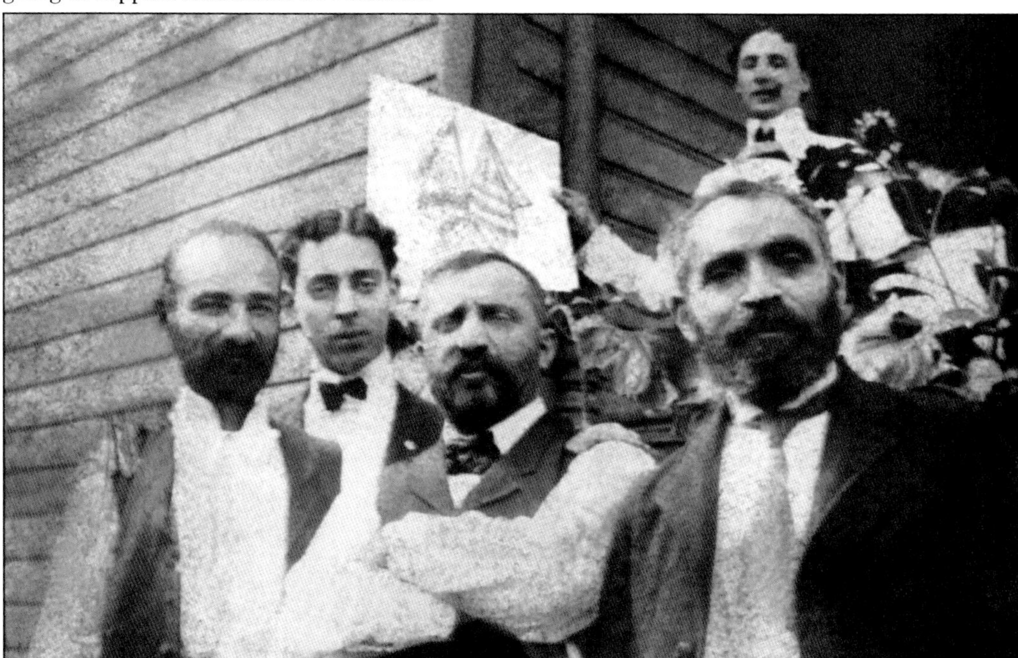

Ralph Raphael (left) was considered the founder of Zionism in Pittsburgh. He wrote a book calling for a Jewish state in 1893, three years before Theodore Herzl's clarion call that was to ignite the modern Zionist movement. Like Herzl, Raphael died in his mid-40s, and his death in 1903 happened just one year before Herzl's own untimely passing.

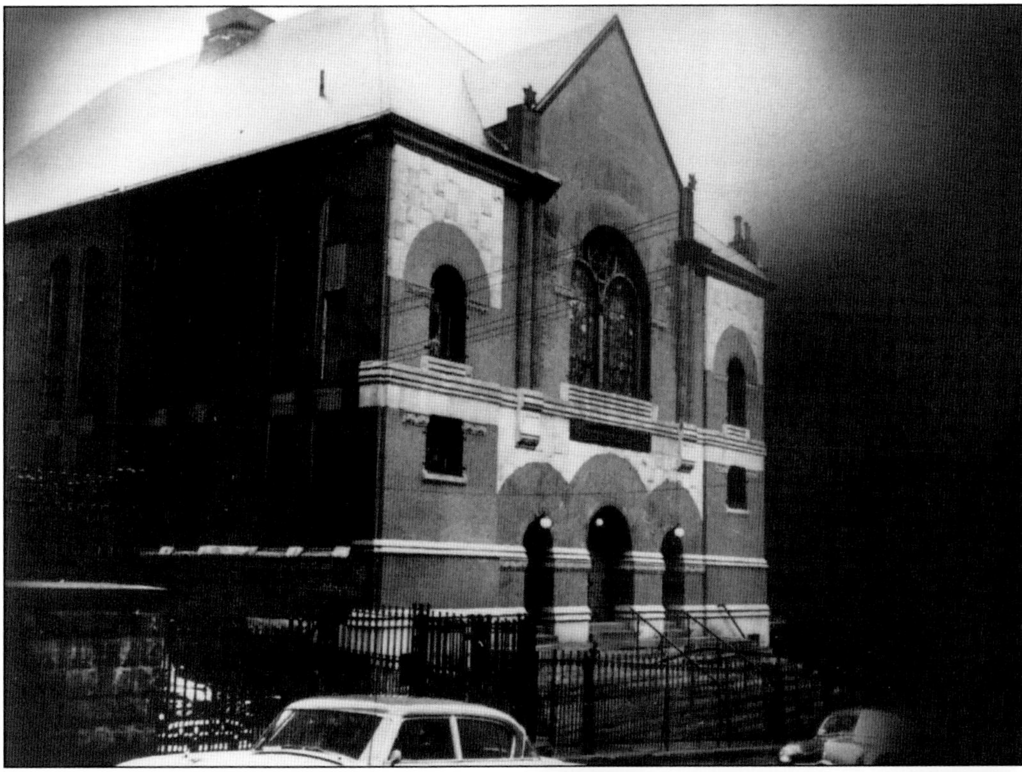

Beth Hamedrash Hagadol, formerly B'nai Israel, was the largest Orthodox synagogue on the Hill. In 1892, the congregation changed its name and moved to a new building on Washington Street that could seat 1,600 people. Its members, largely from the Suwalk and Kovno provinces, were mostly Lithuanian, a Jewish ethnic group that represented at least half of the estimated 5,000 Jews in Pittsburgh at that time.

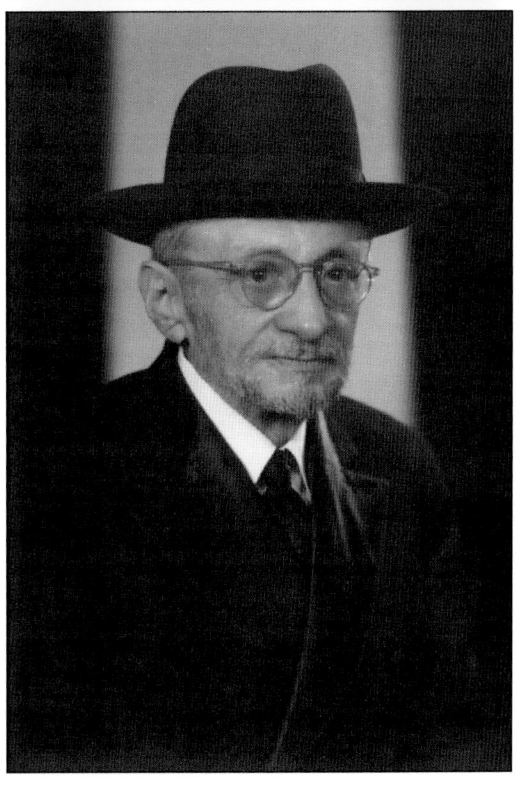

Rabbi Aaron Ashinsky had come to Pittsburgh in 1901 at the age of 35. He became a leader in the community, not only as rabbi of Beth Hamedrash Hagadol, but also as an activist working to establish various Jewish institutions in Pittsburgh, including the House of Shelter and the Jewish Home for the Aged. He was a prominent Zionist sitting on the executive committee of the national Mizrachi Zionist organization.

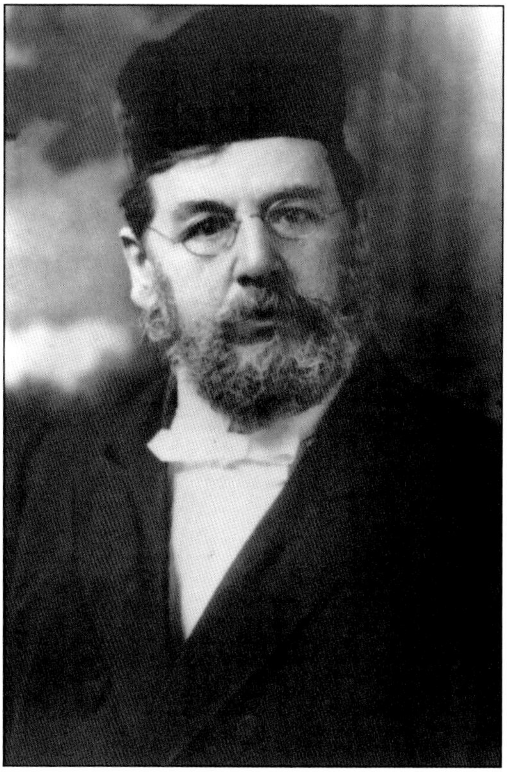

Pittsburgh was home to several renowned Orthodox rabbis. Rabbi Moshe Sivitz (left) was another Orthodox leader in Pittsburgh, the rabbi at Shaare Torah on the Hill. He was the author of a number of books, including a book of poetry and a scholarly commentary on the Jerusalem Talmud. He was a founder of the Union of Orthodox Rabbis. Rabbi Eliyahu Kochin (below) came to Pittsburgh in 1906 to become the spiritual leader of Poale Zedeck and then of Tiphereth Israel Congregation on the Hill. He was working on his fourth volume of sermons when he died of a sudden heart attack in 1945. Not pictured is Rabbi Wolf Leiter of Machsikei Hadas, who was known as "the Rabbi's Rabbi" for his scholarly work and volumes of *responsa*, which are written answers to questions in Jewish law.

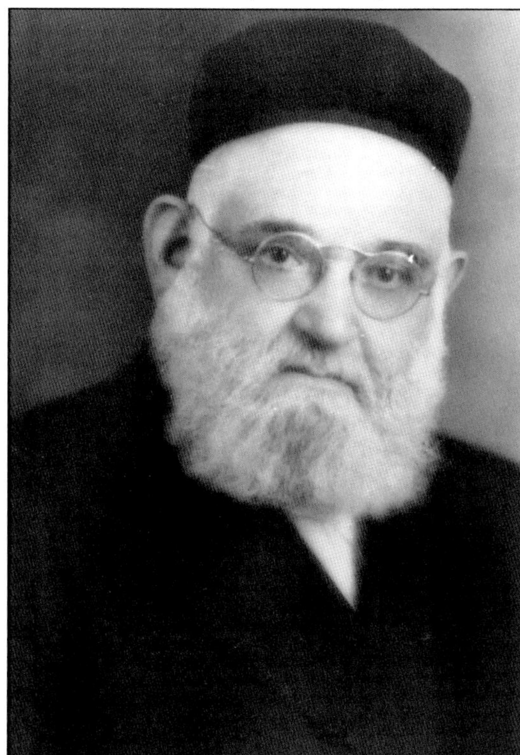

By the mid-1920s, immigration into America was severely restricted by the Johnson-Reed Immigration Restriction Act. (Reed was Sen. David Reed of Pittsburgh). Zena Saul, an immigrant from Suwalk, Lithuania, was tapped by the local chapter of the National Council of Jewish Women to head up their Immigrant Services Department. She worked tirelessly on behalf of would-be immigrants and refugees until her death at the age of 81 in 1967.

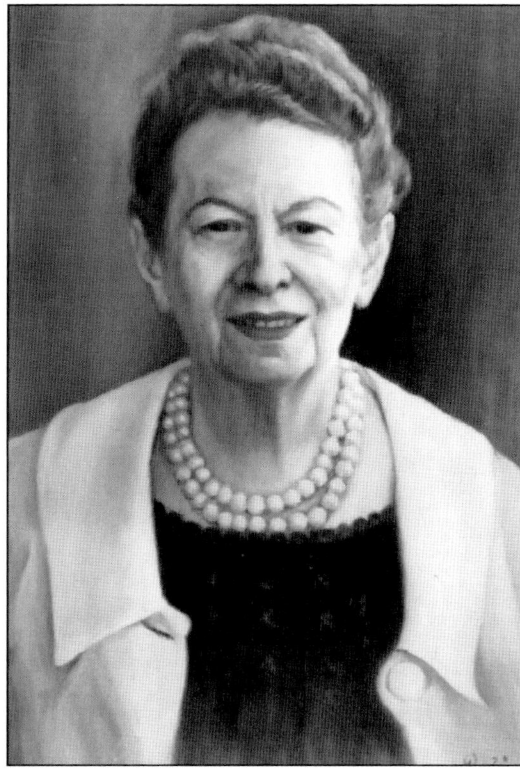

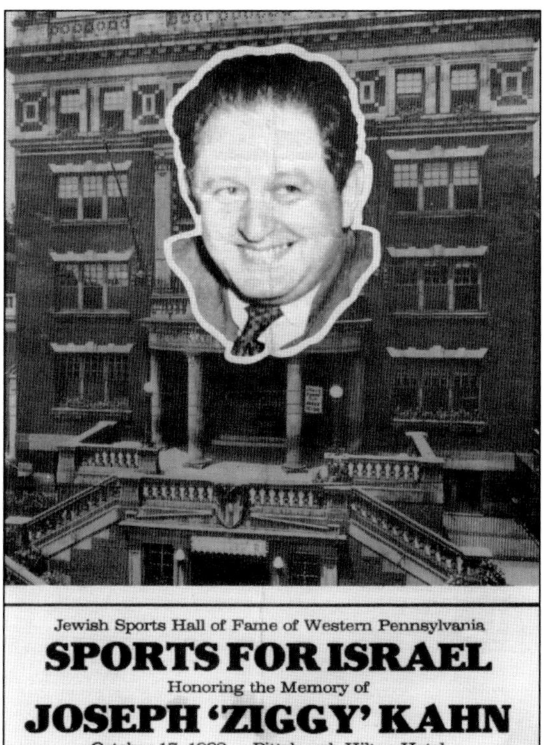

The rise of Hitler provoked a crisis for German Jews. Joseph "Ziggy" Kahn was the longtime athletic director of the Irene Kaufmann Settlement who wanted America to boycott the Olympic Games scheduled for Berlin in 1936. His efforts ultimately failed, but he was diligent in his determination to respond to the crisis. Later on, he became a popular city councilman and was a beloved figure in the community.

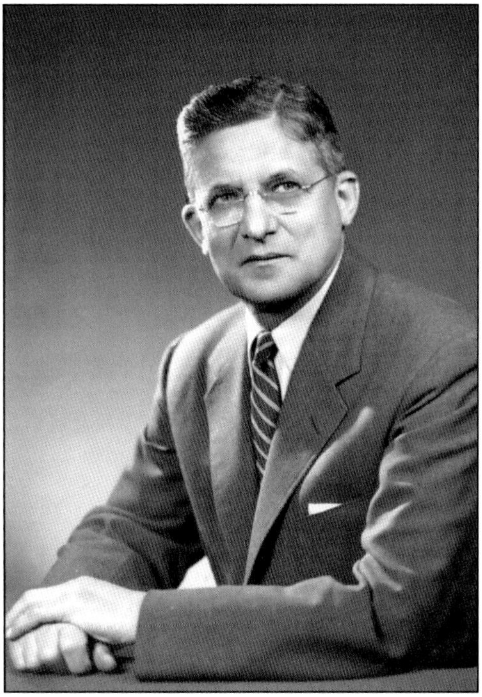

Attorney David Glick of Pittsburgh was another activist trying to respond to the crisis of German Jewry. In 1936, and again in 1938, he went to Hitler's Germany in an attempt to arrange for the emigration of German Jews to South America. He met with Reinhard Heydrich, head of the Nazi Secret Intelligence Service, and traveled throughout Germany secretly reporting on the disaster befalling German Jewry.

This telegram is to Leon Falk, who was called upon by the American Jewish Joint Distribution Committee to oversee refugee resettlement in the Dominican Republic, which offered asylum to desperate Jews. He headed the Dominican Resettlement Association (DORSA) and lived in Sosua in the Dominican Republic for a year. Ultimately, only 500 Jews were able to settle there.

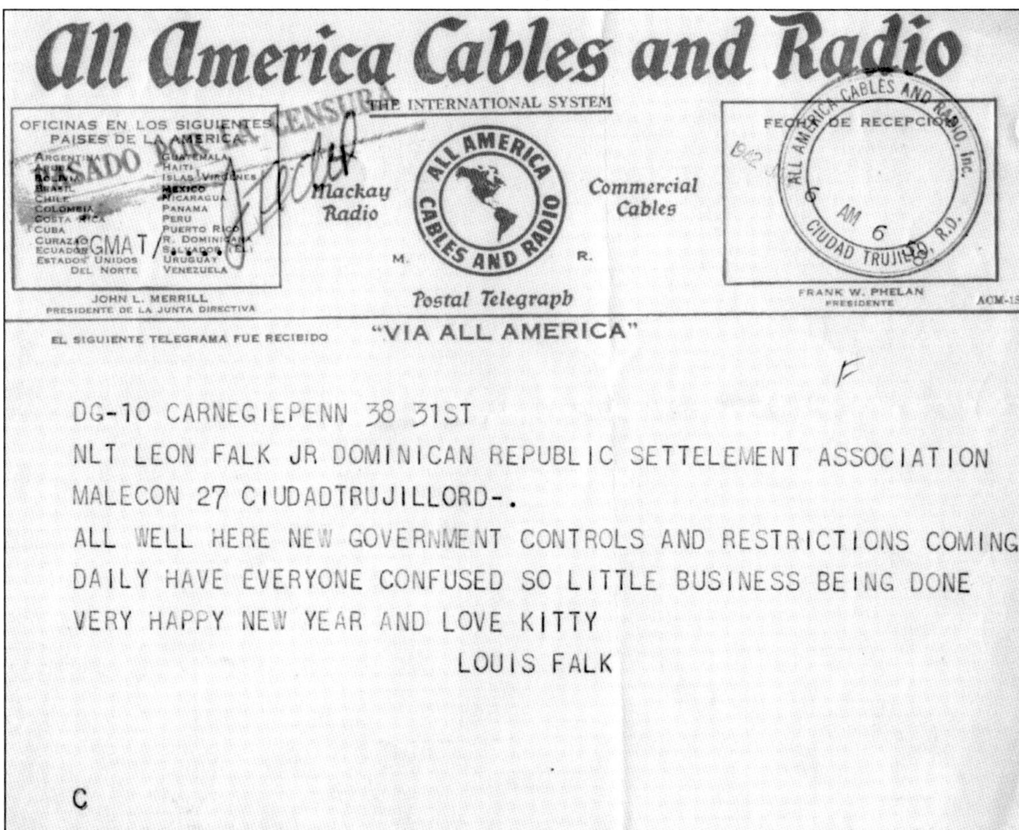

All America Cables and Radio

THE INTERNATIONAL SYSTEM

Mackay Radio — Commercial Cables — Postal Telegraph

JOHN L. MERRILL, PRESIDENTE DE LA JUNTA DIRECTIVA

FRANK W. PHELAN, PRESIDENTE

EL SIGUIENTE TELEGRAMA FUE RECIBIDO "VIA ALL AMERICA"

DG-10 CARNEGIEPENN 38 31ST

NLT LEON FALK JR DOMINICAN REPUBLIC SETTELEMENT ASSOCIATION

MALECON 27 CIUDADTRUJILLORD-.

ALL WELL HERE NEW GOVERNMENT CONTROLS AND RESTRICTIONS COMING

DAILY HAVE EVERYONE CONFUSED SO LITTLE BUSINESS BEING DONE

VERY HAPPY NEW YEAR AND LOVE KITTY

LOUIS FALK

C

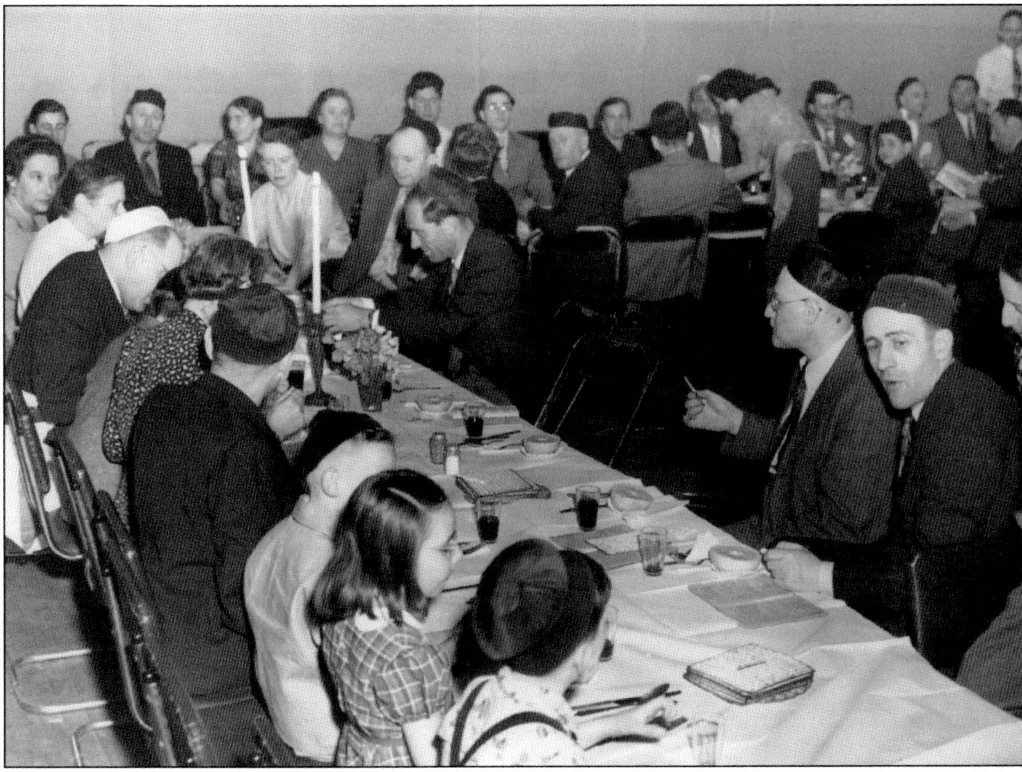

The Friendship Club, observing a Passover seder in this image, was composed of German and Austrian refugees who had escaped from bondage imposed on them not under the Egyptians, but under the Nazis. It had been organized in 1934 for socialization and education. After the Holocaust, they reached out to survivors who were coming to Pittsburgh.

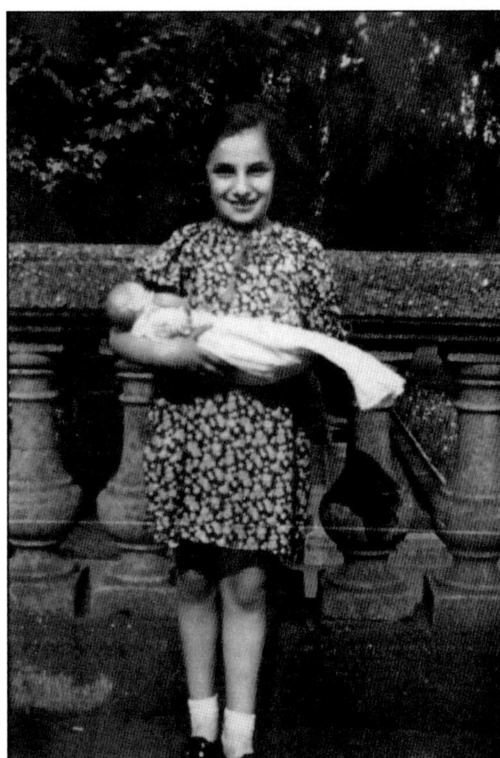

This picture was of happier times for Marga Silberman. She and her mother were among the last Jews to get out of Germany in 1941, but she never saw her grandfather and aunts again. Coming to Pittsburgh with a visa supplied by distant Adelsheimer relatives, she married Jordan Randall and dedicated herself to talking to young people about her experiences. She received an honorary doctorate from Seton Hill University.

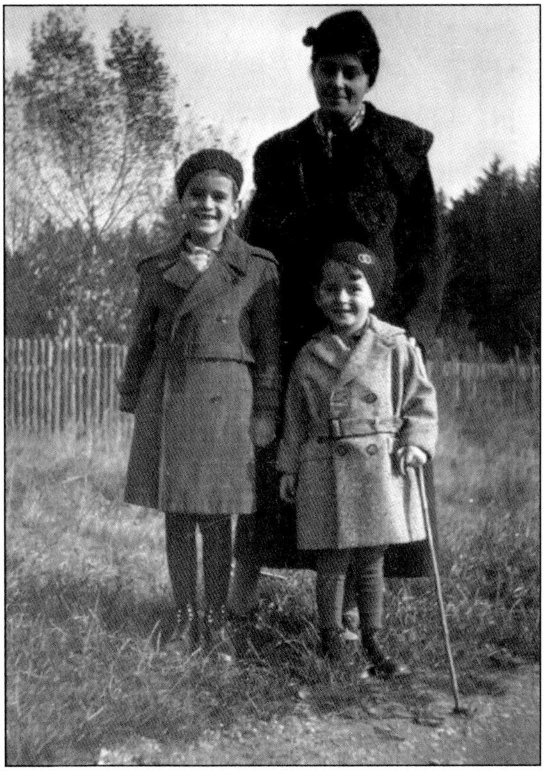

Walter Jacob (left), born in Augsburg, Germany, in 1930, fled to America in 1940. He later was ordained a rabbi at Hebrew Union College and then served as assistant rabbi at Rodef Shalom Congregation. He succeeded Rabbi Freehof as senior rabbi in 1966, a post he held until his retirement in 1997. He has been a major leader in the Reform movement both in America and in Germany. (Jacob family.)

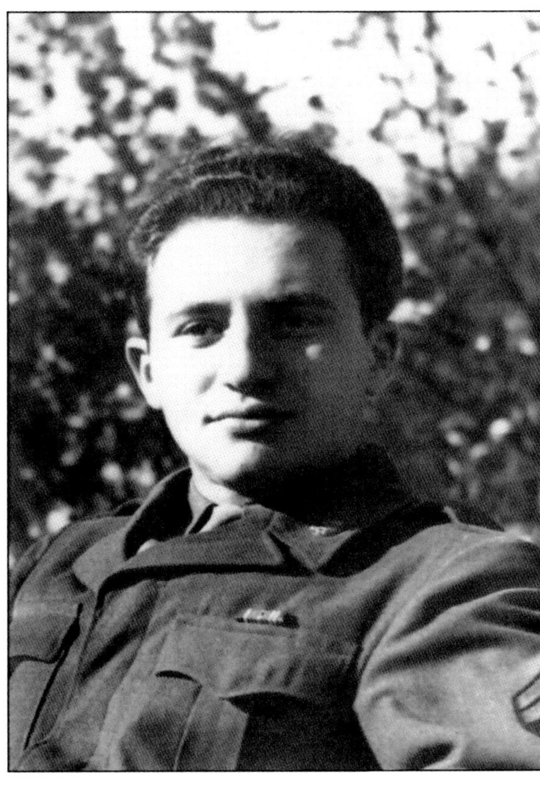

Adolf Grunbaum was born in Cologne, Germany. At the age of 15 in 1938, he immigrated to the United States. As a member of a US Army's Mobile Field Interrogation Unit, he interrogated high-ranking Nazis after the war. He has been the esteemed Andrew Mellon Professor of Philosophy of Science at the University of Pittsburgh since 1960 and is internationally recognized in his field. (Grunbaum family.)

Born in Constance, Germany, in 1925, Fritz Ottenheimer was able to immigrate with his family to the United States in May 1939, just three months before the outbreak of World War II. The author of a memoir, *Escape and Return*, Ottenheimer moved to Pittsburgh in 1950 and worked at Westinghouse for 30 years. He speaks frequently about his experiences and has been the president of the Holocaust Survivors Organization in Pittsburgh.

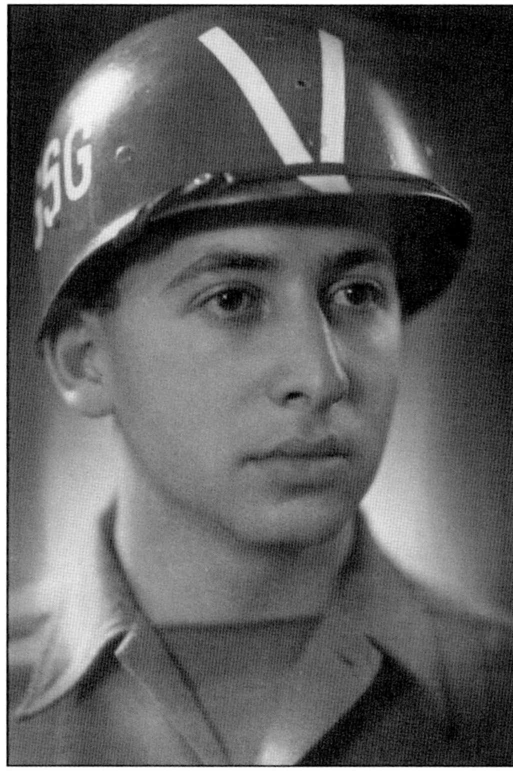

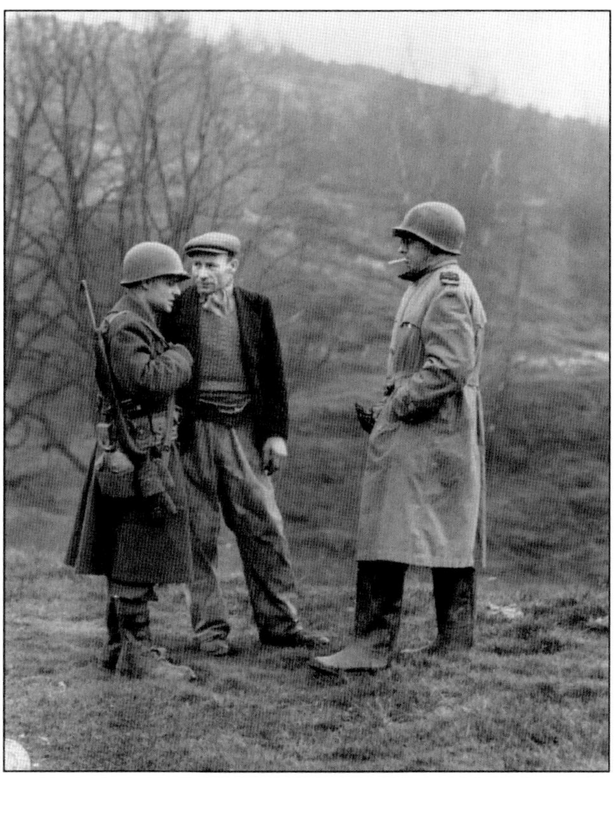

Born Josef Wechsler in Nuremberg, Germany, in 1919, Joseph Eaton (left) escaped his native country only to return with the US Army during World War II. For 52 years, he was a professor in the University of Pittsburgh School of Social Work. He was active in the Jewish Federation's Community Relations Council for many years until his death at the age of 93 in 2012. (Eaton family.)

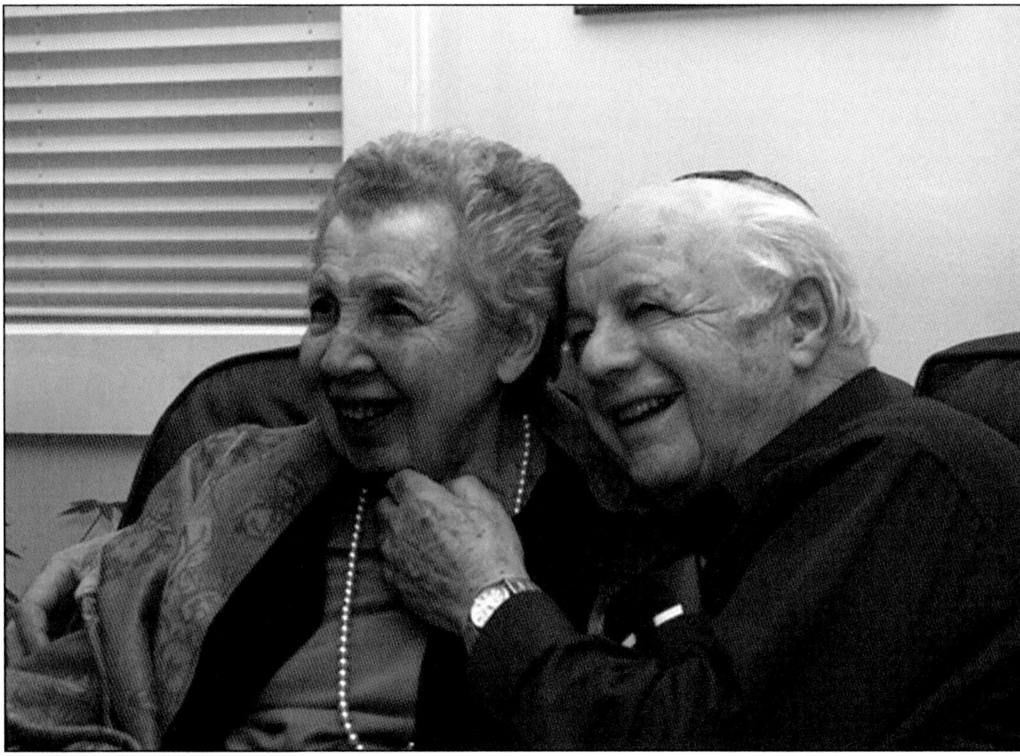

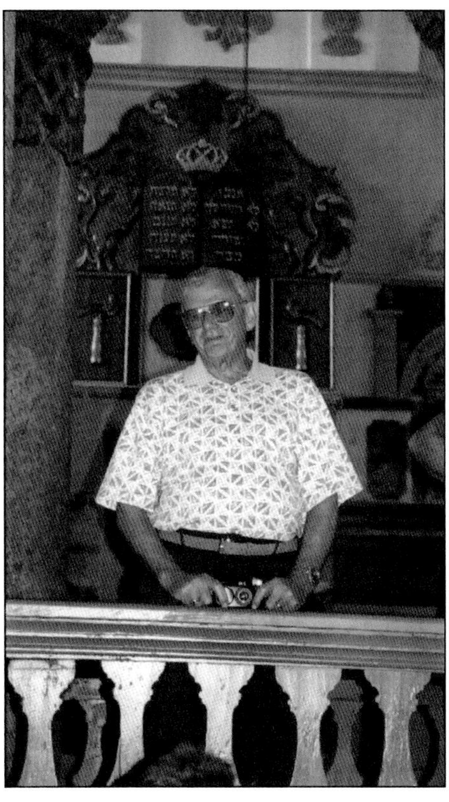

Malka and Moshe Baran were among the several hundred Holocaust survivors who came to Pittsburgh after World War II. Moshe Baran was born in 1920 in Horodok, Poland. He escaped the ghetto to survive the war fighting as a partisan against the Nazis. He married Malka, who was born in Warsaw, Poland, in 1927. All but one of her large extended family—approximately 70 people—were killed. Malka passed away in 2007.

Jack Sittsamer, born in Mielec, Poland, for nearly 30 years shared memories of his struggle to survive multiple concentration camps during the Holocaust. If he had not been liberated May 5, 1945, he believed he would not have been able to survive another week. In 2006, six years before his death in 2012, he was given the Jefferson Award for Public Service. (Sittsamer family.)

Dora Iwler, another Polish survivor, managed to escape the Janowska concentration camp twice, but no one else in her family survived. She met her husband in a displaced persons camp after the war, and three weeks later they were married. The couple operated a dry cleaning store for many years. Dora, who died in 2008, was named a Carlow College Woman of Spirit in 2004. (Iwler family.)

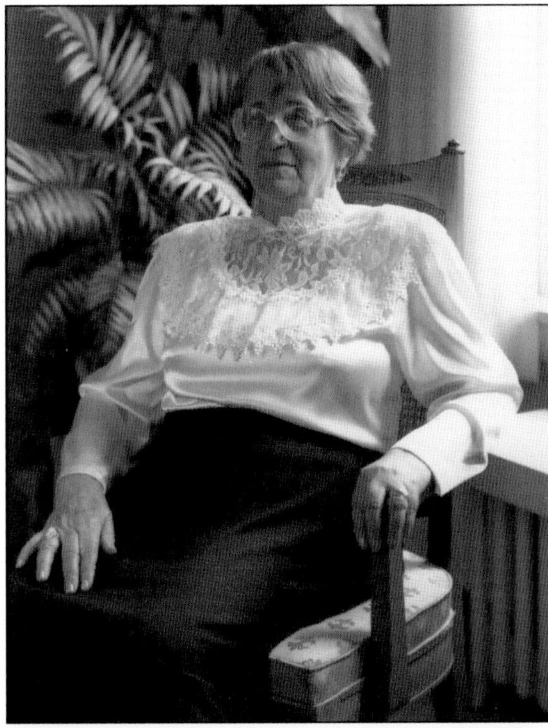

In addition to welcoming Holocaust survivors, Pittsburgh became home to hundreds of refugees from the Soviet Union. This scene at the old Syria Mosque in 1975 is a demonstration against the Soviet Union and a plea for the Communist government to let the Jews emigrate.

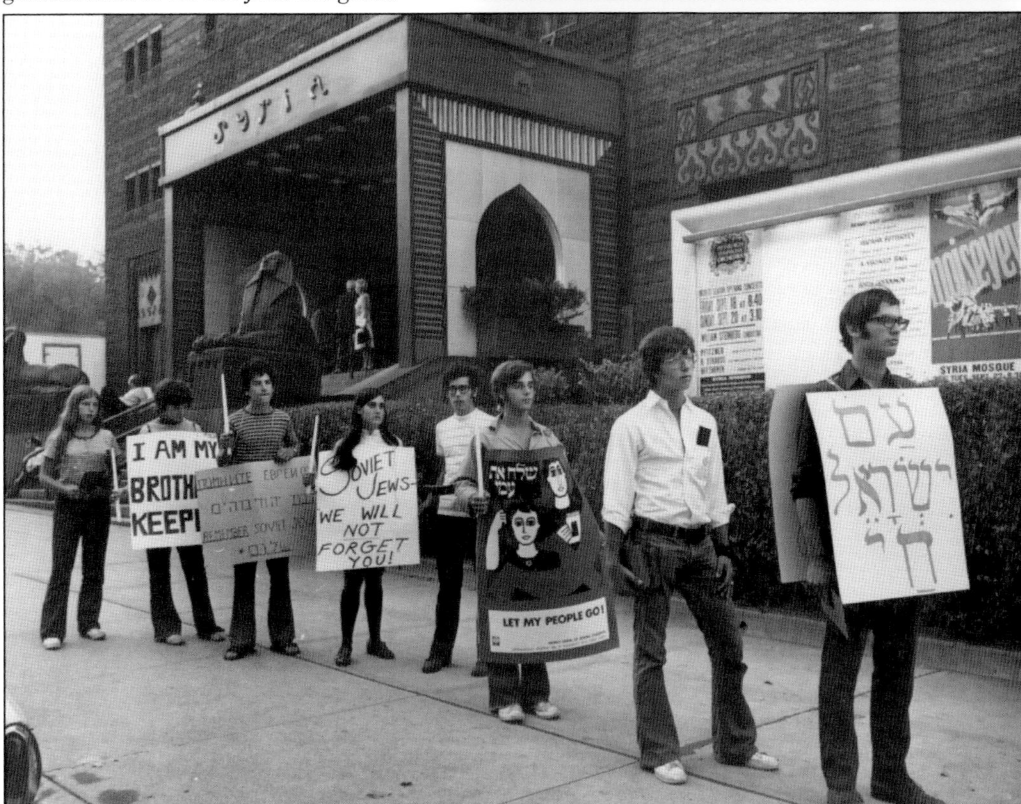

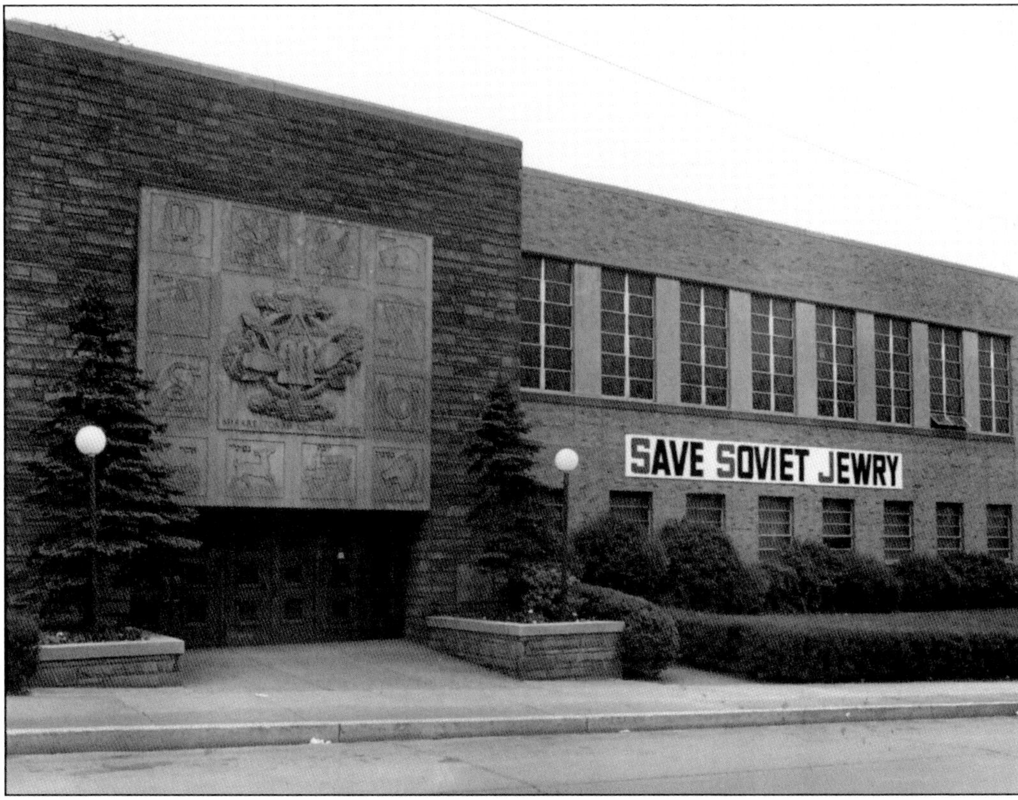

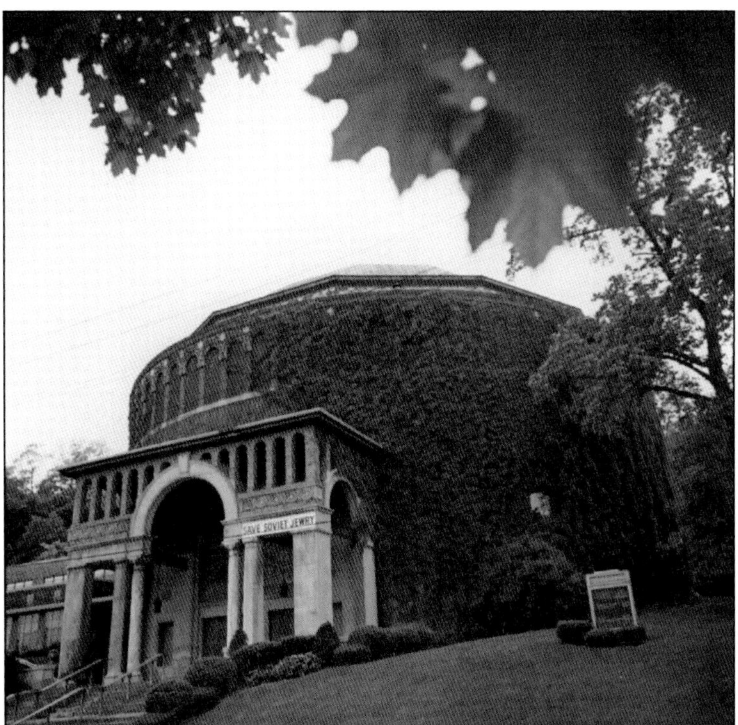

"Save Soviet Jewry" signs hung from synagogues and Jewish buildings around the city. These are pictures from just two of the synagogues in the 1970s that were calling for the release of Soviet Jews. These signs are from the Shaare Torah Congregation in Squirrel Hill and the B'nai Israel Congregation in the East End. Pittsburgh Jews, like Jews around the world, devoted great efforts to win the freedom of Soviet Jews.

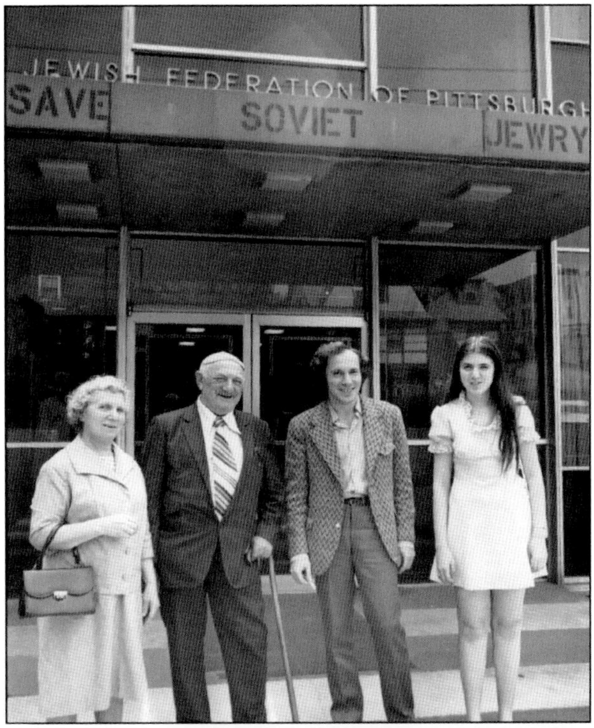

This "Save Soviet Jewry" sign was posted on the United Jewish Federation building on McKee Place in Oakland. The United Jewish Federation spearheaded efforts to encourage the release of Jews from Russia and aid in their resettlement in Pittsburgh, mainly through the auspices of the Jewish Family and Children's Service.

Pittsburgh prepared to welcome and help resettle the Soviet émigrés coming into the city. A New American Resettlement Committee was formed, comprised of representatives from a number of Jewish organizations. This scene is of a dance sponsored by the committee on behalf of Soviet Jewish immigrants in 1981.

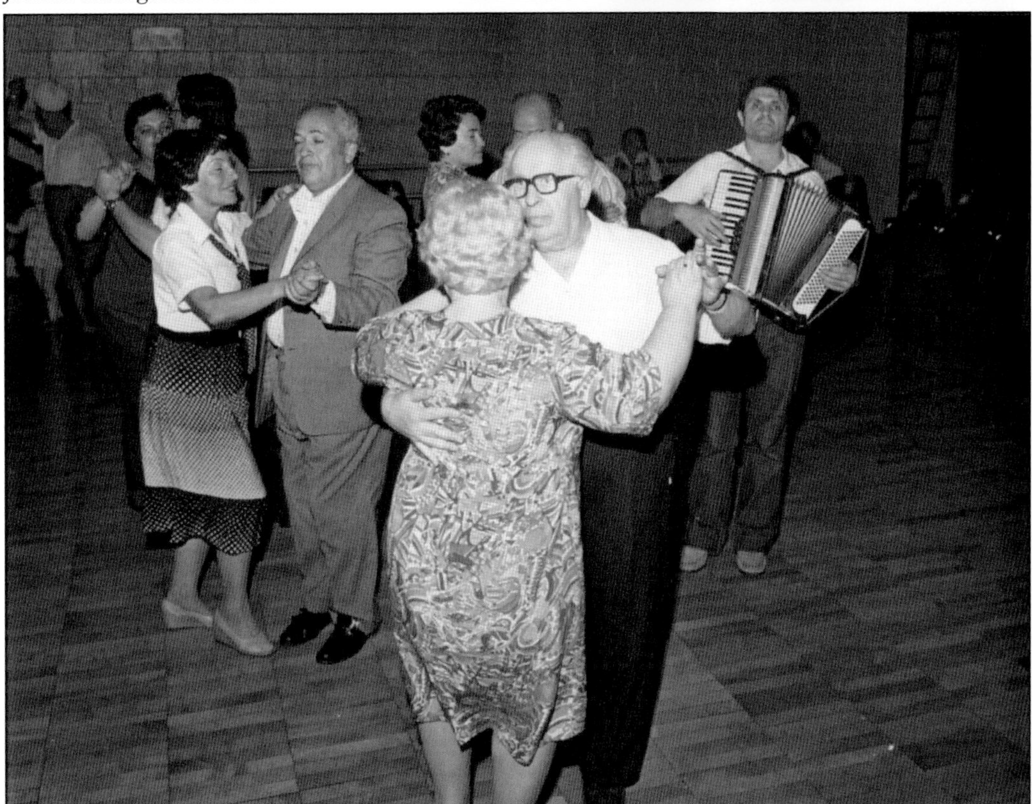

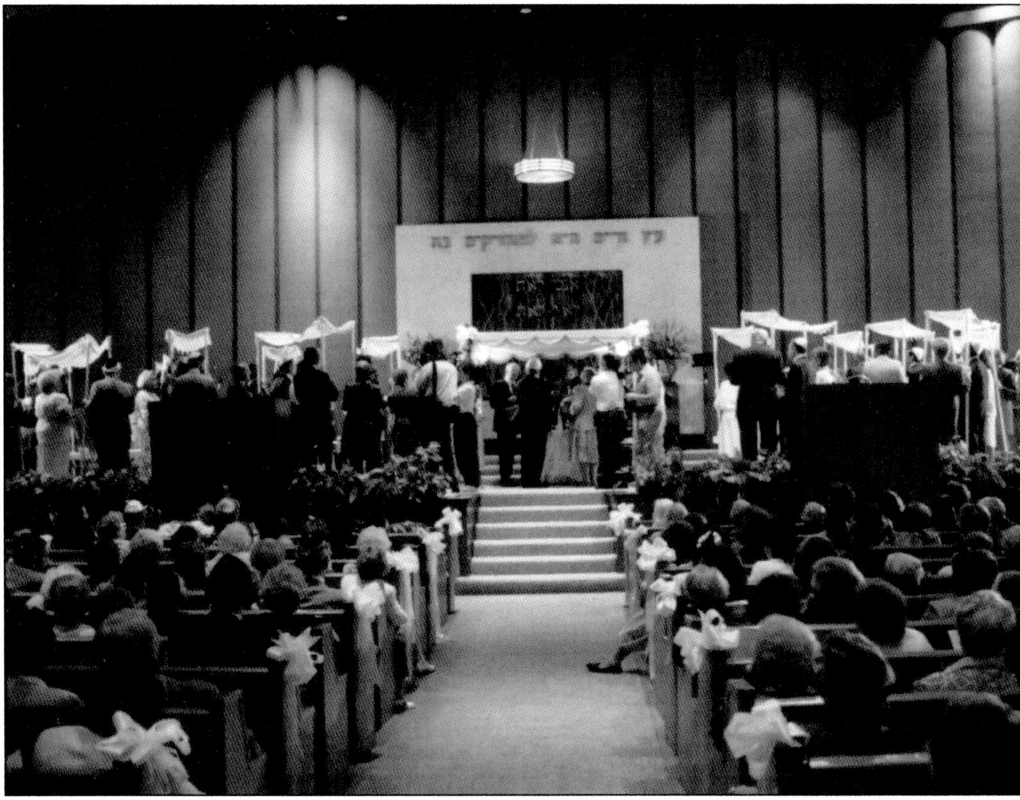

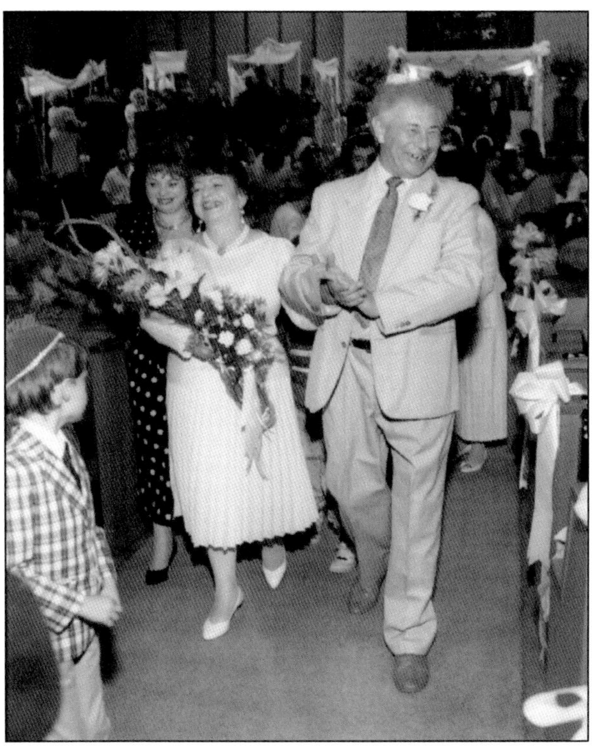

The Geshiktors were one of the families arriving in Pittsburgh from the Soviet Union. They had been married in the Soviet Union in 1952, but when they came to the United States, they wanted a Jewish wedding, something that was prohibited in Russia. The Pittsburgh chapter of the National Council of Jewish Women sponsored a gala evening for those couples who wanted to have a religious ceremony. On September 10, 1990, Svetlana and Semyon Geshiktor stood under the chuppah, or bridal canopy, at the Tree of Life Congregation in Squirrel Hill to be married by Rabbi Morris Landes. An additional 13 other couples that night had their turn as well amid much fanfare and celebration.

Three

Making a Living

Pittsburgh was famous for its mines and mills, but that was not where the Jews were. They were traditionally merchants and shopkeepers. This was certainly true for the German Jewish immigrants of the mid-19th century. The Eastern European Jews who began arriving later in the 19th century took whatever jobs they could find near where they lived, often as peddlers or in the stogie factories that dotted the Hill. These blue-collar workers were able to establish a headquarters by 1919 known as the Labor Lyceum, which was the meeting place for Jewish working-class organizations. Catering to the population on the Hill and the business owners who came on weekends to buy supplies for their stores in small towns outside of Pittsburgh, a corridor of largely Jewish-owned businesses developed by the 1920s. Upper Fifth Avenue and the streets on the lower Hill teemed with shoppers who frequented the stores, from kosher delicatessens and markets to apparel and shoe stores.

Enterprising Jews expanded businesses in traditional fields or ventured into new areas. The fact that four of the five downtown department stores early in the 20th century were Jewish-owned is consistent with the Jewish niche in merchandising. The grocery market was cornered by Giant Eagle. The Levinson Brothers was one of a number of Jewish firms in scrap metal. Herman Fineberg, the Starks, and the Ostrow family all went into the industrial laundry business. Isaac Frank, a trained engineer, established the United Manufacturing Company; the Lehman brothers organized the Blaw-Knox Company. With a determination to achieve a higher education, Pittsburgh had its share of Jewish doctors, lawyers, and dentists. Some of these people became major players in their respective fields, and their success enabled them to become important philanthropists. This was certainly the case with the Falks, Lehmans, Kaufmanns, Robinsons, Posners, Katzes, and others. Both the Jewish and non-Jewish communities have benefitted from their largesse.

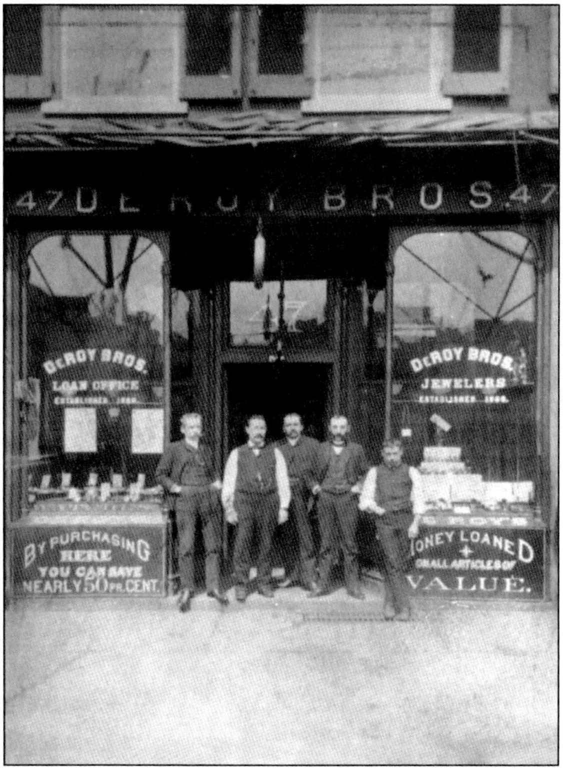

The DeRoy brothers, Joseph, Israel, and Abraham, were part of a contingent of more than 10 families from Holland in the 1850s and 1860s. These three diamond cutters opened a jewelry store downtown at 47 Smithfield Street that was a fixture for over 100 years. The original business was renamed Joseph DeRoy & Sons after a split in the partnership.

Cass Sunstein had come to America around 1866 from the Suwalk province of Lithuania. Like the Guckenheimer and Wertheimer families before him, Sunstein got into the business of producing high-quality rye whiskey. His son A.J. Sunstein, who succeeded him in 1913, became a state legislator and prominent member of the Jewish community. The firm closed as a result of Prohibition in 1920.

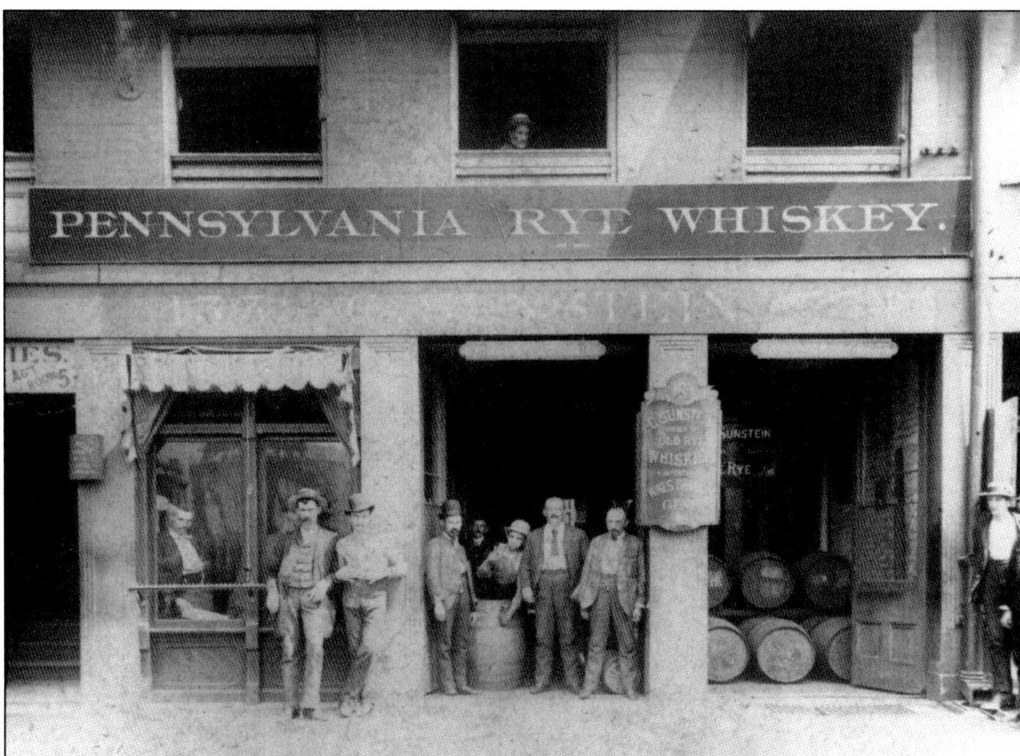

This 1861 bottle was produced by the glassworks of William Frank & Sons, originally known as the Frankstown Glass Works. H.J. Heinz would buy a dozen bottles at a time for his homegrown horseradish when he first started out in 1869. Isaac Frank, William's son, and Howard Heinz, H.J. Heinz's son, became lifelong friends. In 1876, the glassworks burned down and was not rebuilt.

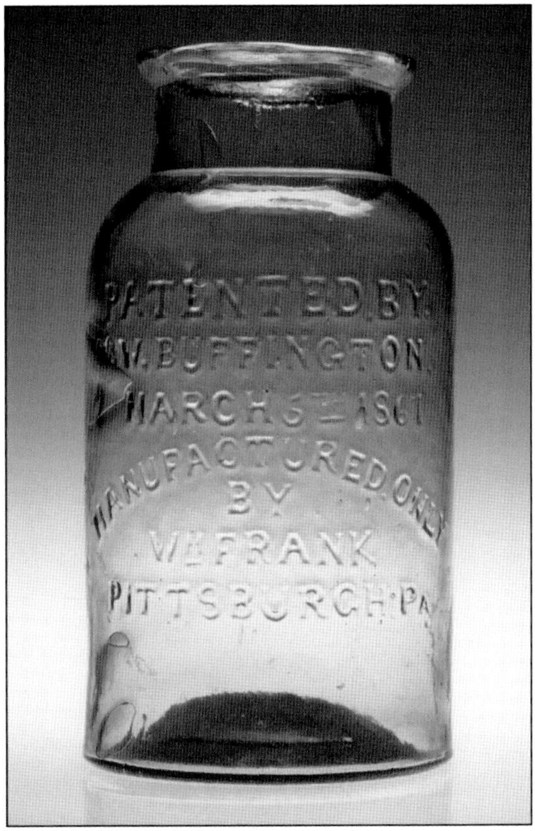

Charles Reizenstein, a German immigrant who came to Pittsburgh in 1866, opened a glass and china store on Federal Street in Allegheny City. The business ultimately moved into its own, much larger building on Liberty Avenue in downtown Pittsburgh. Every year, either he or his son Louis traveled to Europe to purchase items for import. Louis Reizenstein was decorated by the Belgian government for his support of a factory in Liege, Belgium.

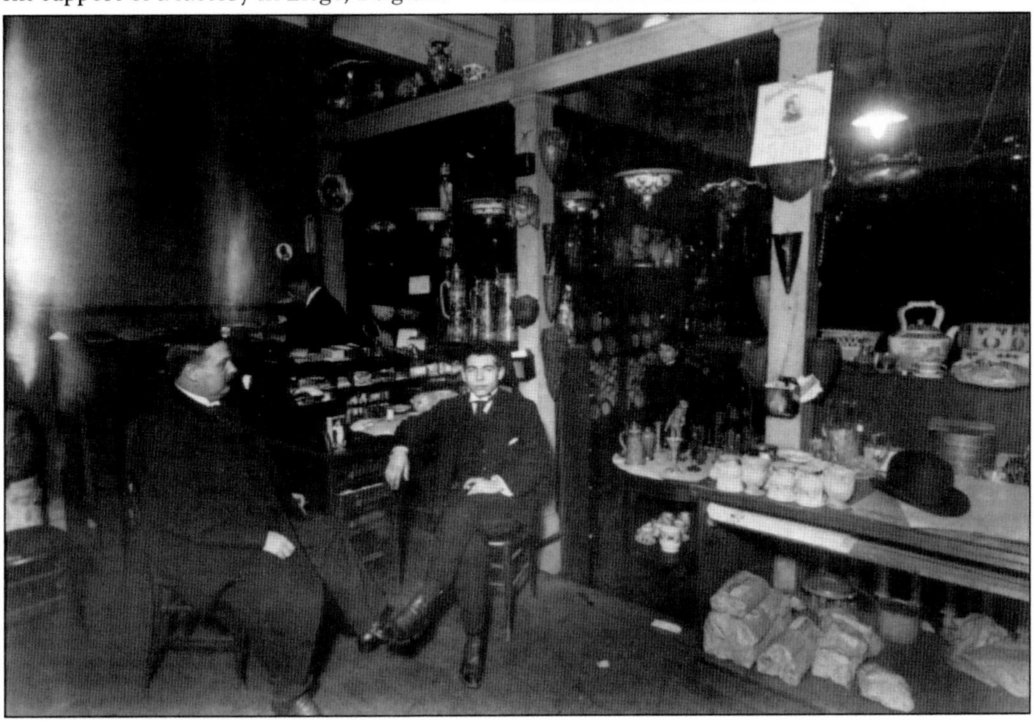

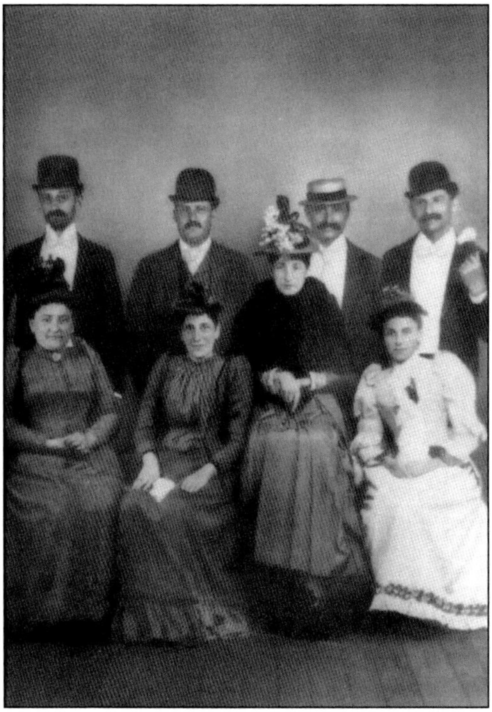

These are pictures of the four Kaufmann brothers and their wives (left) and their first store (below). Jacob came first from Germany in 1868 and was soon followed by Isaac, Morris, and Henry. Initially peddling notions to farmers in western Pennsylvania, they were soon able to open a tiny store on Carson Street on the South Side in 1871. This was the beginning of the Kaufmanns' rise to department store fame. By the early 20th century, Kaufmann's, "the Big Store," was the largest Jewish-owned department store in the city. Its only rival was the Joseph Horne Company. It employed 3,000 people and grossed $10 million a year. Edgar J. Kaufmann, the son of Morris Kaufmann, took over the management of the company in 1914. He married Liliane, who was Isaac Kaufmann's only daughter.

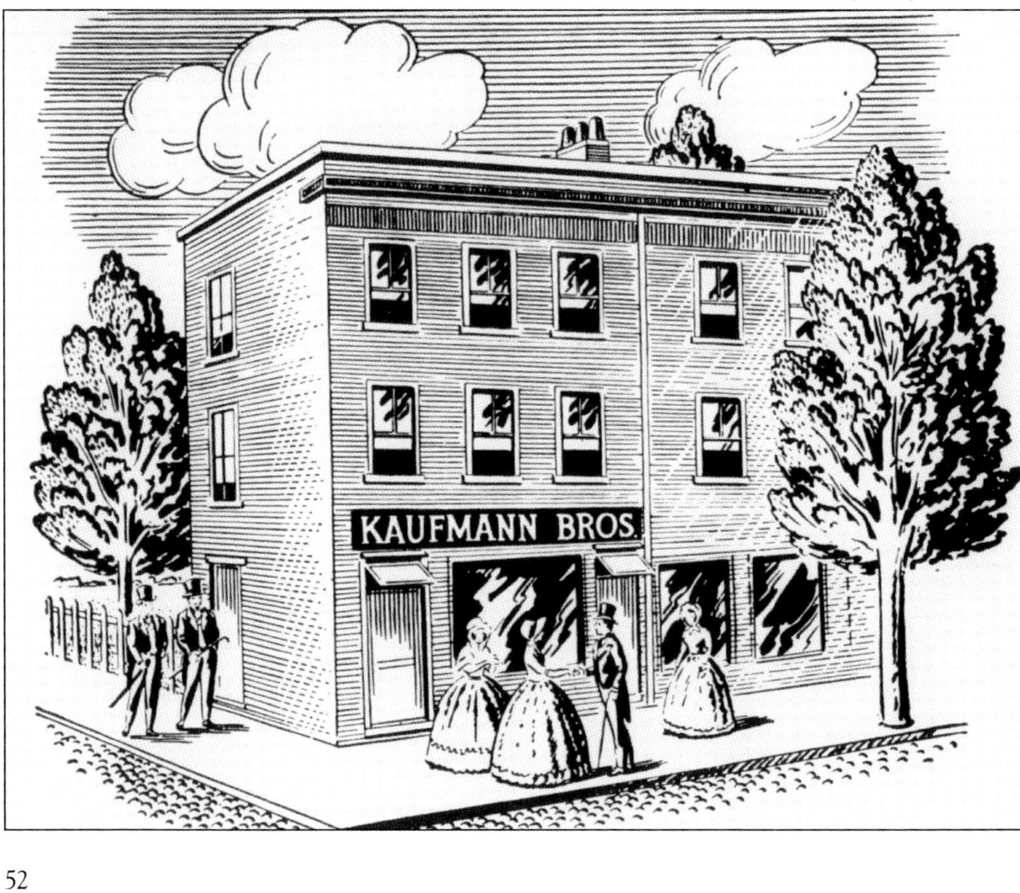

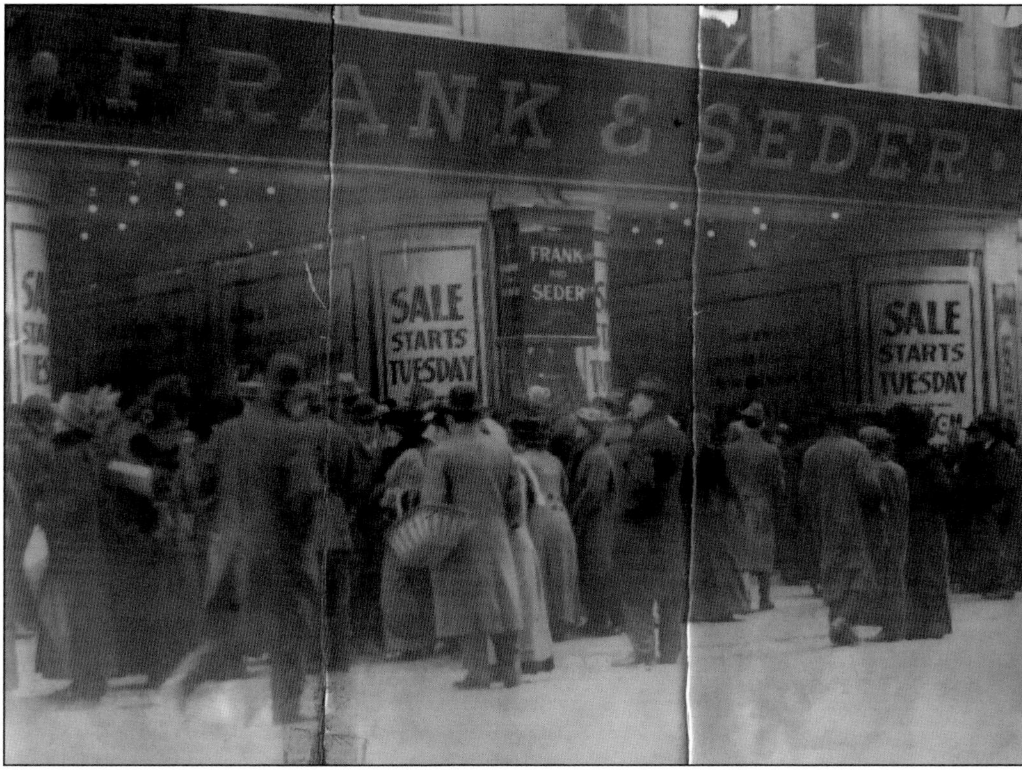

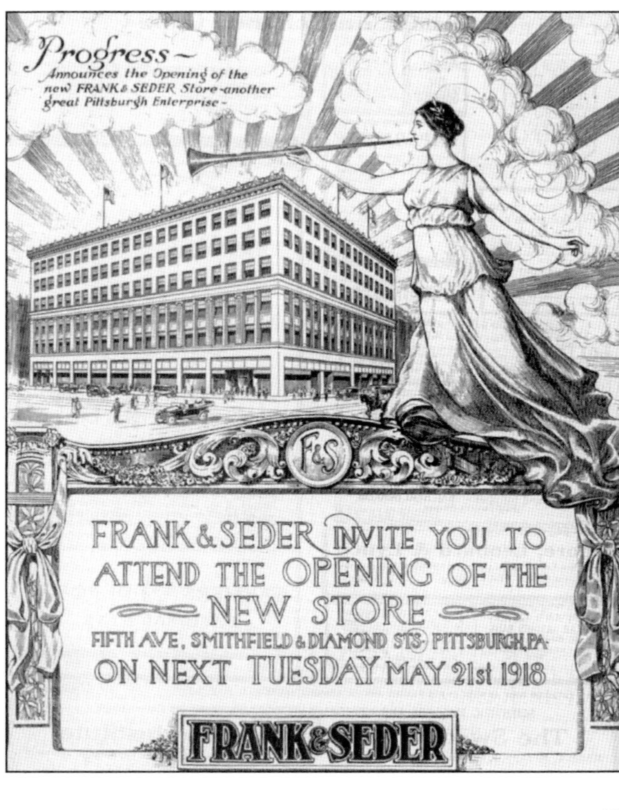

Jacob Frank and Isaac Seder both were immigrants from Russia. In 1907, they opened a retail store on Fifth Avenue and Smithfield Street, but by 1918, they had expanded into an eight-floor store covering the entire block at Fifth Avenue and Diamond (now Forbes) and Smithfield Streets, directly across the street from Kaufmann's. Both Frank and Seder were active in the Jewish community. They were major contributors to the campaign to build Montefiore Hospital and were trustees of Tree of Life Congregation. This Frank & Seder advertisement is from May 17, 1918.

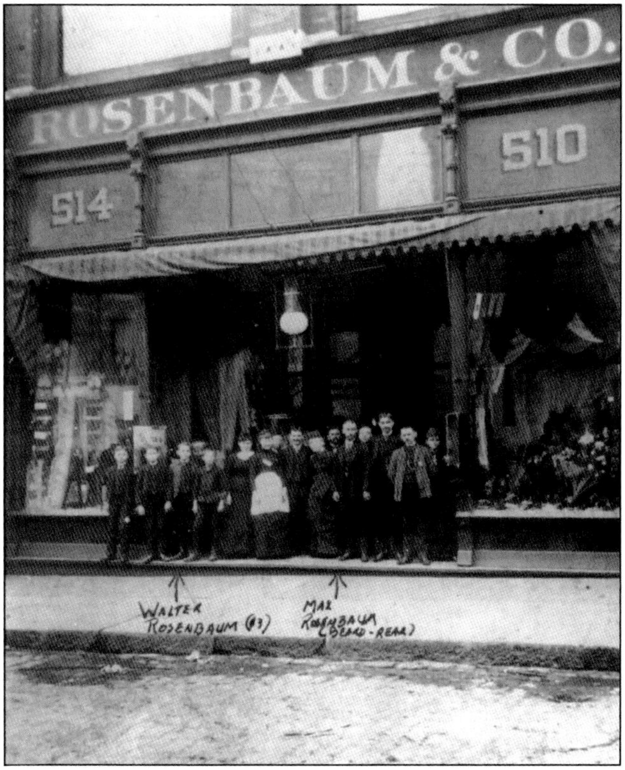

Rosenbaum & Co. was founded in 1868. Max Rosenbaum and his brother-in-law Max Rothschild were both emigrants from Germany. When Rosenbaum died in 1908, Rothschild became president of the firm. In 1915, he built a new department store on Sixth Street between Liberty and Penn Avenues downtown. The store had 2,000 employees. Like the other department store executives, Rothschild was very active in the Jewish community. The advertisement below from October 9, 1925, is for shirts worn by the Pittsburgh Pirates, who had just won the National League pennant on their way to a World Series victory. Barney Dreyfuss, the team owner, is in pictured on the third row, eighth from left.

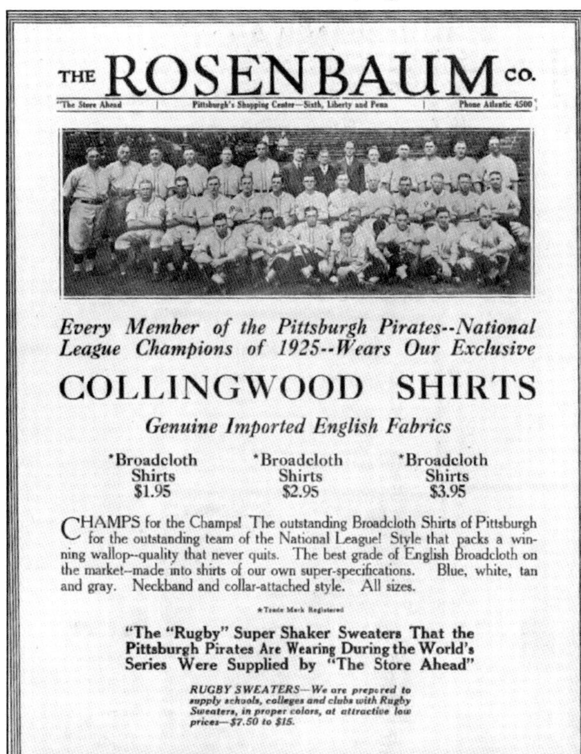

After a dispute with Edgar Kaufmann, several disgruntled executives and Kaufmann relatives opened a new department store in 1913 known as Kaufmann & Baer. Theodore Kaufmann was vice president, and Max Blum, the son-in-law of the late Jacob Kaufmann, was secretary. Morris Baer, who had started at the original Kaufmann's as a stock clerk, was named president of the new company. In 1928, the company was sold to Gimbels.

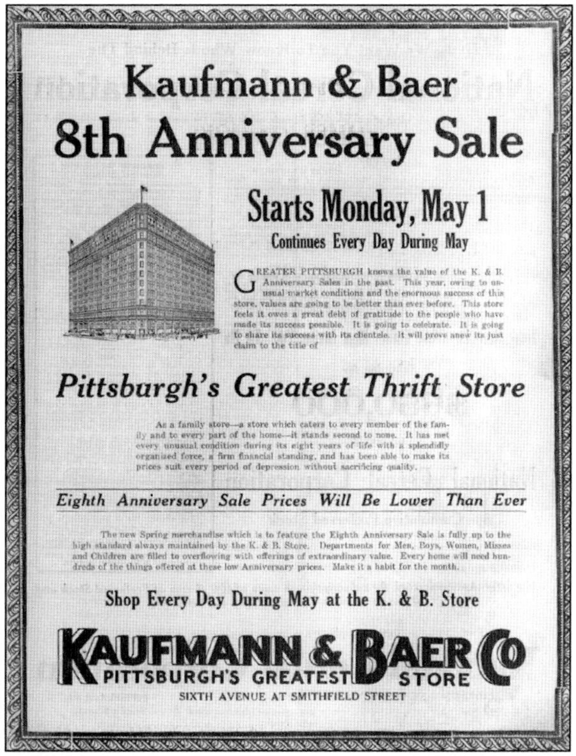

While most Jewish businessmen tended to gravitate to light industry, several Jews went into heavy industry. In 1917, the Blaw-Knox Company was formed when brothers Albert and Irwin Lehman merged their respective business interests. In its heyday, the company was one of the largest producers of specialty steel products. Albert and Irwin were major philanthropists in the Jewish community and beyond.

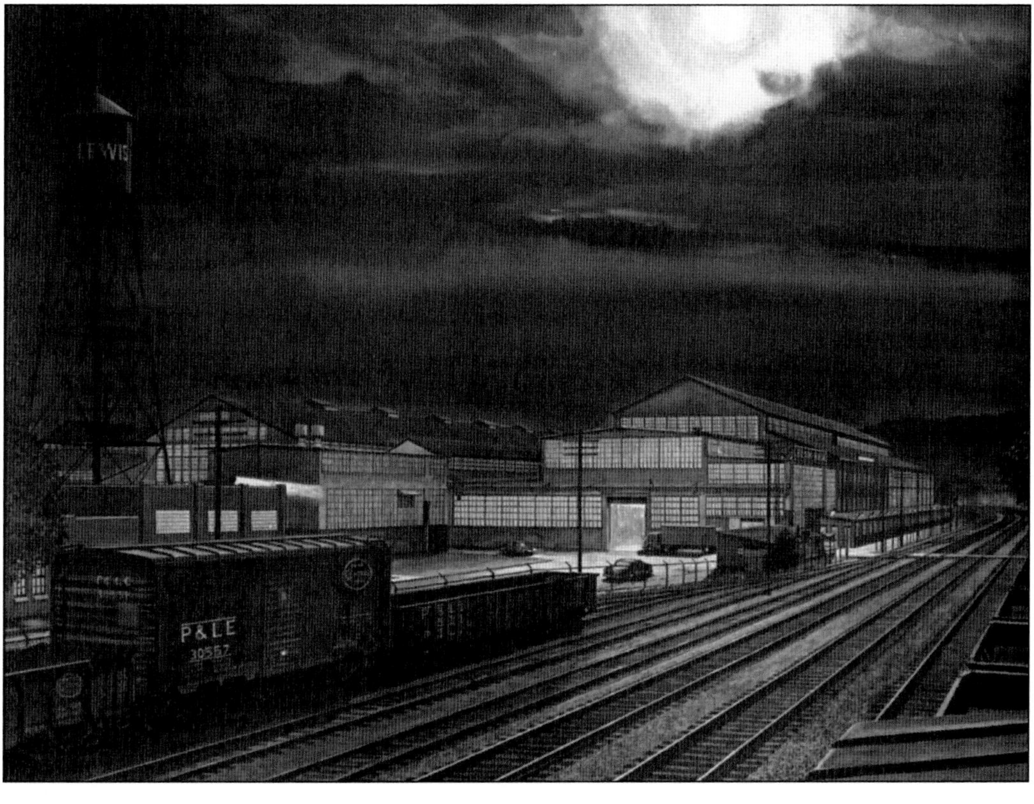

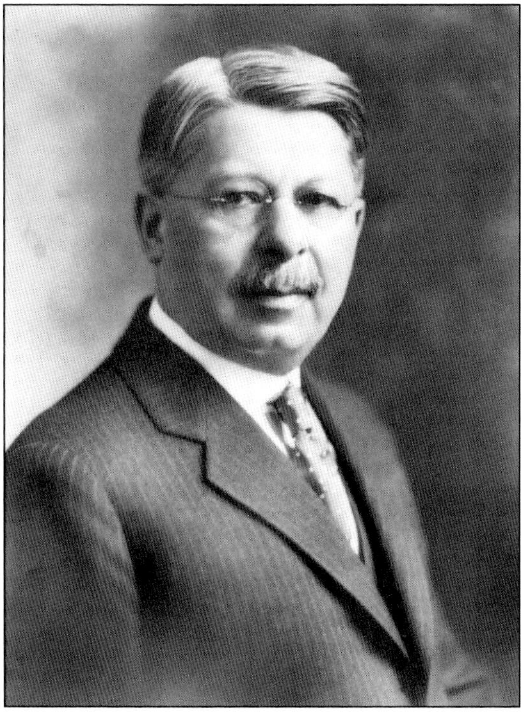

Isaac Frank was the son of Pauline and William Frank. A graduate of the Rensselaer Polytechnic Institute with a degree in civil engineering, he went on to found the United Engineering and Foundry Company in 1901 and later helped form the Weirton Steel Company. A 1908 publication reported that United built the largest rolling mills in the world. It employed 70 engineers and draftsmen and 900 production workers. Frank died in 1930.

The Workmen's Circle (Arbeiter Ring), first organized in New York, was established in Pittsburgh in 1904 by Eastern European immigrants. It had, at one time, more than 1,600 members. It represented the Jewish proletariat on the Hill and provided benefits as well as support for Jewish and non-Jewish strikers. This is a picture of the Workman's Circle 35th Anniversary Committee in 1939.

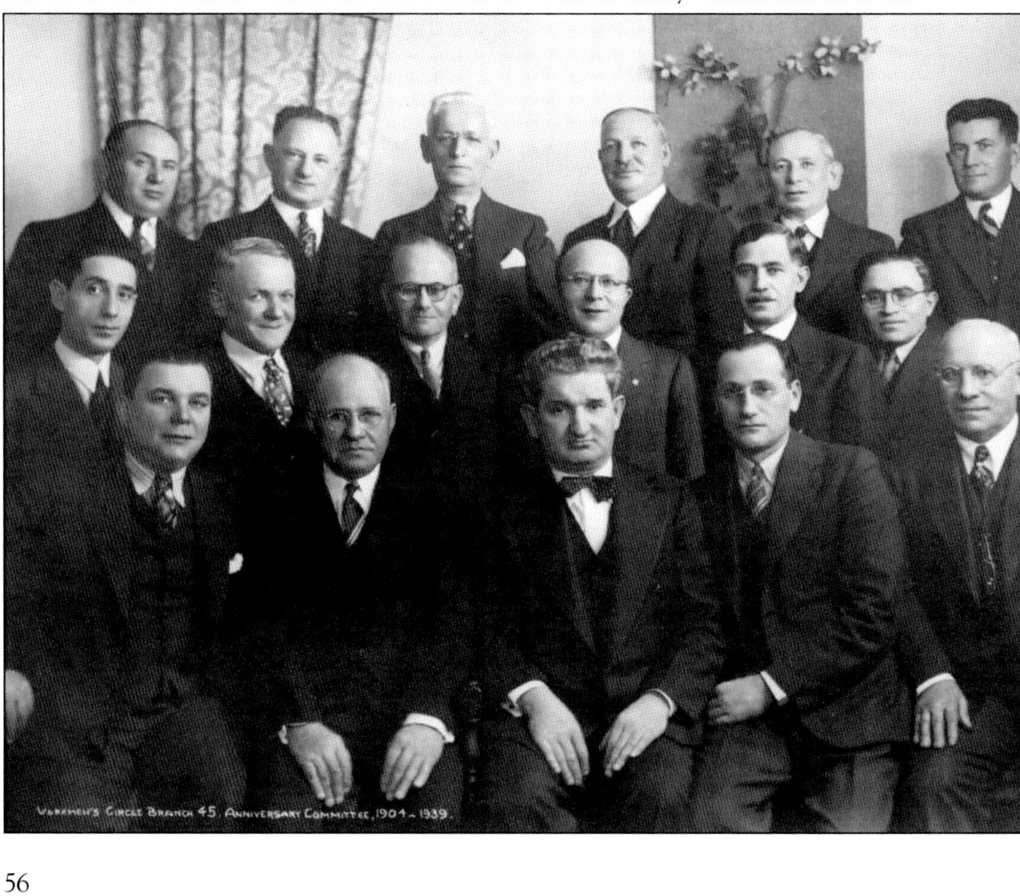

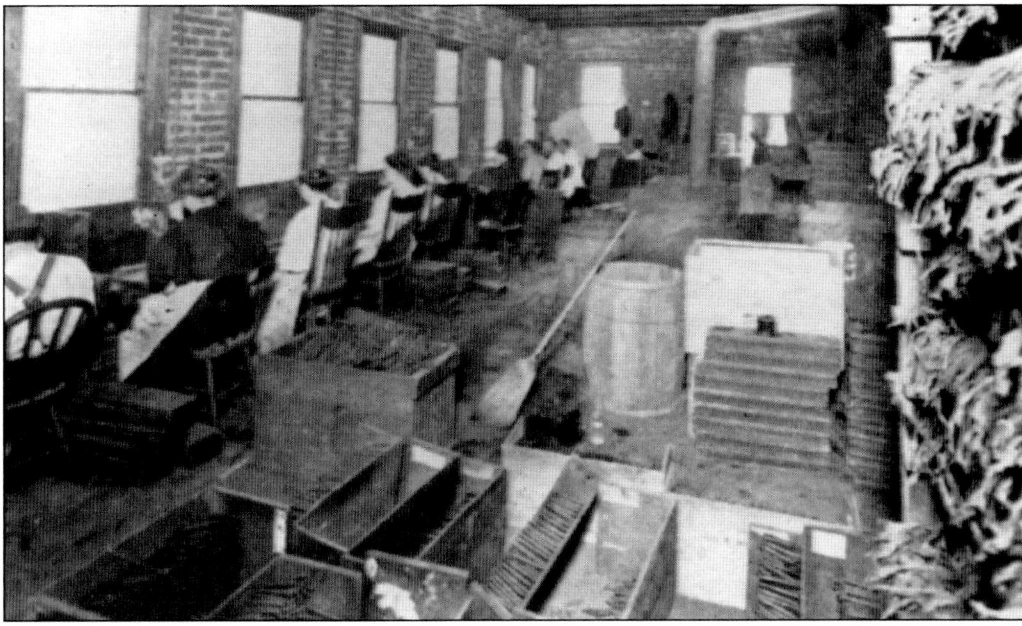

Stogie manufacturing, as seen in this picture, was a common occupation for poor Eastern European Jews, particularly women. The stogies, which were inexpensive cigars, were very popular. These sweatshops blanketed the Hill.

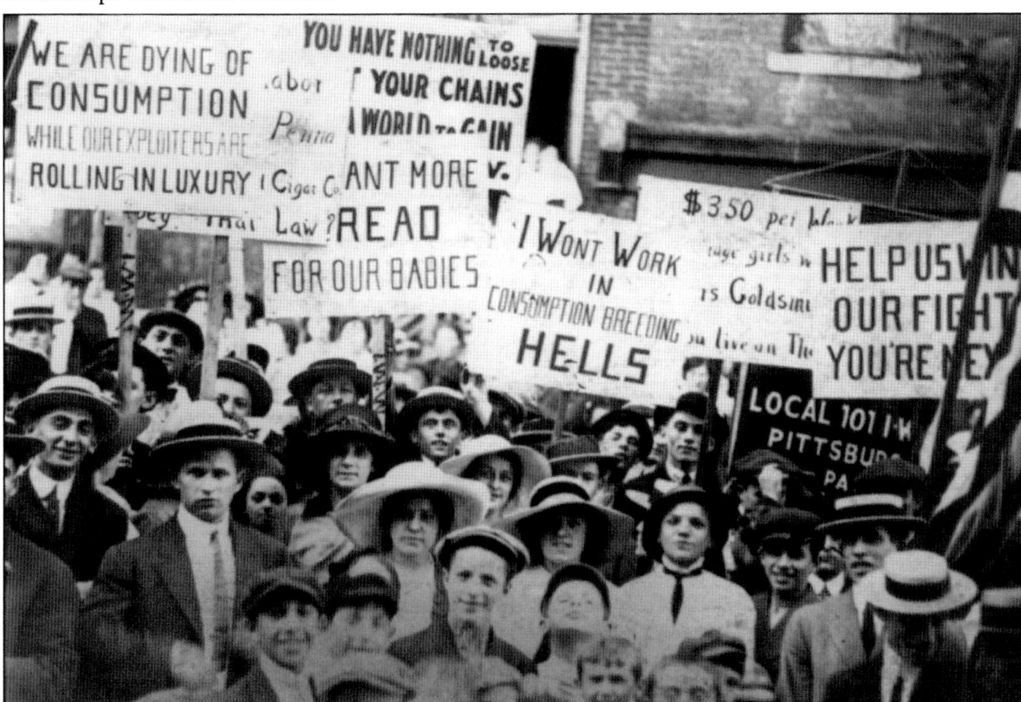

In 1912 and again in 1913, stogie workers went on strike to improve their working conditions. These are strikers at the Penn Cigar factory. While a four-month strike in 1913 was considered a success, it was a Pyrrhic victory since the strike crippled the industry in Pittsburgh, giving Cleveland a much greater market share. (Walter P. Reuther Library, Wayne State University.)

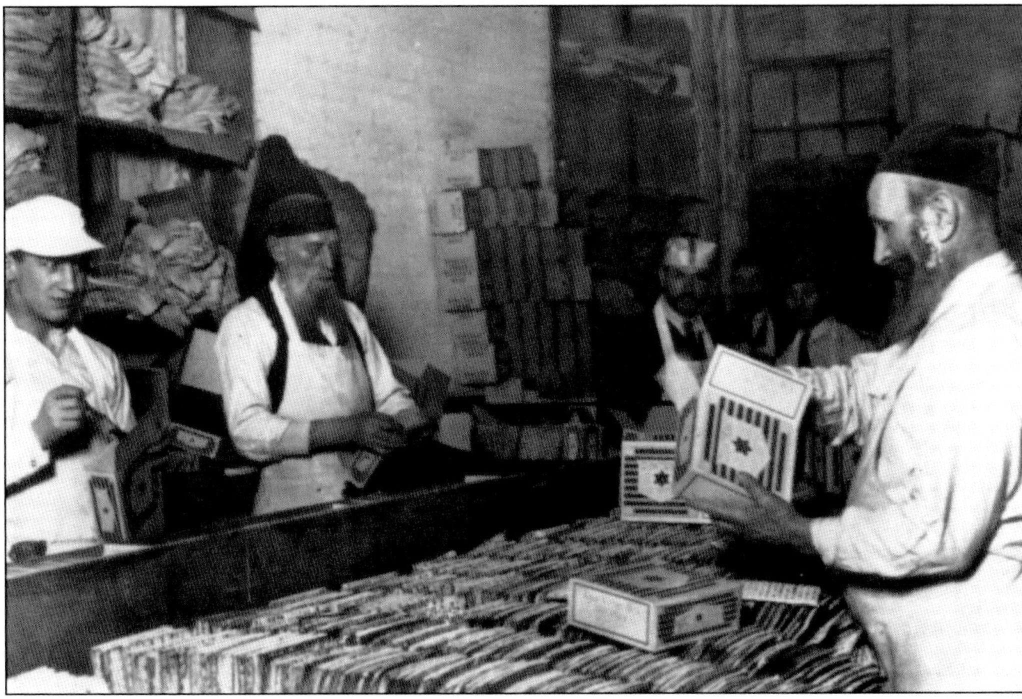

The men are working in Caplan's Bakery, a popular bakery on the Hill. Jacob Radford (second from left, Gloria Elbling's grandfather) is baking matzo, the traditional food on the Jewish holiday of Passover. In addition to the Stogie Workers Union with which Jews were affiliated, Jews had organized the Hebrew Bakers Union.

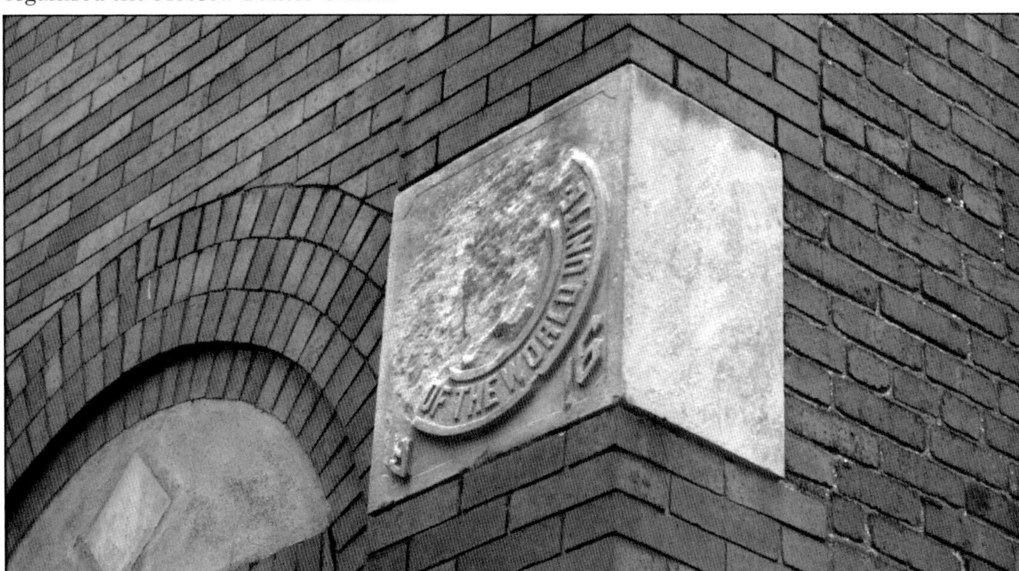

The Labor Lyceum was built in 1916 on the Hill after a nearly 10-year fundraising campaign. It housed all the activities of the various Socialist organizations and trade unions in the city. By 1930, with labor bitterly split between Socialists and Communists and with the onset of the Depression, the building was sold. However, the money from the sale was lost when the bank holding the funds failed.

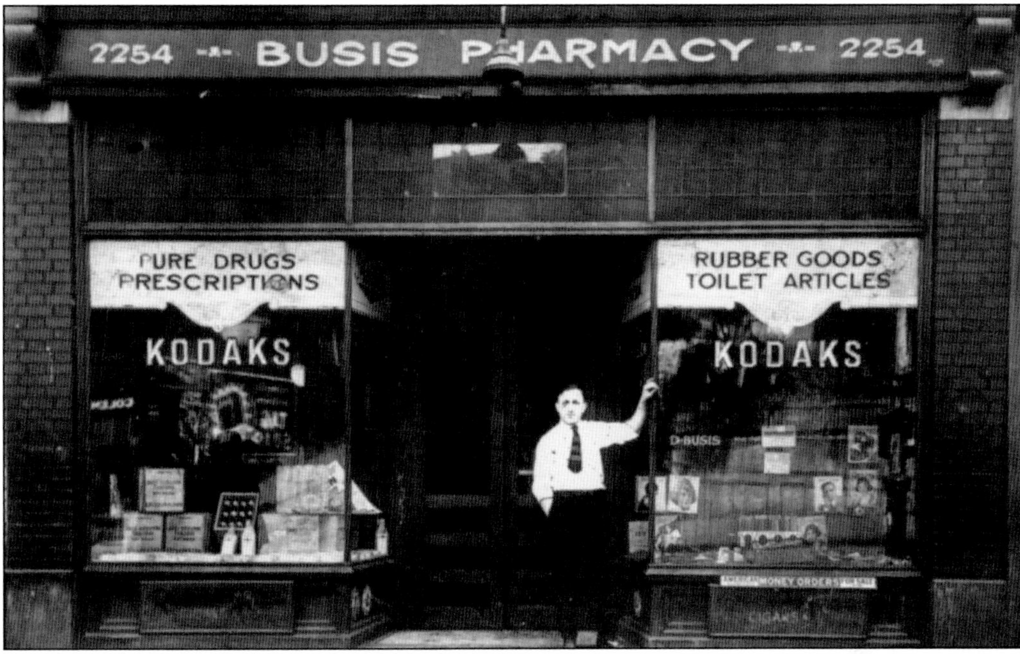

While many Jews were factory workers, others were able to open up small shops, often after peddling. David Busis had a pharmacy on the Hill. He organized a boycott of German pharmaceuticals in response to Hitler's attack on Jewish businesses in Germany. His son Sydney became a highly respected physician.

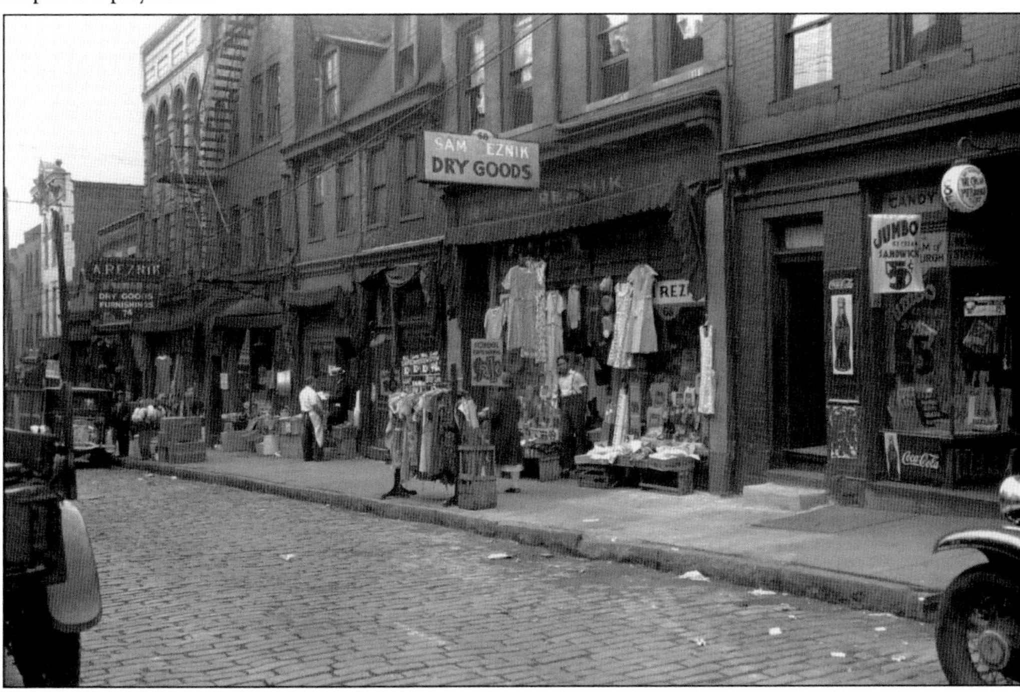

Sam Reznik had a small store on Logan Street on the Hill, in the same block as Caplan's Bakery. He sold dry goods and later moved to Fifth Avenue. Abe Reznik, his brother, had a dry goods shop down the street. Sam's granddaughter is Rochelle Blumenfeld, the artist.

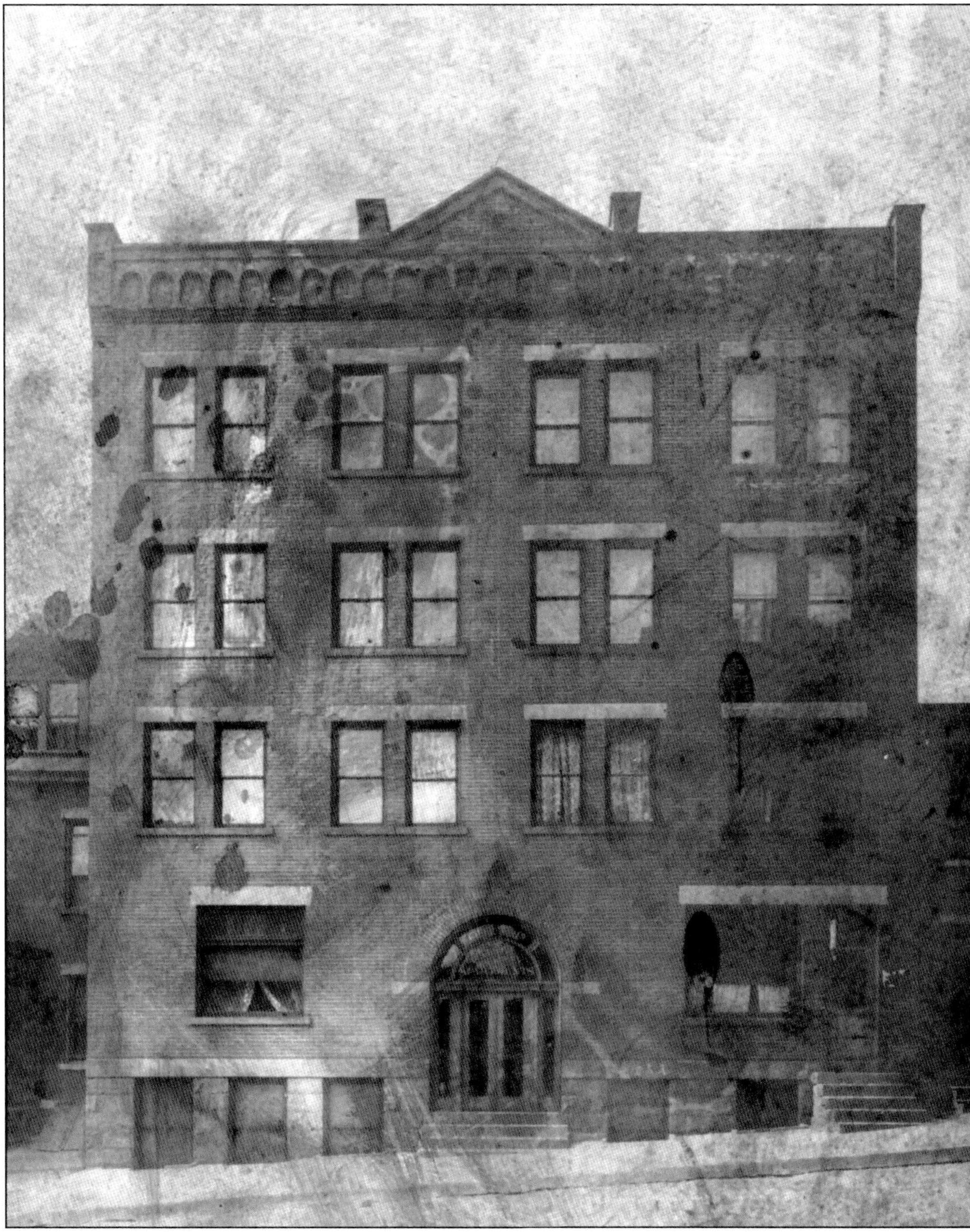

The Kalson Bath House, or Kalson's Natatorium as it was formally known, was a community institution on Franklin Street in the lower Hill, which was the site of the Civic Arena's parking lot. Since most apartments in the early 20th century did not have indoor plumbing, bathhouses were of great importance on the Hill. Men and women went on separate days. Elhanan (Huna) Kalson and his wife came to Pittsburgh from Lithuania in 1891. In 1895, he was the first Jew to receive a master plumber certificate.

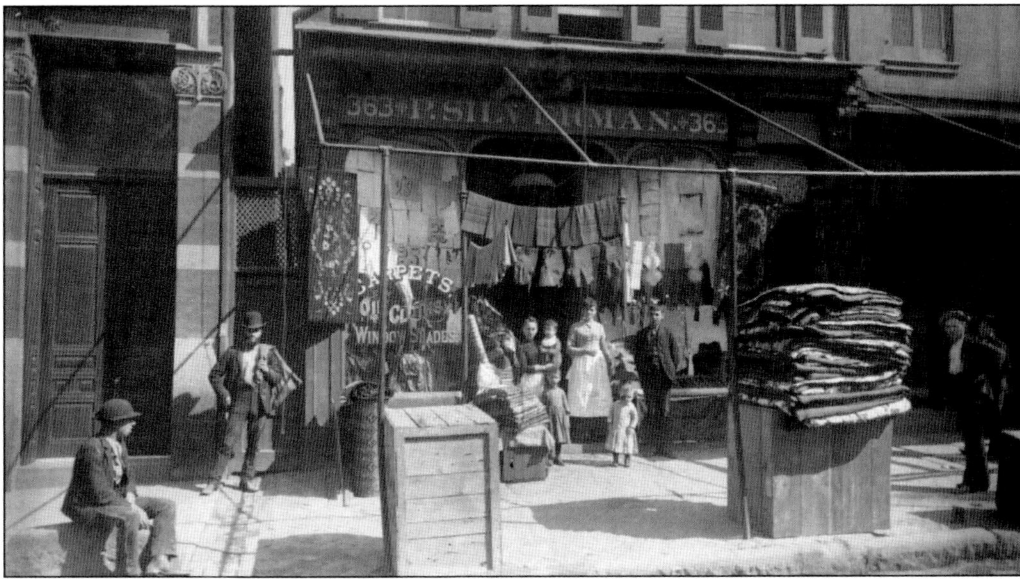

The Silverman store was on Fifth Avenue. While his immigrant father made a living as a small shopkeeper on the Hill, Alexander, born in 1881, became head of the Department of Chemistry at the University of Pittsburgh at a time when there were few Jews on the faculty. He also was a consultant to some of the biggest glassmakers in America and an expert on the art of glassmaking.

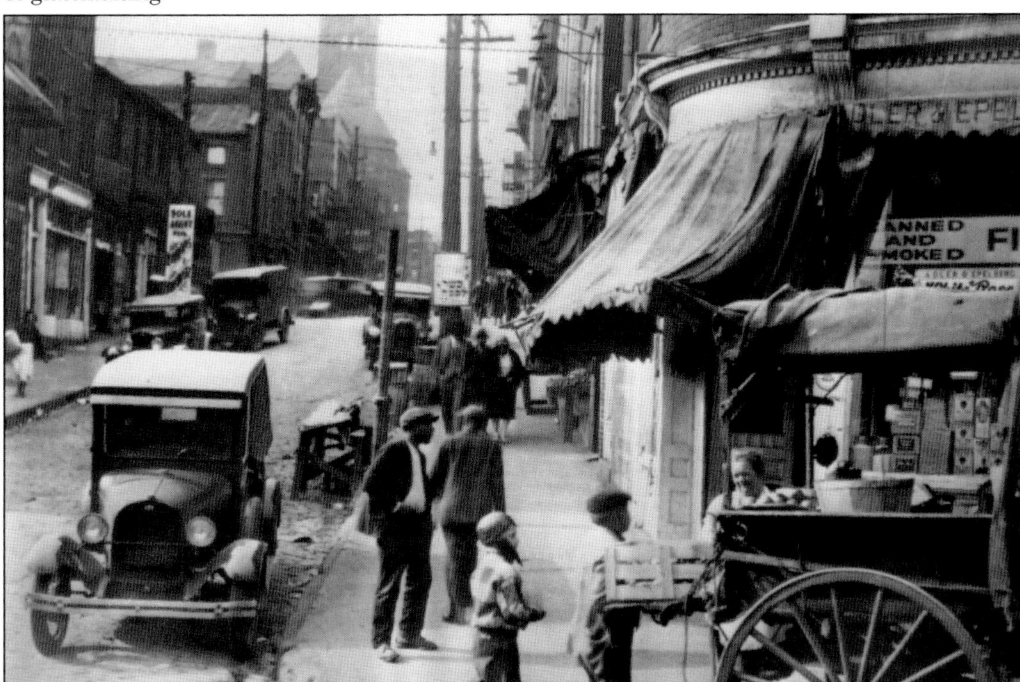

Colwell Street in the lower Hill in 1927 was teeming with all manner of shops catering to its Jewish-immigrant customers. It also was notorious for its "houses of ill repute," which caused Jewish communal leaders at the Irene Kaufmann Settlement much consternation. Anna B. Heldman and others attempted, mostly unsuccessfully, to close the prostitution business down.

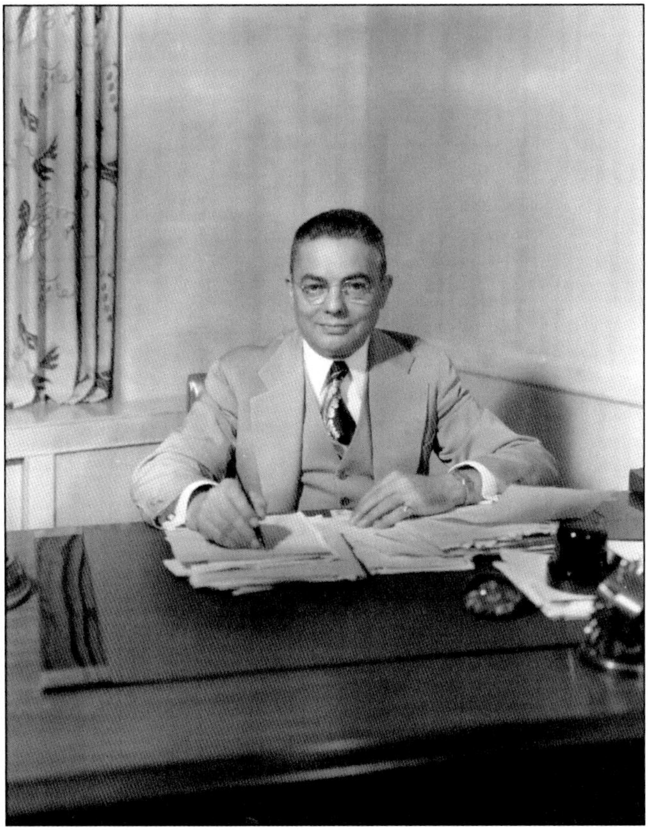

Julius Halpern became the banker to many local businessmen who could not get loans from more established Pittsburgh banks. Immigrating to the United States in 1907, he became an importer and manufacturer of toys and costumes. In 1944, he joined the Washington Trust Bank and increased the bank's loan portfolio twentyfold. His sons Irving and Bernard joined him in business. Active in the Jewish community, Halpern died in 1962.

As Jews moved off the Hill, they took their businesses with them or established new ones. Harry Wald opened a grocery store at 2134 Murray Avenue in Squirrel Hill in 1920. Wald's, Steinberg's kosher butcher, and Benkovitz's fish store were the earliest food shops on Murray Avenue.

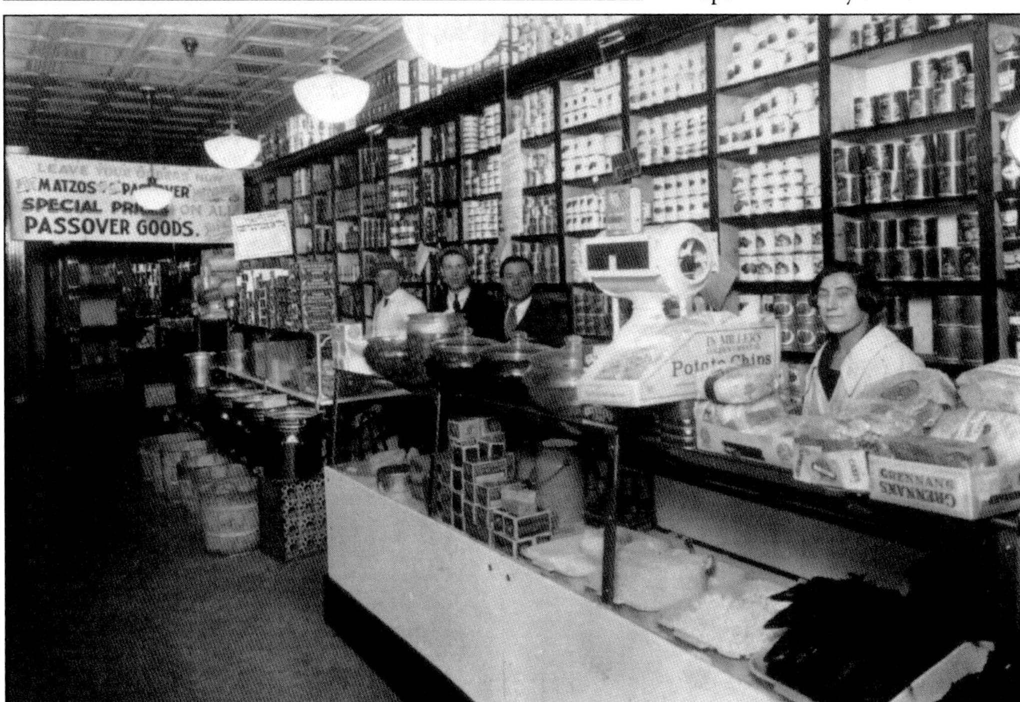

Catering to the Jewish community in Squirrel Hill is this kosher wines store in 1947. (Pittsburgh City Photography Collection, Archives Service Center, University of Pittsburgh.)

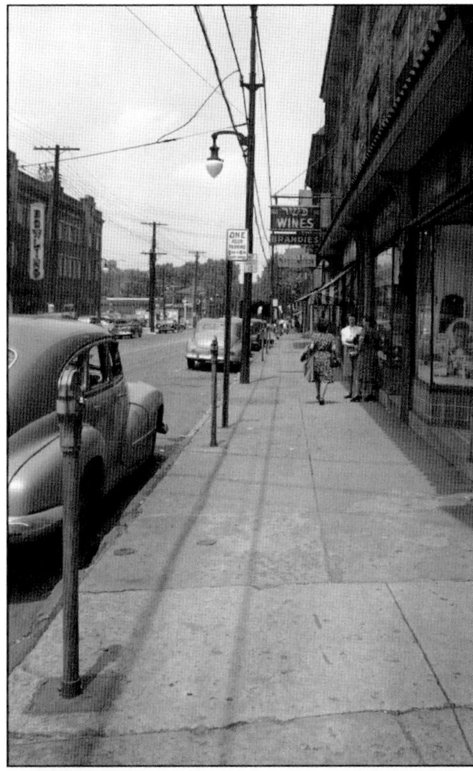

Lee Byron Foster was born in 1881 and started the L.B. Foster Company in 1902 with $5,000 lent to him by his father, who had an oil field supply company. Brothers Sidney, Reuben, and Byron were brought in as the business expanded from selling abandoned rail lines to coal companies to the manufacture of steel sheet pilings used in foundations.

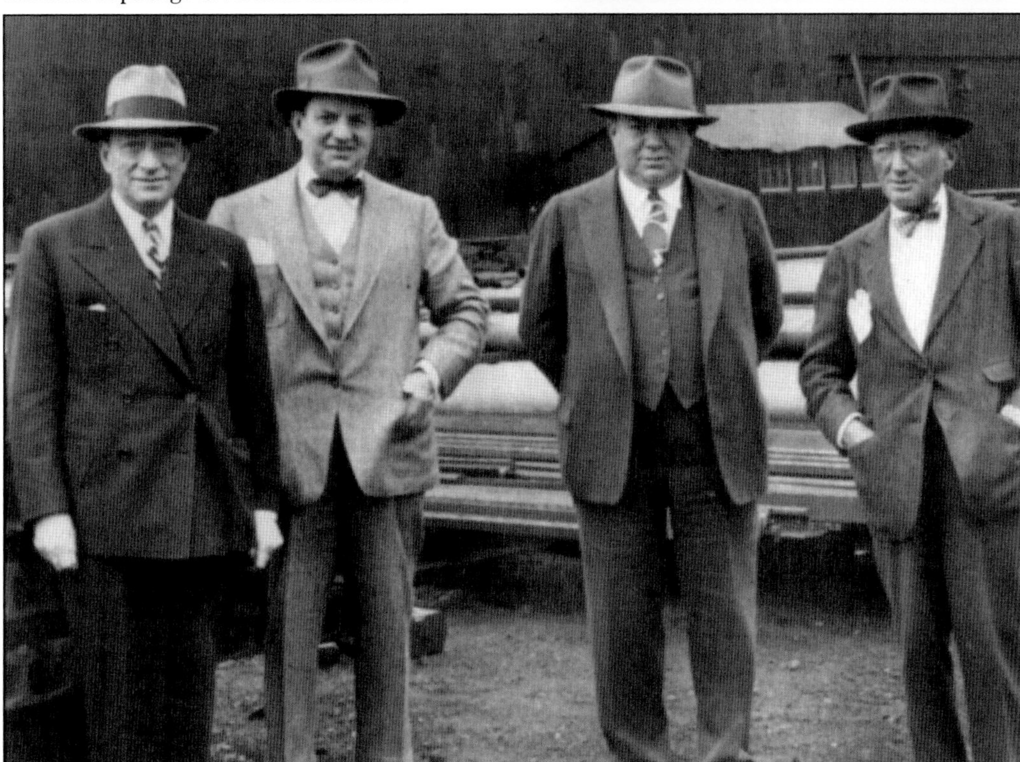

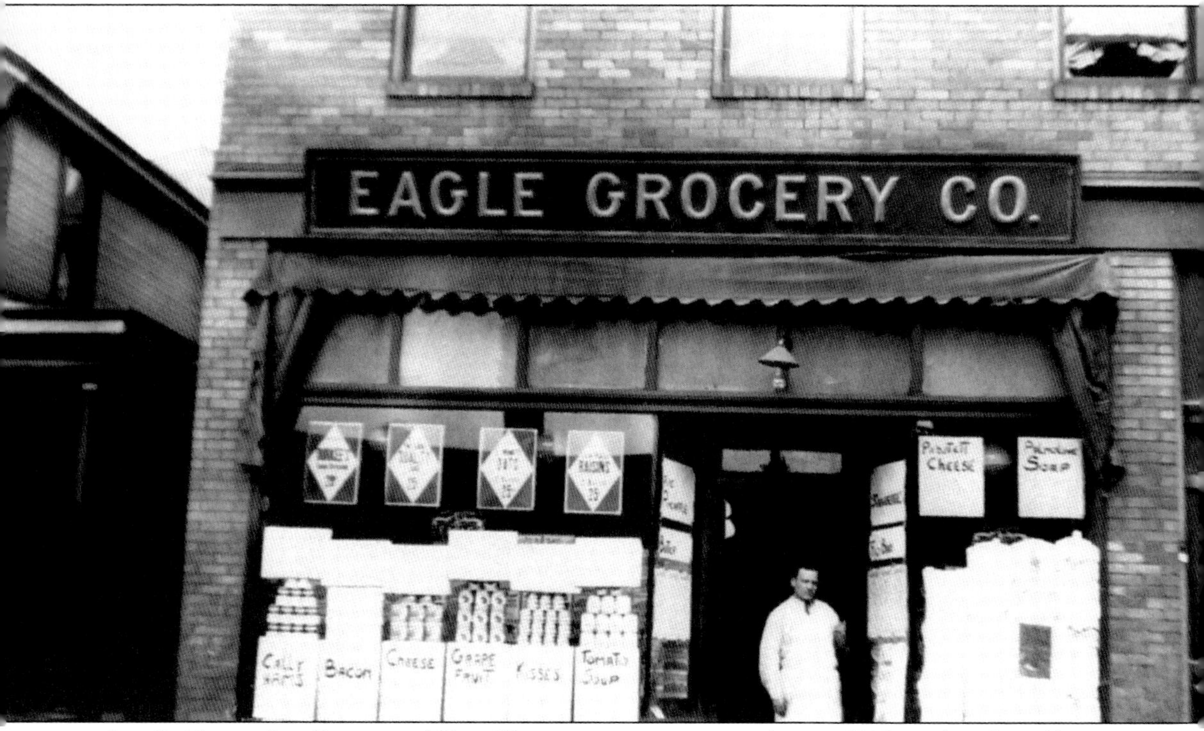

Joe Goldstein, Joe Porter, and Ben Chait went into partnership in 1918, and within 10 years, their 125 Eagle Grocery stores were sold to the Kroger Company. Meanwhile, Hyman Moravitz and Morris Weizenbaum were building the successful OK Grocery stores. These five, who had all struggled just to make a living, went into business together in 1931, and Giant Eagle was born.

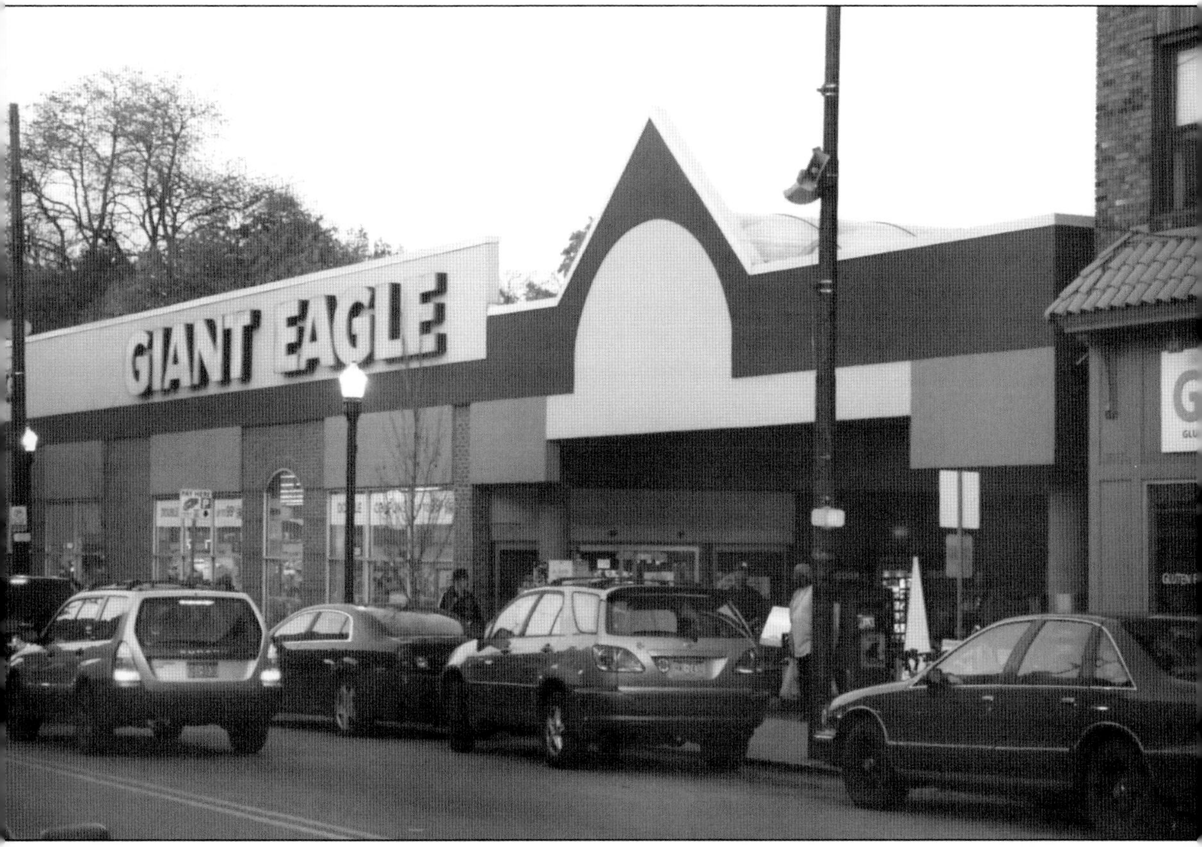

Today, Giant Eagle is a household name. Its brand is in 420 locations, with 220 supermarkets and 200 GetGo stations. It has 36,000 employees, does $9.6 billion in annual sales, and is the 21st-largest privately owned company in the United States. The Giant Eagle Foundation has contributed millions of dollars and tons of food to a host of communal causes and organizations, largely in the Pittsburgh area.

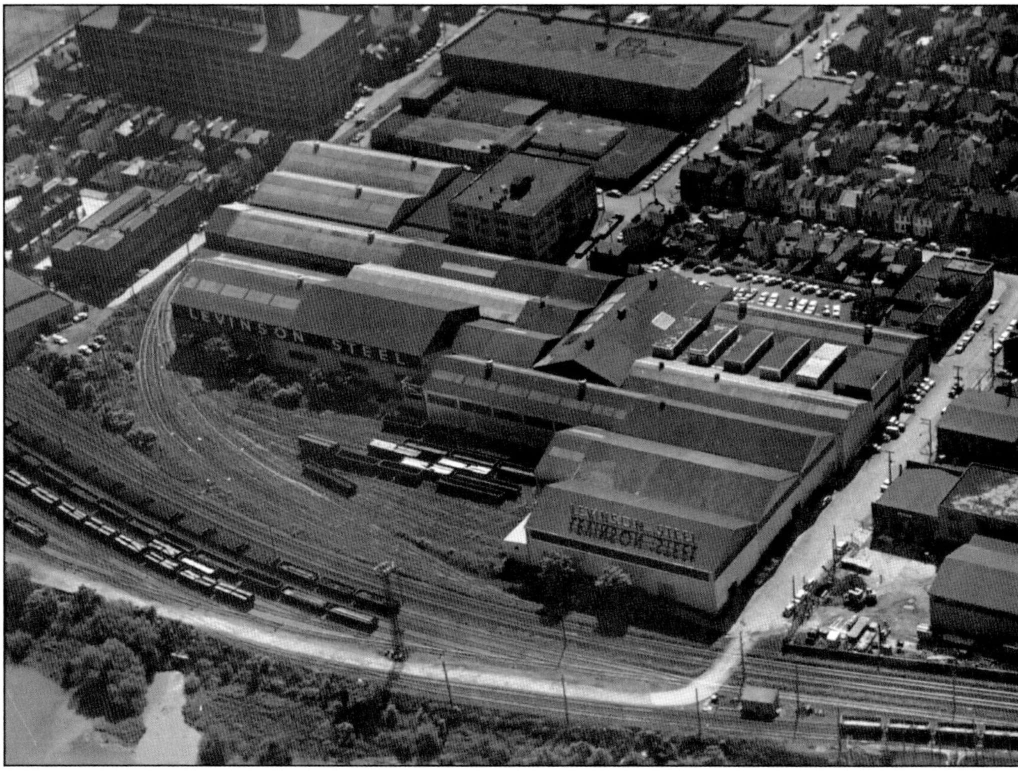

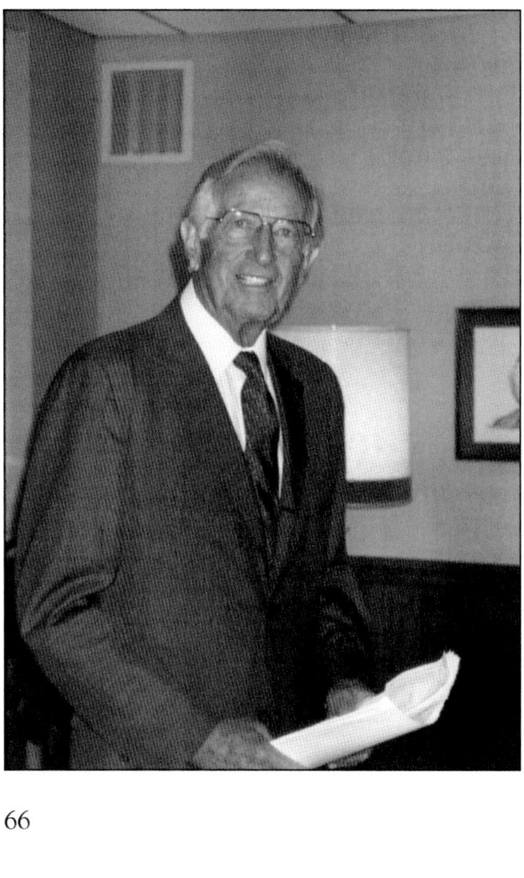

James Levinson started as a scrap metal dealer with a horse and wagon on the Hill. By 1926, he was in the steel-fabricating business on the South Side, becoming the nation's 11th-largest steel fabricator, employing some 3,000 people. Levinson did work on the World Trade Center in New York City. Foreign competition forced the business to close in 1980. Aaron Levinson, James's eldest grandson, was a prominent civic leader.

The son of Russian immigrants, Jack Buncher rose from a scrap metal dealer to real estate tycoon. At the time of his death at age 90 in 2001, the *Pittsburgh Post-Gazette* noted that he had acquired "one of the largest real estate portfolios ever accumulated in Pittsburgh." In 1974, he established the Buncher Foundation, which has supported multiple nonprofits in and out of Pittsburgh. (Buncher Foundation.)

Henry Posner Jr. was born in 1918. He graduated from Shady Side Academy and Princeton University. His father was in the outdoor advertising business, which Henry Jr. joined in 1946. He later established the Pittsburgh Outdoor Advertising Company. Posner, who died in 2011, gave millions to Carnegie Mellon University, Shadyside Hospital, the Children's Rehabilitation Institute, Rodef Shalom, and to Jews in the former Soviet Union. (Posner family.)

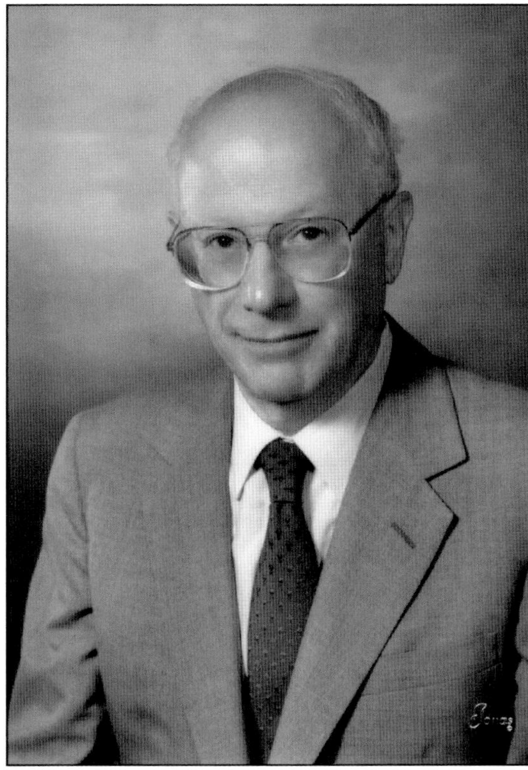

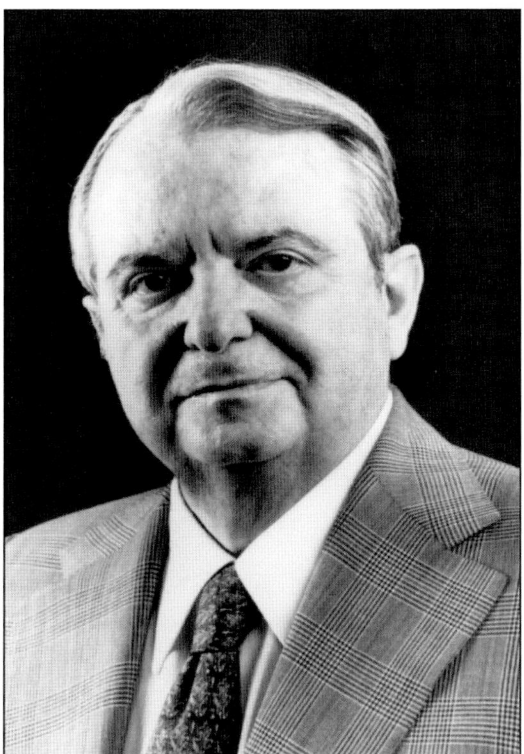

In 1914, eleven-month-old Joe Katz fled the pogroms of Czarist Russia with his parents just one month before the start of World War I. Raised on the Hill, he started designing and printing handbills, ultimately founding PaperCraft, which became a publicly held corporation listed on the New York Stock Exchange. Katz was an art collector and was a major contributor to the University of Pittsburgh School of Business, which is now called the Katz School of Business. (Katz family.)

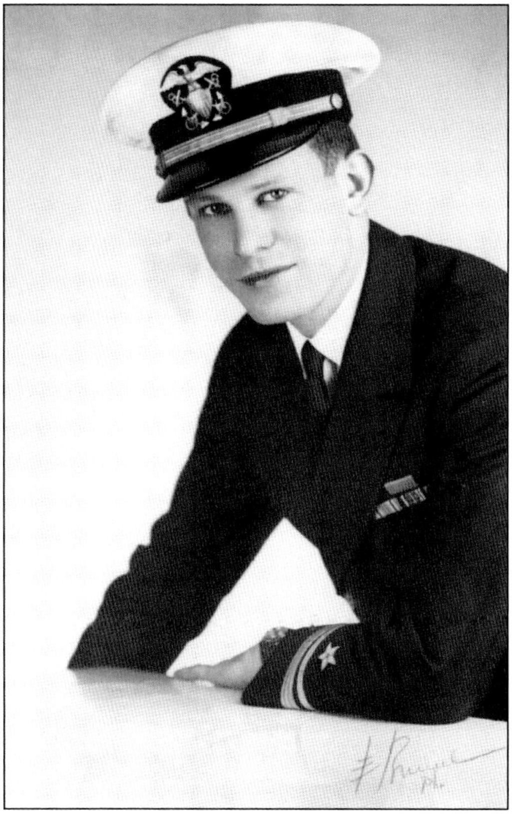

Ray Rackoff was in the Navy during World War II. After completing metallurgical engineering studies at Carnegie Tech, Rackoff joined the company founded by his father-in-law, Benjamin Weinberg. The company, started during the Depression in 1933, provides specialty industrial tools and replacement parts and today has hundreds of employees worldwide. Rackoff, who became president in 1962, died in 1996.

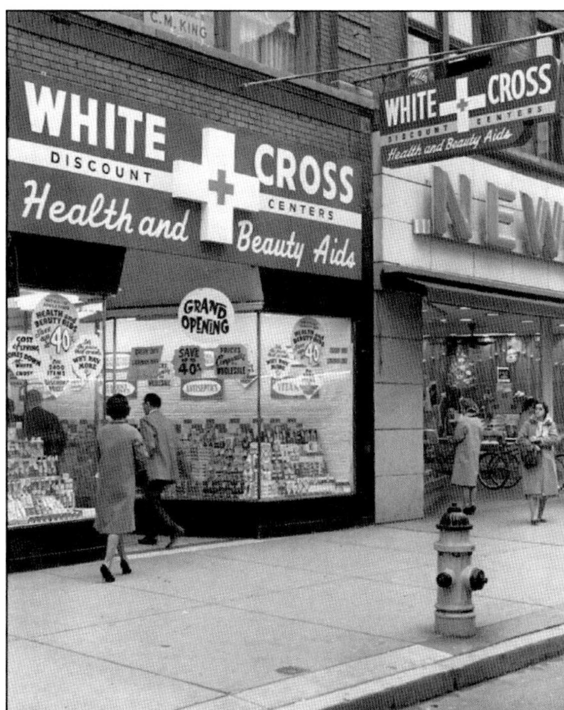

After World War II, Alex Robinson, a Lithuanian immigrant, was joined by his sons Harold, Donald, and Sanford in the wholesale tobacco and candy business. They pioneered health and beauty-aid departments in supermarkets, with A&P as a major customer, and developed the White Cross discount drugstore concept. Within 11 years, White Cross grew from a single store to 200 stores and merged into Revco. (Robinson family.)

Four

Community Institutions

At one point in the 1920s, there were more than 300 Jewish organizations and agencies of various sizes in Pittsburgh. The extent of the Jewish communal infrastructure was (and still is) impressive. This plethora of organizations, agencies, and institutions has long characterized Jewish communities, and Pittsburgh is no exception. Jewish educational establishments have been very important in the life of the community. Earlier efforts in after-school education included the Hebrew Institute, the School of Advanced Jewish Studies, and the Yiddish Yehoash Folk School. The 1940s saw the founding of two day schools—the Yeshiva and the Hillel Academy—and in the 1970s, the Community Day School was established. In the realm of health care, the establishment of Montefiore Hospital was a major accomplishment. The Irene Kaufmann Settlement and the Jewish Y, with its building on Bellefield Street in the Oakland district of the city, provided educational, recreational, and social opportunities. The Gusky Orphanage, the Jewish Home for the Aged, and the Hebrew Free Loan were all institutions or organizations that met the needs of the community. These were some of the major institutions, but there were many other organizations, like Zionist groups and women's organizations, including the Pittsburgh chapter of the National Council of Jewish Women. There was a multitude of synagogues, large and small, on the Hill, in the East End, in Squirrel Hill, and elsewhere around the city on the north shore and in Beechview. There were the sisterhoods in all these congregations and the *landsmanshaften*, informal groups of Jews emanating from the same hometown area who were devoted to providing social and economic help to their members. The community, even through the Depression, sustained a myriad of organizations manned by volunteers and Jewish communal professionals.

The Federation of Jewish Philanthropies, organized in 1912 in Pittsburgh, was established to streamline and make more efficient the raising and distribution of funds to some of these major Jewish institutions. Today, what is now known as the Jewish Federation of Greater Pittsburgh includes agencies and organizations devoted to Jewish learning, aging and human-welfare needs, Jewish communal life, community relations, and a partnership with Israel.

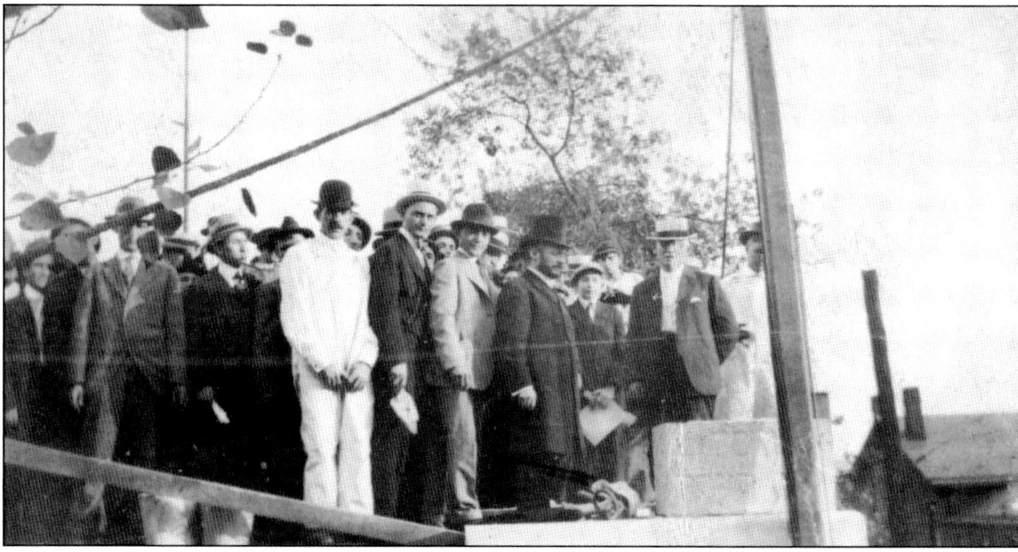

In 1915, ground was broken for the Hebrew Institute. Rabbi Ashinsky had not been happy with the quality and quantity of Jewish education in the city and had diligently led the effort to build a citywide school for hundreds of children. With funds raised from many donors—Louis Aaron in particular—Ashinsky's dream finally became a reality. Sol Rosenbloom was a major benefactor and president.

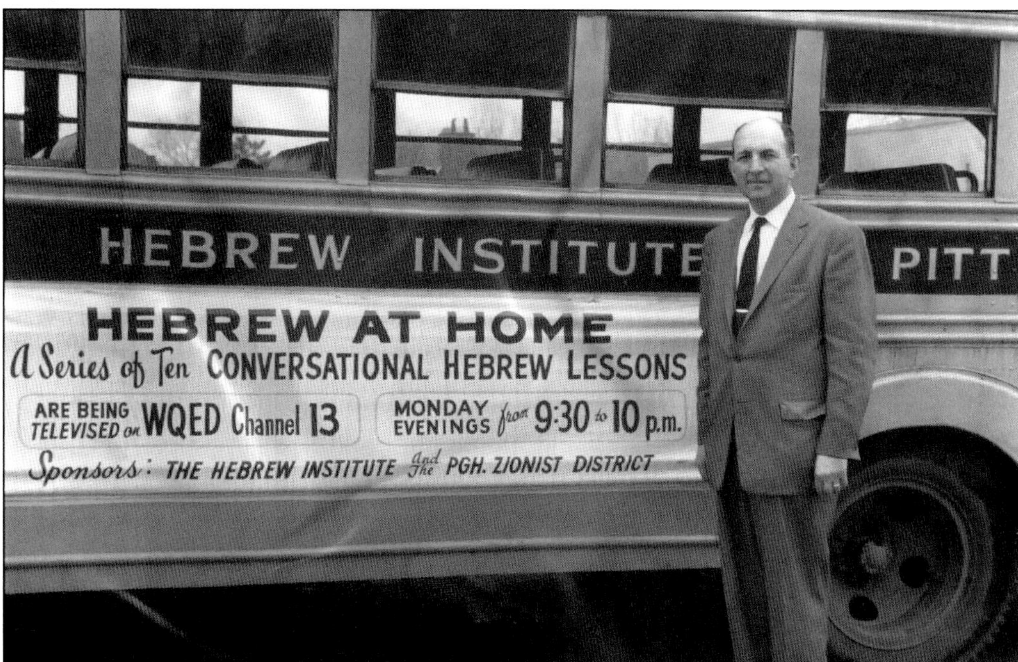

Dr. Solomon Abrams was the second principal of the Hebrew Institute, succeeding his father, Israel Abrams, a graduate of the Vilna Yeshiva and City College of New York. The Hebrew Institute building on the Hill was sold in 1943, one of the last Jewish institutions to leave the area. Its new site was at the intersection of Forbes and Denniston Avenues in Squirrel Hill, which is now the site of the Yeshiva Girls' School.

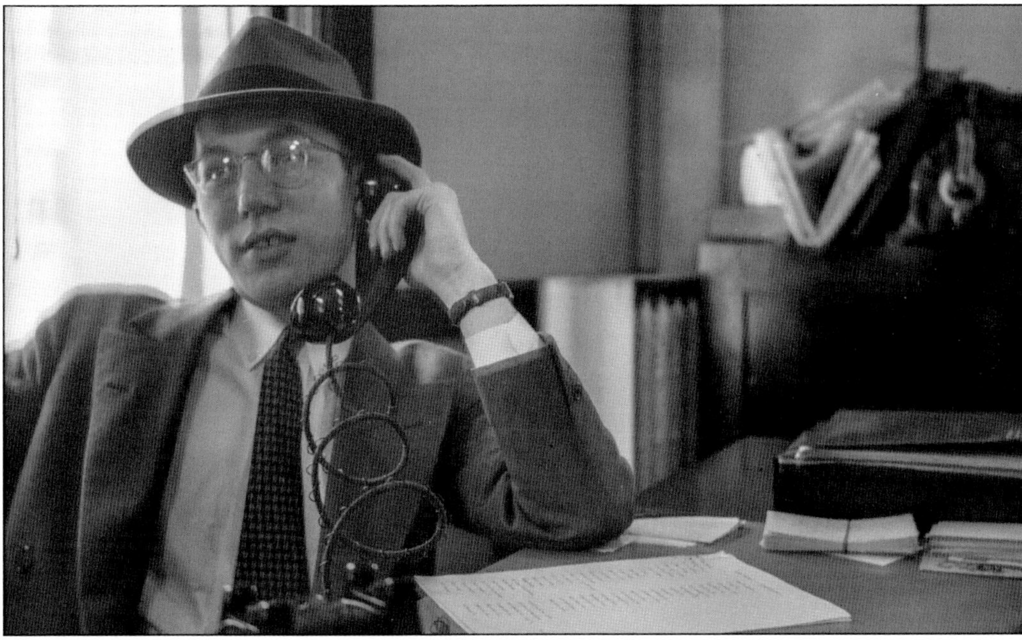

Hillel Academy, an Orthodox day school, was founded in 1947 by five men—Rabbi Dr. Joseph Shapiro of Poale Zedeck, Rabbi Dr. Bernard Poupko of Shaare Torah, Adolph Schoenbrun, Abraham Butler, and Donald Butler. Schoenbrun became the first president. Donald Butler (pictured) was a staunch supporter of the school for over 65 years until his death at the age of 93 in 2013. (Hillel Academy.)

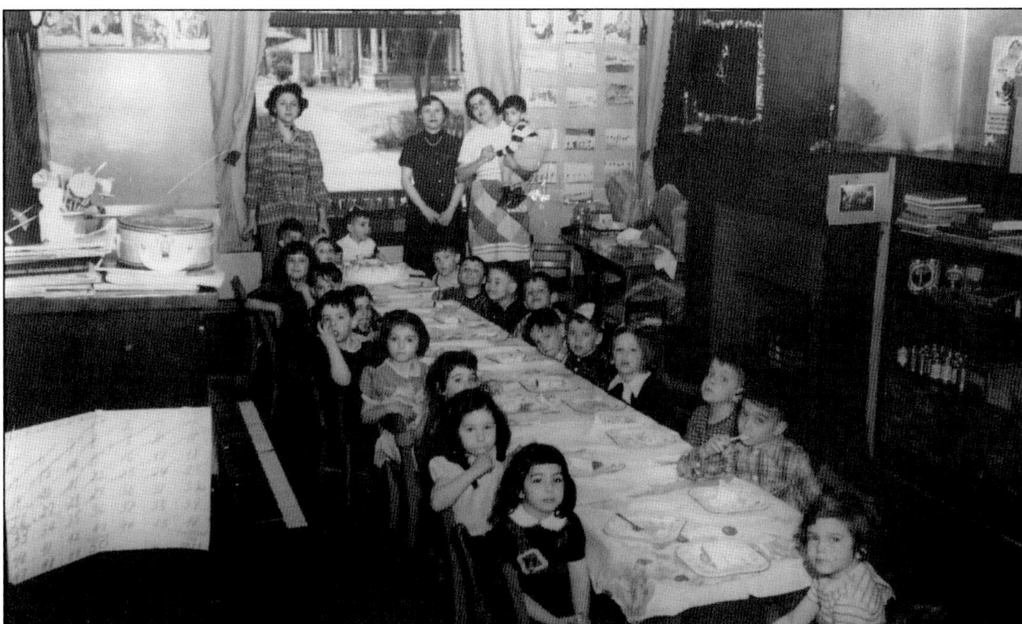

This is a picture of an early class at Hillel Academy. Initially, the school was housed in the automobile showroom of David Horvitz in the Morrowfield Apartments on Murray Avenue. Today, the Hillel building is on Beacon Street in Squirrel Hill and has more than 300 pupils. An expansion is under way.

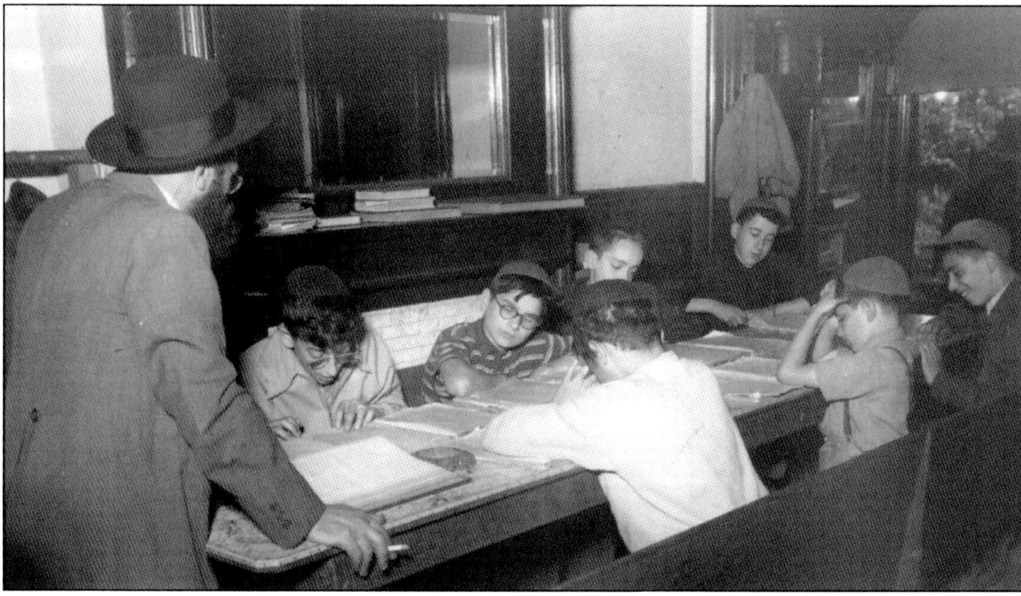

In 1943, Rabbi Sholom Posner came to Pittsburgh from Chicago at the behest of his teacher, Rabbi Menachem Mendel Schneerson, to found a Jewish day school. The Yeshiva School, which started with five students, was the first Jewish day school in the city since the 1860s, when Rodef Shalom experimented briefly with a day school.

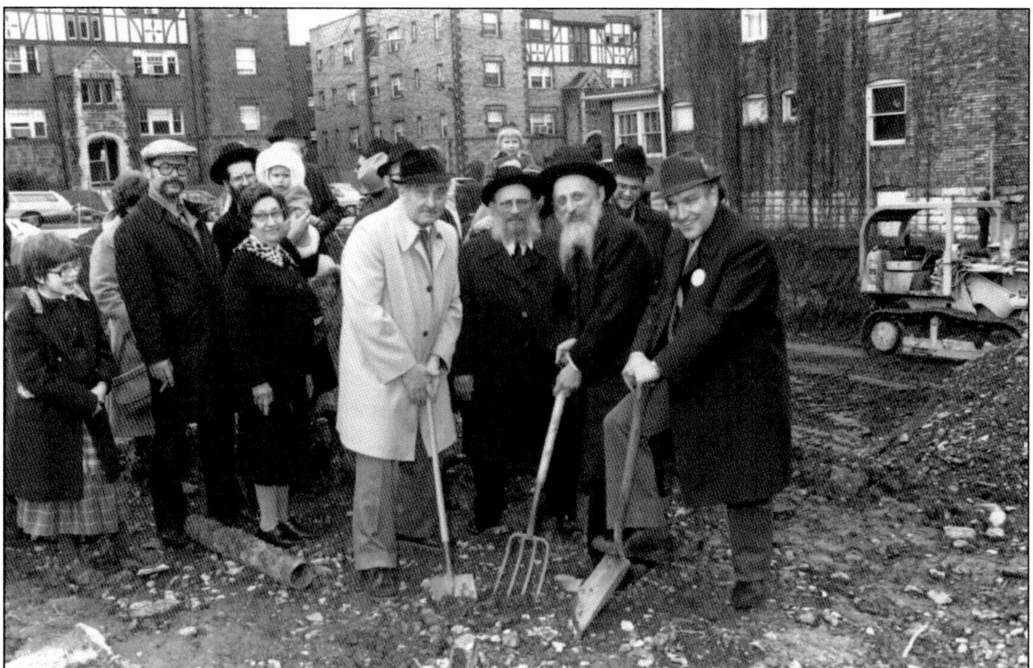

The Yeshiva School has grown today into two schools, one for boys and one for girls. This picture is of the 1978 ground breaking for the building that is now the boys' school on the corner of Hobart and Wightman Streets in Squirrel Hill. Pictured from left to right are Meyer Cohen, Rabbi Posner, Rabbi Abraham Twersky, and Rabbi Howard Balsam. In the background is Rabbi Yisroel Rosenfeld (behind Twersky), the current dean.

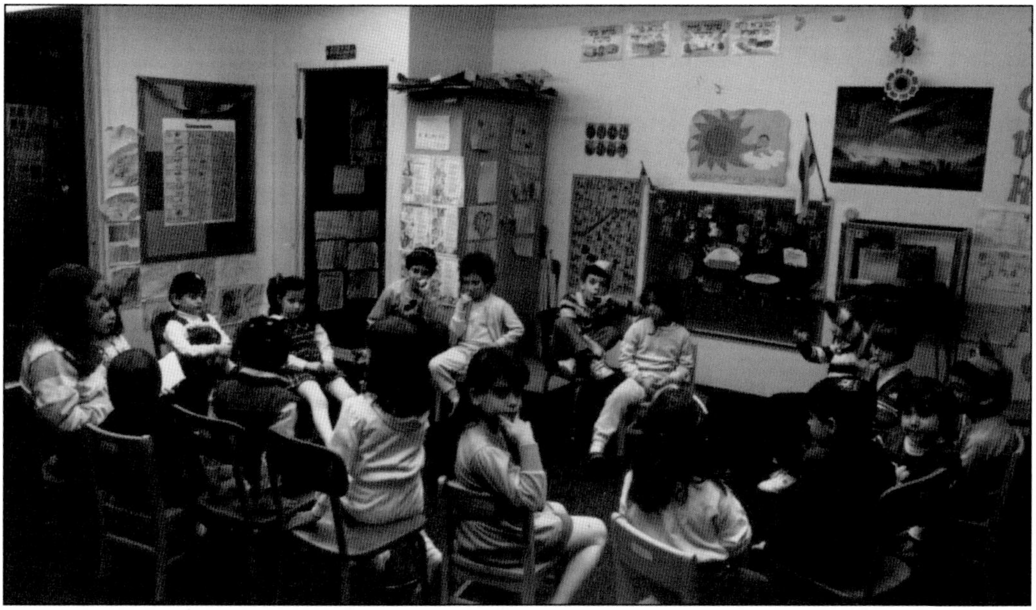

The Community Day School was the third Jewish day school established in Pittsburgh after World War II. It opened in 1972 as a nondenominational Jewish day school. It met for years at the Hebrew Institute but in 1996 moved into the former St. Philomena Church and School at the corner of Forward Avenue and Beechwood Boulevard. Today, it is an independent school, the only non-Orthodox day school in the city.

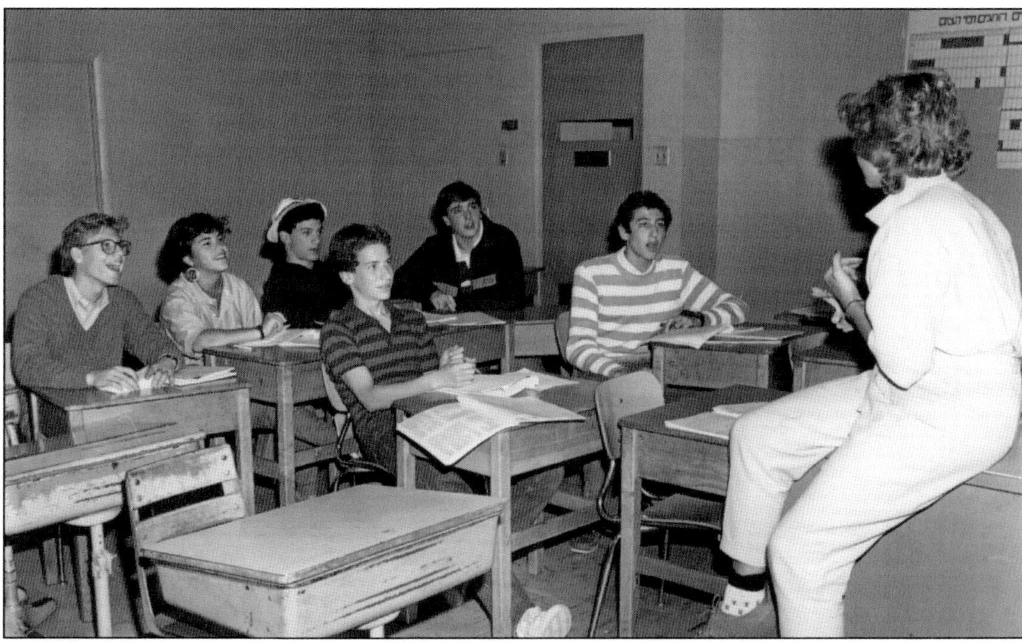

This picture from 1985 shows a class at the School of Advanced Jewish Studies (SAJS). The school was founded in 1969 with the merger of the College of Jewish Studies and the secondary and teacher-training programs of the Hebrew Institute. Dr. Aharon Kessler, who had come to Pittsburgh to oversee Jewish education in the early 1950s, became the dean of the school. The program is now called J-Site

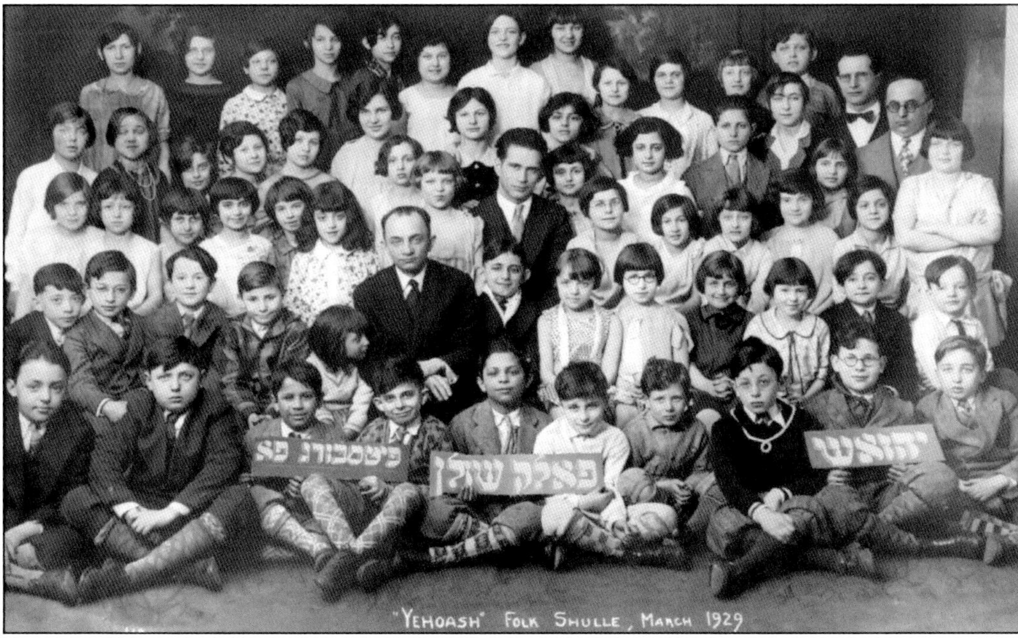

Yehoash Folk School was a Yiddish school organized in 1925 at the IKS. In the early decades of the 20th century, at least eight schools offered Yiddish classes in an attempt to keep the language alive. However, with the passing of the Eastern European immigrant generation and the impact of the Great Depression, the Yiddish schools all closed in the 1930s.

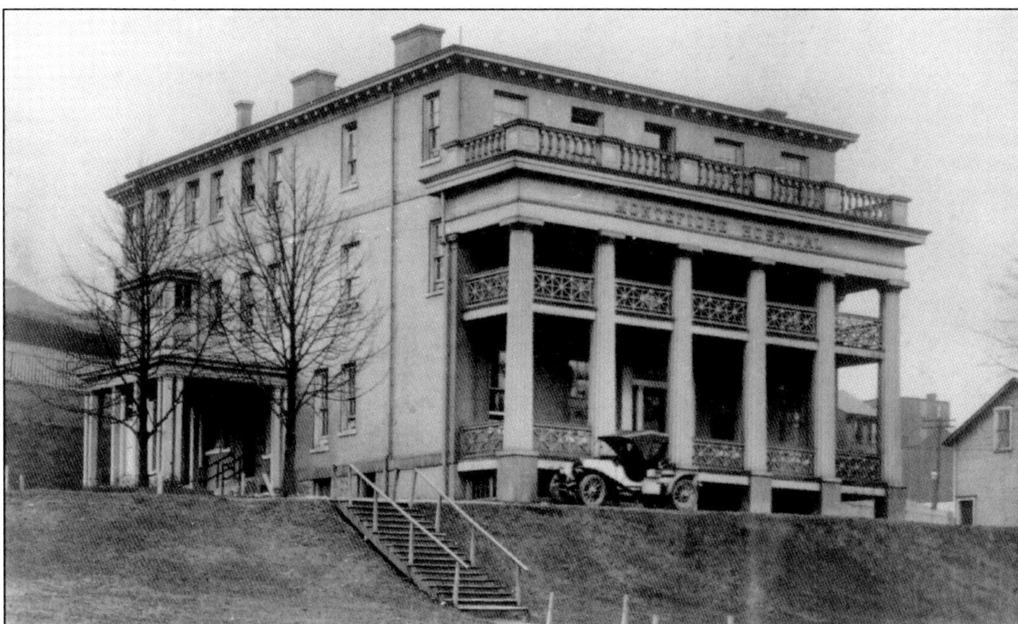

After years of fundraising, the first Montefiore Hospital was opened on the Hill at Centre and Herron Avenues in 1908. Henry Jackson was the first president. Having a Jewish hospital meant that Jewish hospital patients had kosher food and Jewish doctors could get hospital staff positions. Earlier, in 1897, Isaac Kaufmann had established in memory of his wife the Emma Kaufmann Clinic, which became part of the University of Pittsburgh.

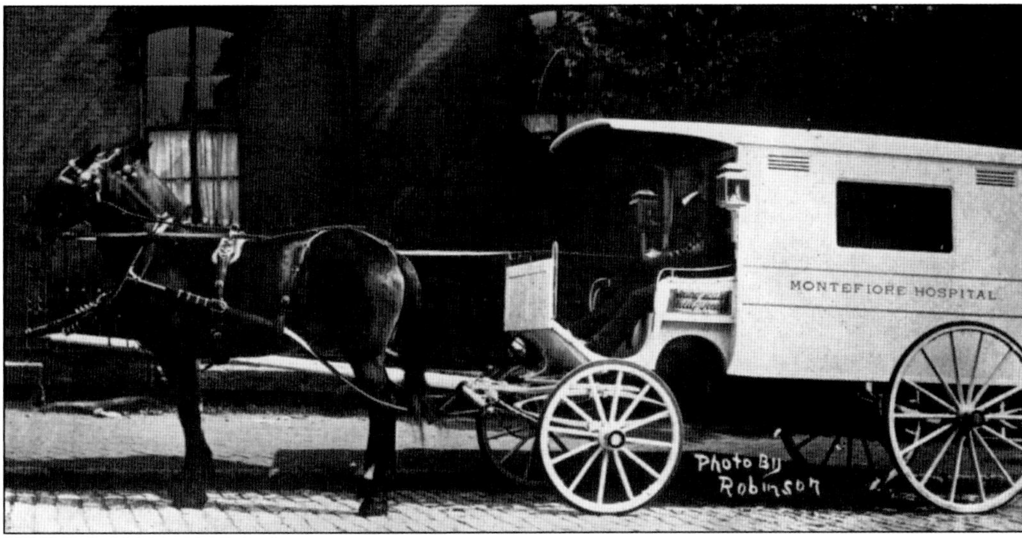

The Young Ladies' Sick and Relief Society was organized in 1905. They donated a white ambulance pulled by horses to Montefiore Hospital, as seen in this undated photograph. The first motor-powered ambulance was not in operation until after 1929.

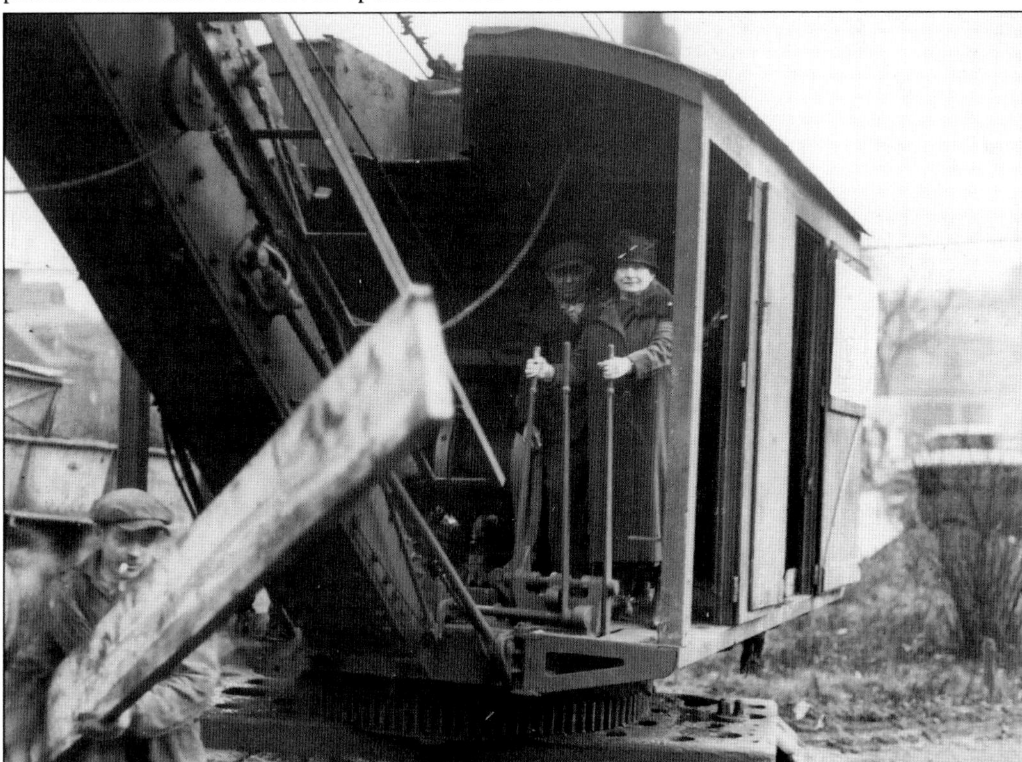

Annie Jacobs Davis was the driving force behind the creation of Montefiore Hospital. A Lithuanian immigrant, she married Barnett Davis in 1883 and soon gave birth to 11 children. At the urging of Dr. Albert Blumberg, she determined to build a hospital to extend the healing work of the Bikur Cholim Society. She is pictured on a steam shovel at the ground breaking for the second hospital in 1927.

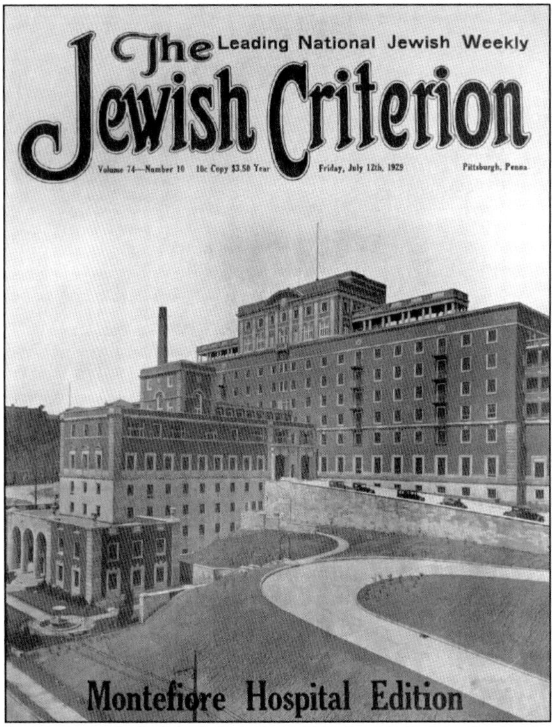

The first hospital was overcrowded, so another major drive was jump-started by Dr. K.I. Sanes and Isaac Seder of Frank & Seder's, with Albert Lehman as the chair. In 1929, the second Montefiore Hospital opened on Fifth Avenue in Oakland. Maurice and Leon Falk had previously gifted the Falk Clinic, an ambulatory dispensary, to the University of Pittsburgh.

In 1890, Esther Gusky donated $30,000 to build the Gusky Orphanage, named in honor of her husband, Jacob Gusky. Jacob Gusky came to Pittsburgh in 1864 to work for the clothier Meyer Hanauer. His stepfather, Simon Cohen, bought Hanauer's business at Gusky's urging, and when Cohen retired, the store was Gusky's. He was known for his many charities, including orphanages and hospitals, and he provided turkeys for the poor on Thanksgiving Day every year.

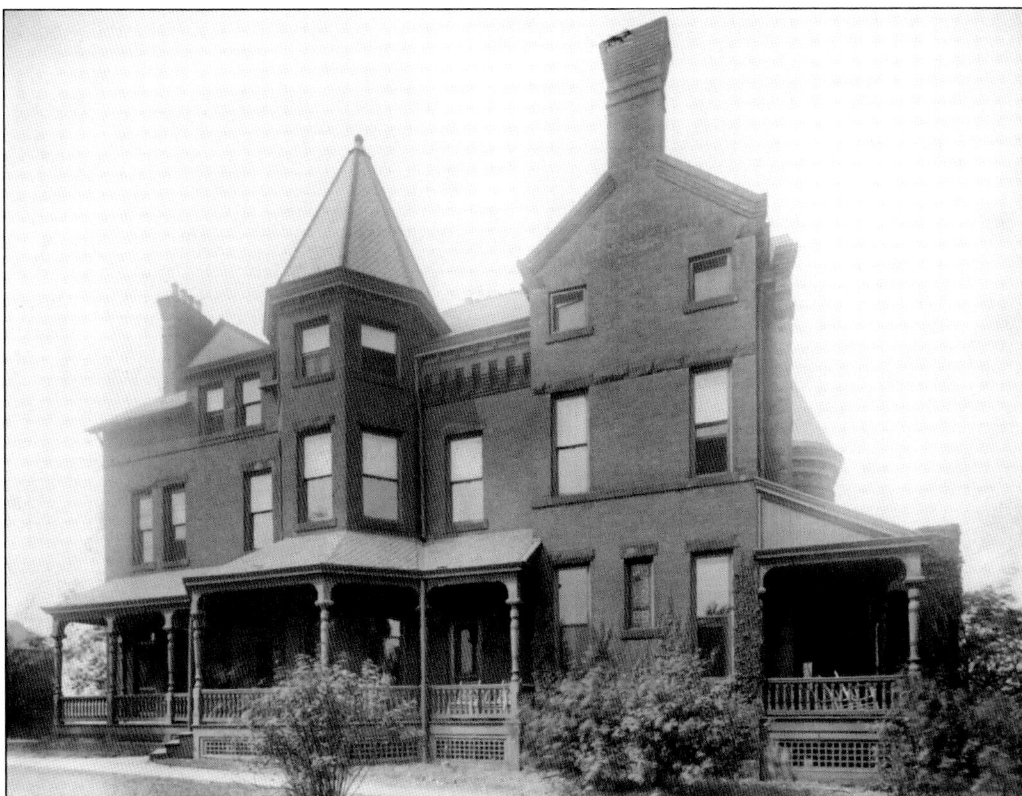

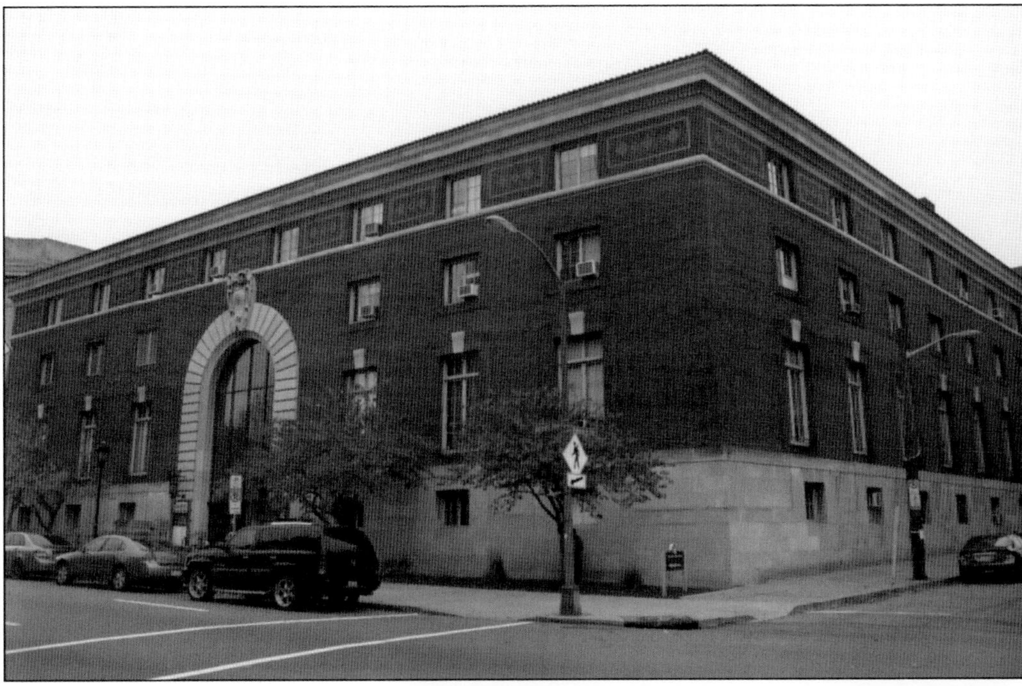

After fitful starts and no permanent space, the Young Men and Women's Hebrew Association (Y) opened their new facility on Bellefield Avenue in Oakland in 1926. The fundraising had been led by Irwin Lehman, with major donations by Edgar Kaufmann, Mrs. Isaac Seder and Mrs. Morris Baer. Herman Passamaneck was the executive director, serving from 1925 until his retirement in 1954.

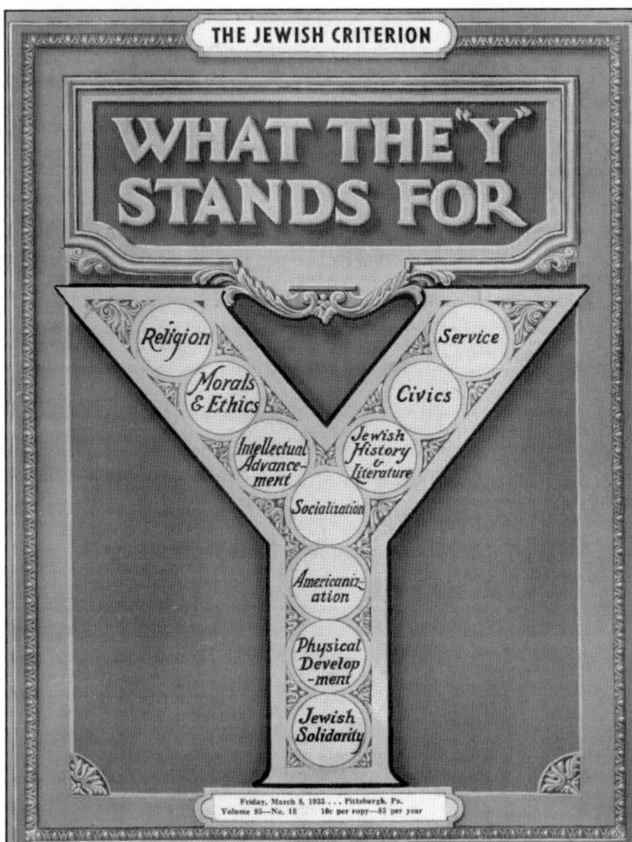

The Y provided extensive recreational, educational, and social activities, as seen in this 1935 picture. In 1960, it merged with the Irene Kaufmann Settlement and later became known as the Jewish Community Center, now located in Squirrel Hill. (*Jewish Criterion*, Pittsburgh Jewish Newspaper Project.)

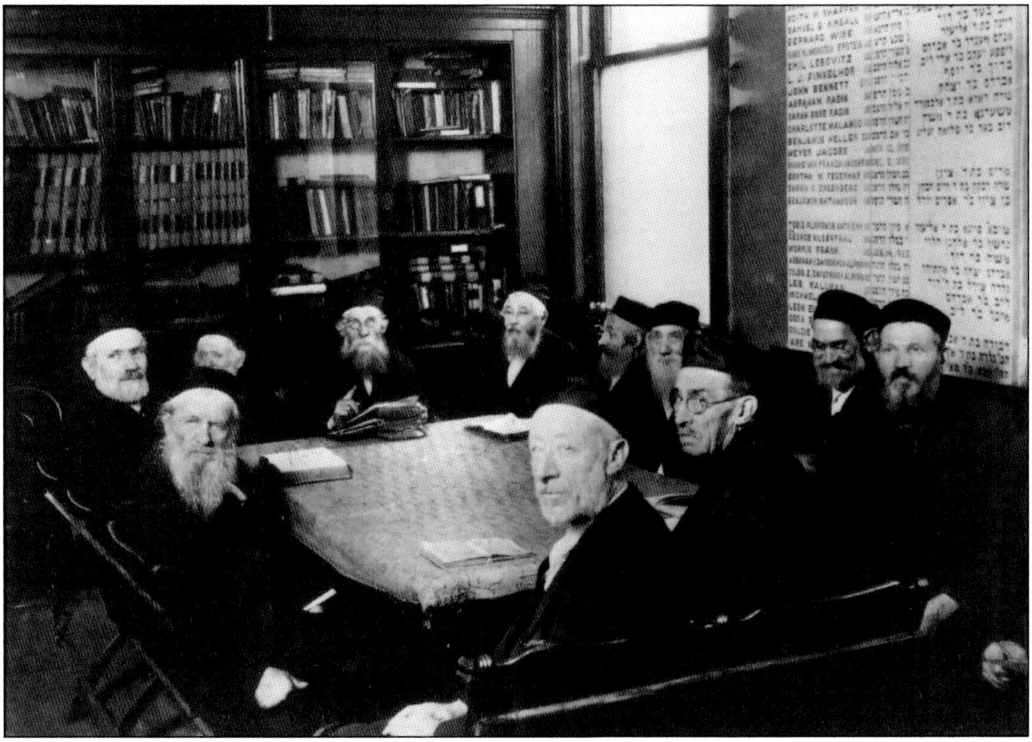

More than 700 donors from Pittsburgh and surrounding areas contributed to the purchase of a home on Brackenridge Avenue on the Hill to house the Jewish Home for the Aged in 1906. Rabbi Ashinsky was a key organizer, and Henry Jackson was the first president. The picture is of a study group at the home in 1920.

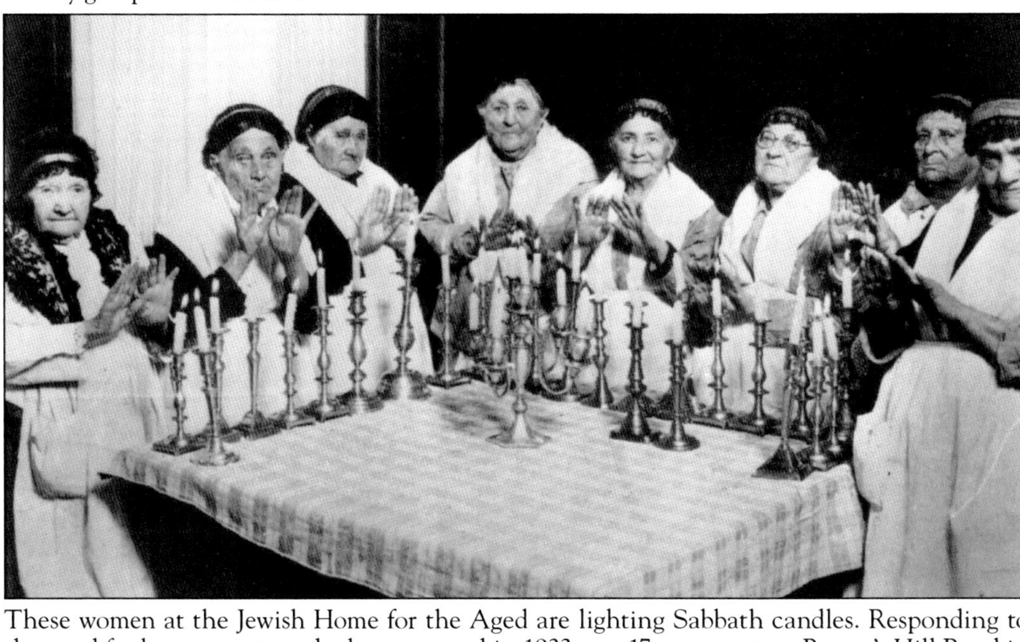

These women at the Jewish Home for the Aged are lighting Sabbath candles. Responding to the need for larger quarters, the home moved in 1933 to a 17-acre tract on Brown's Hill Road in Squirrel Hill.

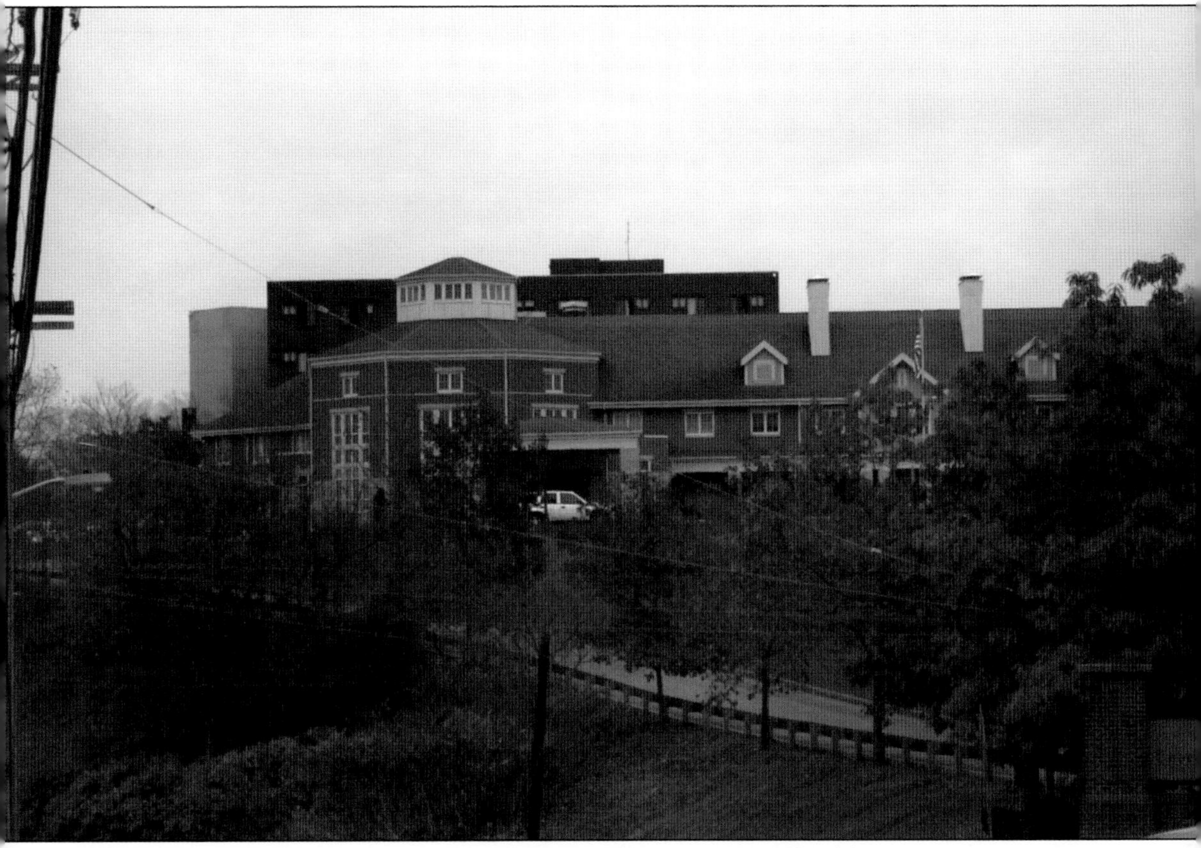

Today, the Jewish Association on Aging offers a full continuum of health care services, serving tens of thousands of seniors in various residential facilities, including the Charles Morris Skilled Nursing & Rehabilitation Center, Weinberg Village, and Weinberg Terrace. There are also a variety of nonresidential programs, including the Sivitz Jewish Hospice, the JAA Home Health and Outpatient Rehabilitation, Anathan Club Adult Day Service, and Mollie's Meals, which provides home-delivered kosher meals. The main facility is located on Brown's Hill Road, where the Jewish Home for the Aged was first located after it had moved from the Hill in 1933.

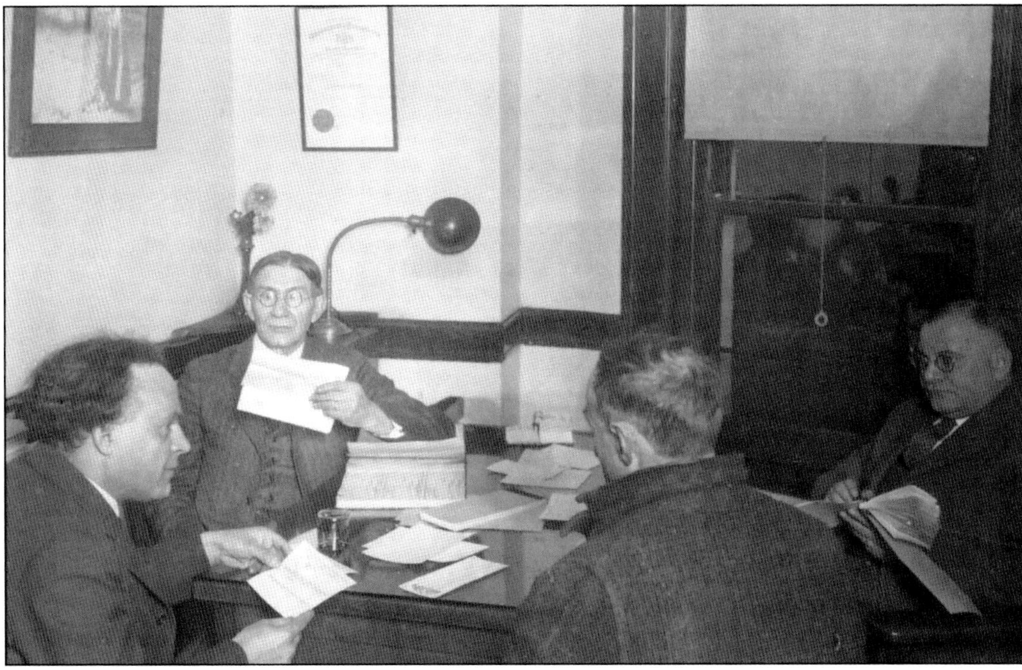

The Hebrew Free Loan Society is an organization that lends money at no interest to worthy applicants. It was organized in 1887 by Simon Shupinsky and other Eastern European Jews and to this day is the oldest functioning free loan society in America. This is a picture of free loan volunteers reviewing applications at the Irene Kaufmann Settlement in 1924.

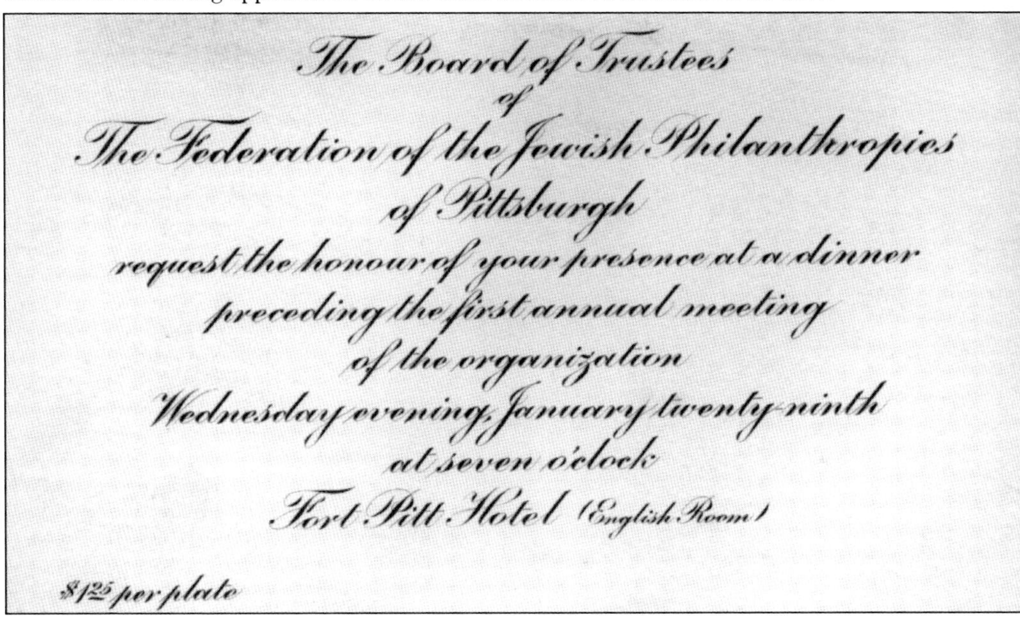

The Board of Trustees
of
The Federation of the Jewish Philanthropies
of Pittsburgh
request the honour of your presence at a dinner
preceding the first annual meeting
of the organization
Wednesday evening, January twenty-ninth
at seven o'clock
Fort Pitt Hotel (English Room)

$1.25 per plate

By 1912, the momentum to consolidate and make more efficient the raising and distribution of funds in the Jewish community culminated in the establishment of the Federation of Jewish Philanthropies. This advertisement was for the first annual meeting of the federation, with Aaron Cohen as chair of the board. Receipts that year totaled $71,745.78 to be distributed to 14 beneficiaries, including Montefiore Hospital, the Gusky Orphanage, the IKS, and the Hebrew Free Loan.

Five

Jews in Social Justice, Civic Reform, Politics, and Education

"Justice, Justice Shall Thee Pursue" reads Deuteronomy 16:20. Over the generations, Jewish professionals and volunteers have dedicated themselves to this Biblical imperative. It is part of their tradition, but Jews have also felt the sting of discrimination and prejudice, which has only underscored for them the need to get involved to protect the rights of minorities and promote equal opportunities. Many activists were lawyers like Josiah Cohen and A. Leo Weil. Weil was determined to fight city corruption early in the 20th century. Attorneys Henry Ellenbogen and Samuel Weiss both became US congressmen. However, lawyers were not the only ones committed to public service. Rabbis like J. Leonard Levy of Rodef Shalom Congregation were outspoken proponents of social causes. Businessman Emmanuel Wertheimer and Adolph Edlis were state legislators, with Edlis later serving as city treasurer. Enoch Rauh served on the first nine-member city council, and his wife, Bertha, a consummate volunteer, was appointed by Mayor William A. Magee to head up the Department of Public Charities. Marcus Aaron led the Pittsburgh City School Board, followed by his daughter-in-law Maxine Aaron and his granddaughter Elinor Langer. Dr. Adolph Lewin was on the school board for over 40 years. Maurice Falk in 1929 established the Falk Foundation that for 85 years supported projects promoting a "tolerant, just and inclusive" society. Harold Ruttenberg was the research director for the Steel Workers Organizing Committee in the 1930s. City councilman Abe Wolk led the effort to clean up the city's smoke pollution. In a much later era, Sophie Masloff served the public as the first female mayor of the City of Pittsburgh. Several women—including Sadie Alter and her sister Florence Reizenstein, Lillian Friedberg, and later Frieda Shapira and Dr. Barbara Shore—were known in their time as crusaders for social justice, particularly with regard to combating discrimination and improving the lives of African Americans in Pittsburgh. And recognizing the importance of education, Philip Chotsky founded three trade schools, Dorothy Finkelhor founded what became Point Park College, and David Kurtzman became Pennsylvania's secretary of education.

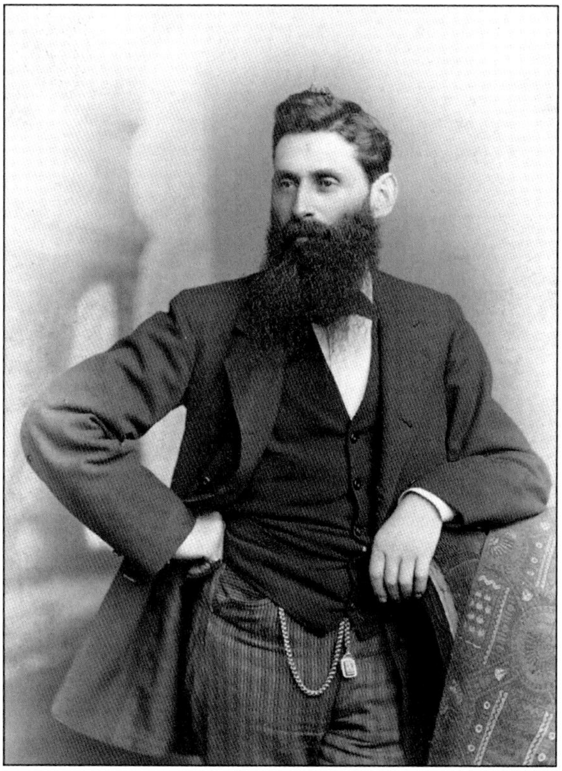

Emanuel Wertheimer was a wealthy liquor distiller and one of the earliest Jews in politics from the area. He was a councilman in Allegheny City from 1879 to 1892 and served in the state legislature from 1893 to 1894. He also served as president of Rodef Shalom from 1871 to 1886 and was a member of the Concordia Club.

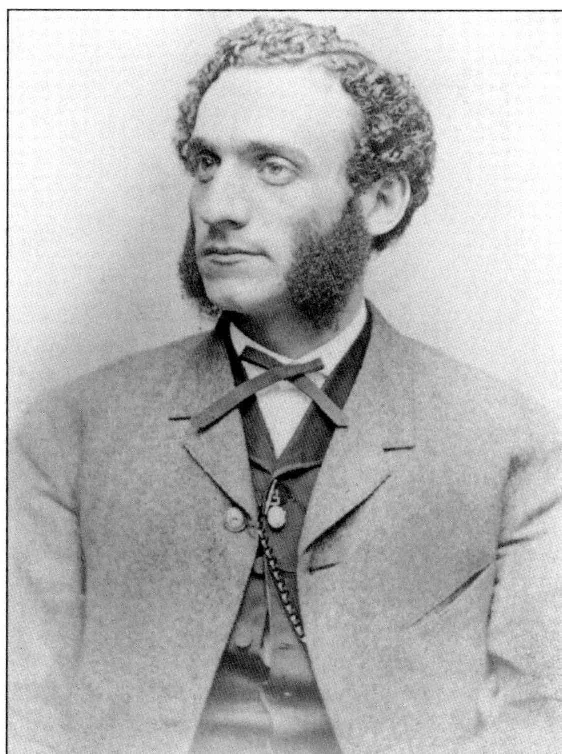

Judge Josiah Cohen came to Pittsburgh in 1860 at the age of 20 to teach at Rodef Shalom. He gave up teaching to go into law and ultimately became a highly respected judge of the Court of Common Pleas. Noted for his eloquence, he was a frequent speaker and major player in the Jewish and non-Jewish worlds until his death at the age of 90 in 1930.

A. Leo Weil was a highly successful corporate lawyer who, as head of Voters League, attacked city government and school board corruption in the early 1900s. He was likened to the fiery prophet Amos for his zeal. During his lifetime, he gave generously of his time and money to the "welfare of humanity." He died in 1938, and two years later, the Pittsburgh Board of Education named a school after him.

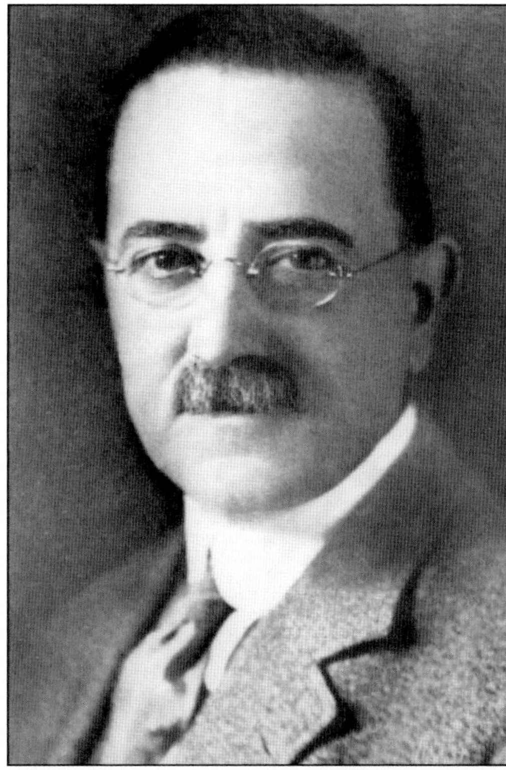

Enoch Rauh (first row, second from left), along with his brother Marcus, by 1882 had established a wholesale clothing business on Liberty Avenue. Rauh married Bertha Floersheim in 1884 and in 1911 was selected by Gov. John Tener to sit on the newly created nine-member city council. He died suddenly while in office on Thanksgiving Day 1919.

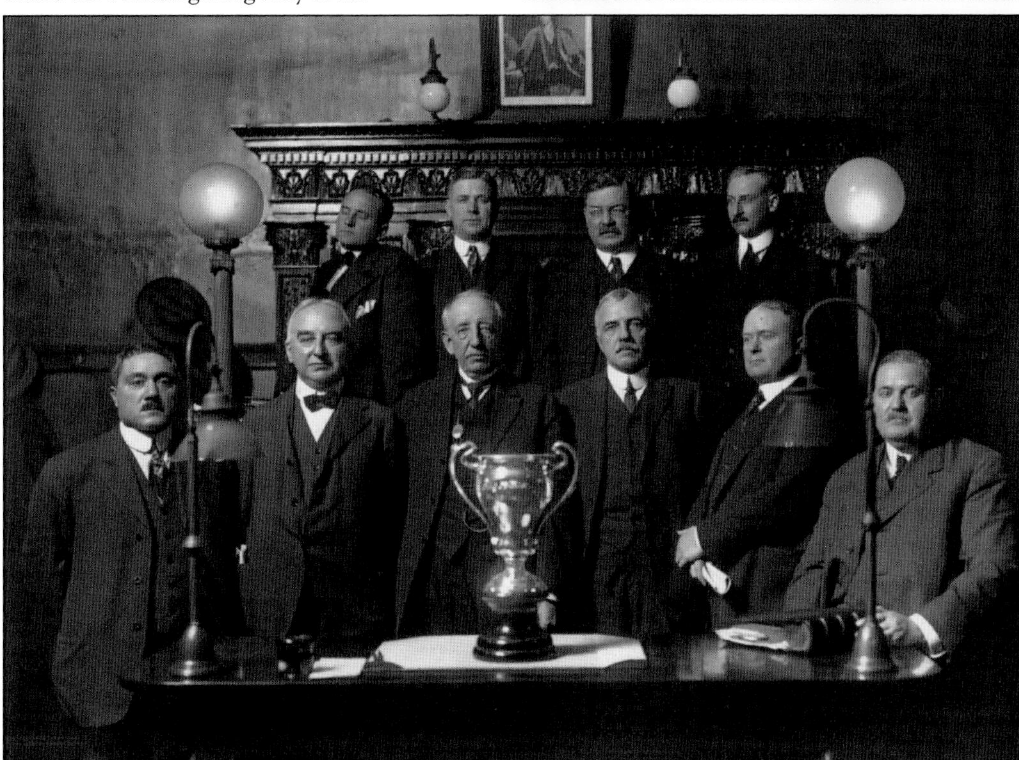

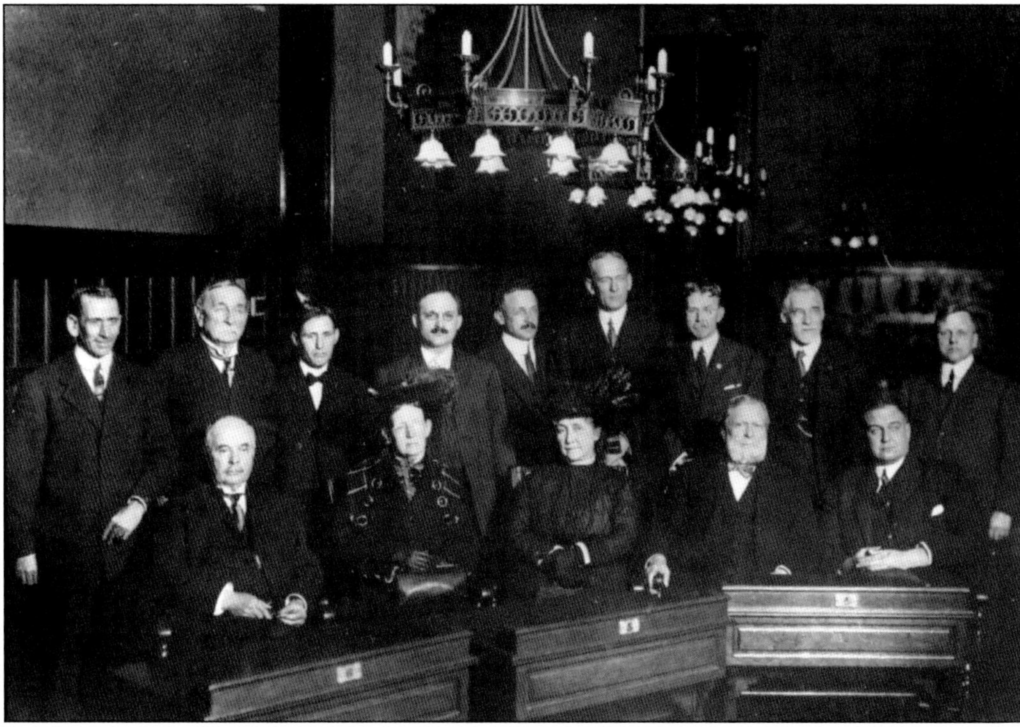

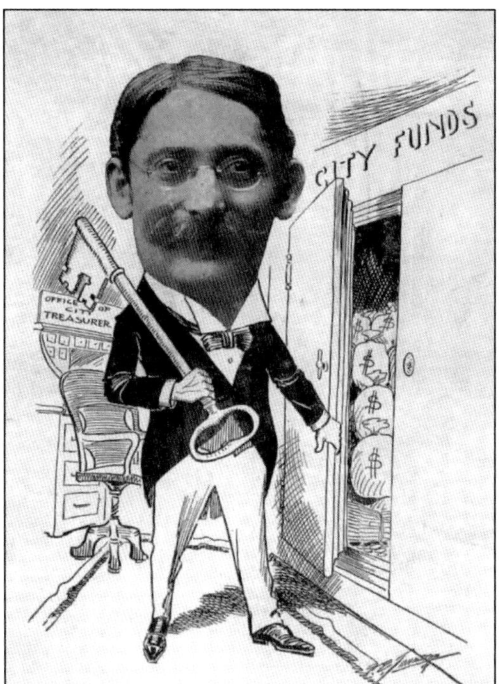

ADOLPH EDLIS

This picture is of the new 15-member school board set up in 1911. It included two Jews. Marcus Aaron (second row, fifth from left) served for 36 years and was president from 1922 to 1942. Dr. Adolph L. Lewin (second row, fourth from left) served until his death in 1953. Aaron was a prominent businessman, the president of the Homer Laughlin China Company, and Lewin was a practicing physician.

Adolf Edlis was a Hungarian Jew who was elected in 1897 to the Pittsburgh Common Council and then to the Pennsylvania House of Representatives in 1904, becoming the first Jewish immigrant from Eastern Europe to be elected to the state legislature. He was responsible for the Edlis Act, which attacked "white slave" trafficking. In 1909, he was appointed city treasurer by mayor-elect William Magee and continued in office until 1914.

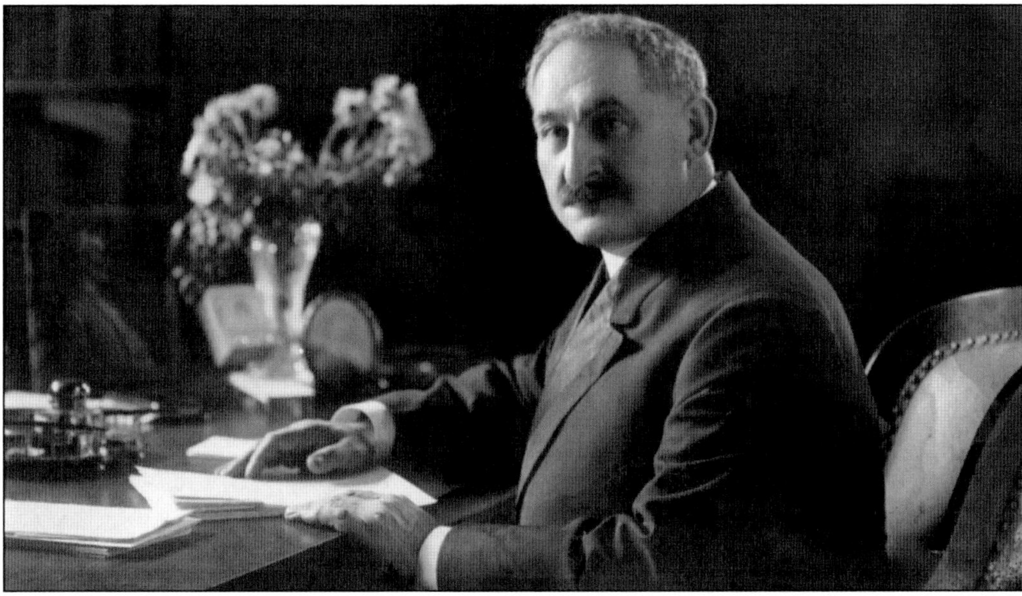

Rabbi J. Leonard Levy of Rodef Shalom was a major force in the Pittsburgh community from the time of his arrival in town in 1901 until his sudden death in 1917. In 1905, the *Pittsburgh Post* listed Levy as one of the 12 Pittsburghers who had attained a national and international reputation along with the likes of Andrew Carnegie and George Westinghouse. (Rodef Shalom Congregation Archives.)

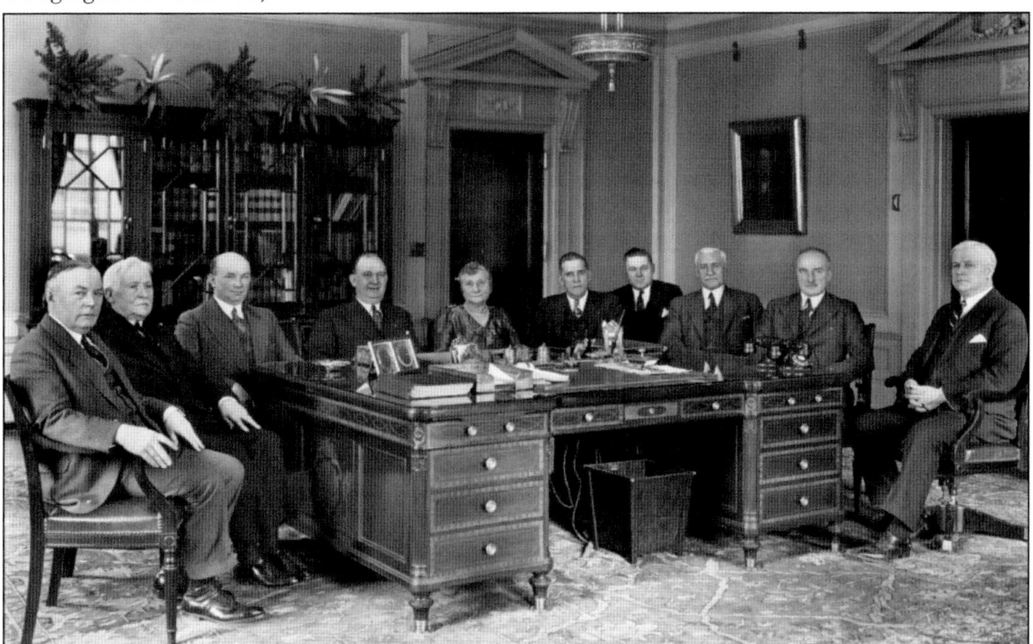

Bertha Rauh became the first woman appointed to a mayor's cabinet in the state of Pennsylvania when she became the director of Department of Public Charities under Mayor William Magee. She had been president of the Pittsburgh chapter of the National Council of Jewish Woman for 20 years and a founder and active volunteer in an astonishing number of organizations, earning her various titles, including "Mother Pitt" and "Pittsburgh's Best Citizen."

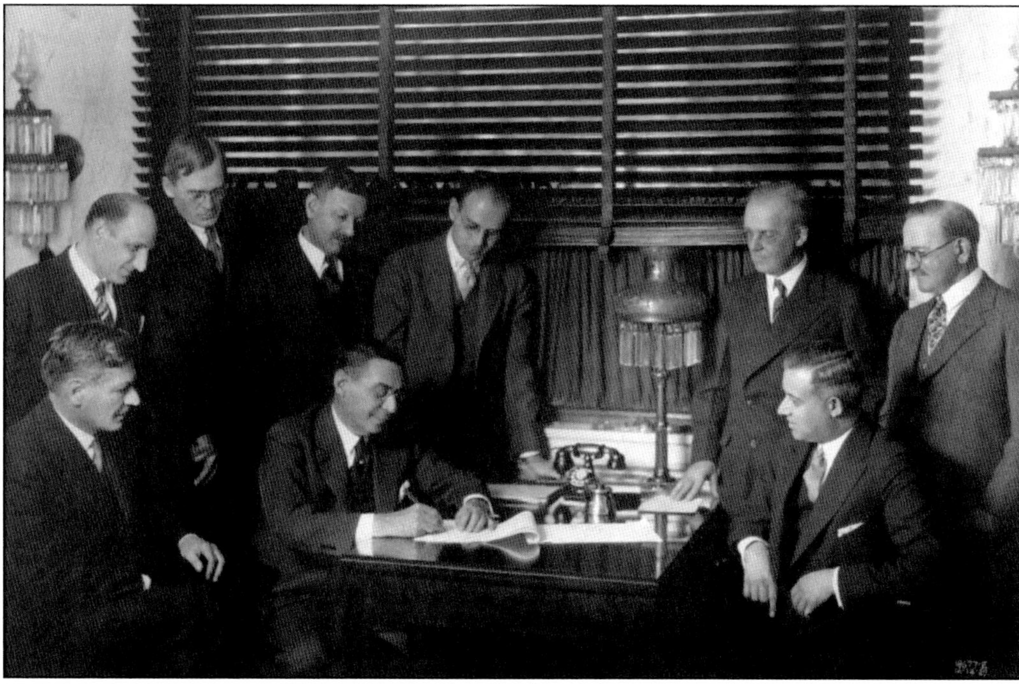

In 1929, Maurice Falk established the Falk Foundation in memory of his first wife, Laura, with securities valued then at $10 million, an unprecedented gift at the time. He explained, "It is my firm belief that any surplus of material wealth which may come to a man is properly to be regarded as a trust to be employed for the welfare of mankind."

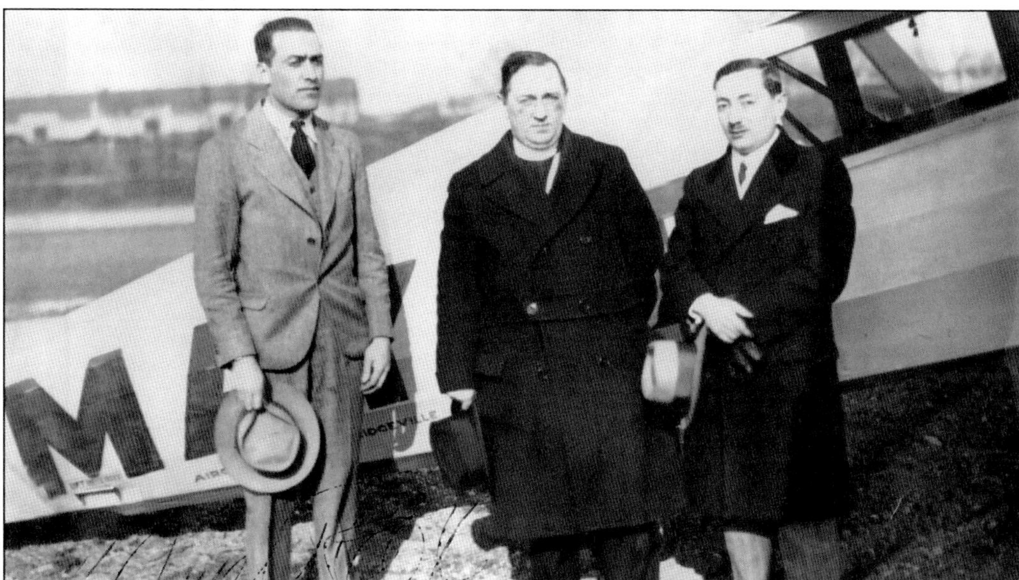

Henry Ellenbogen (far right), an Austrian immigrant and graduate of Duquesne Law School, in 1929 was hired by the Pittsburgh American for Civil Liberties Union to defend a Pitt student who was expelled for defending striking coal miners. He soon met Fr. James Cox, a popular priest who helped propel Ellenbogen into Congress when Franklin Roosevelt and the Democrats swept into power in 1932. Ellenbogen later became a judge.

Abraham Wolk was born on the Hill, served in World War I, and was elected for five terms as a Pittsburgh city councilman. He was behind landmark legislation on smoke control and the establishment of the University of Pittsburgh School of Public Health and the Allegheny Department of Health. Along with Edgar Kaufmann, he founded the Civic Light Opera, was president of B'nai Brith in Pittsburgh, and started "I Am an American Day."

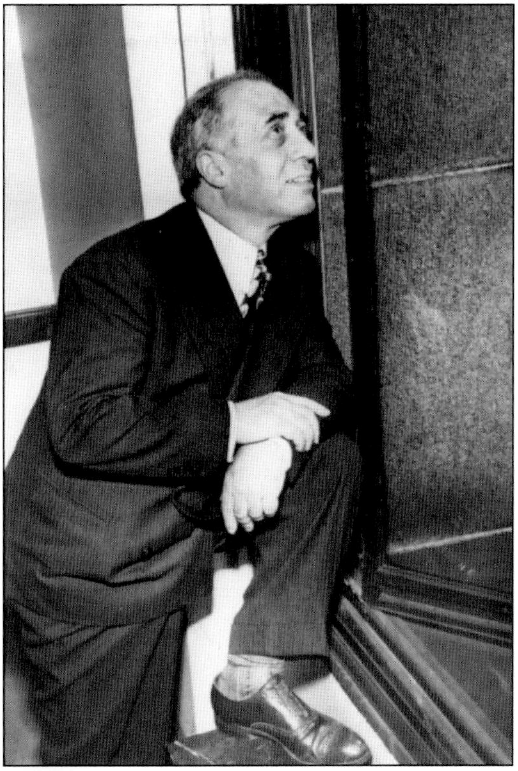

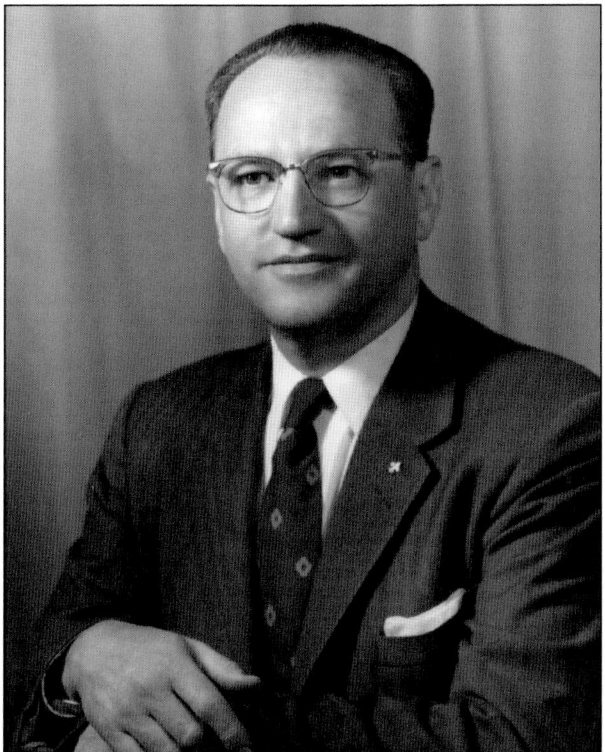

At the University of Pittsburgh, Harold Ruttenberg became involved with organized labor. In 1936, when he was just 22, he became the research director of the Steel Workers Organizing Committee. He was considered the right-hand man of Philip Murray, the president of the Steelworkers Union from 1942, when the union was founded, until 1952. He and his wife, Kitty, later amassed a significant art collection.

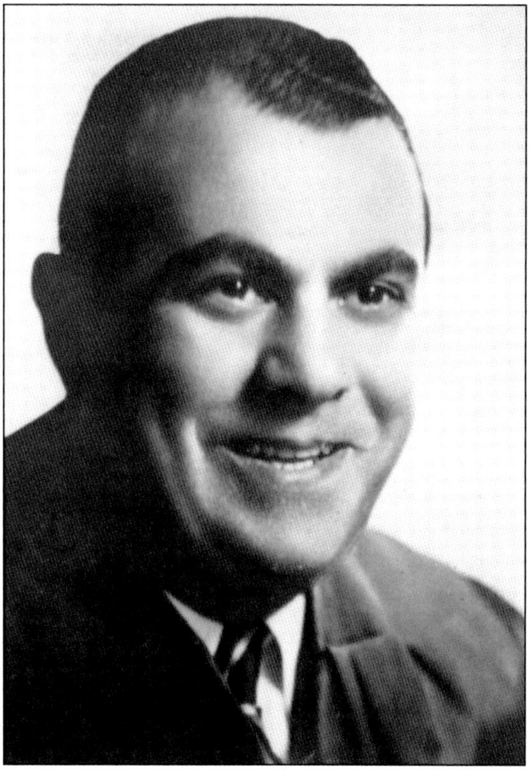

A graduate of Duquesne University and the University of Pittsburgh Law School, Samuel Weiss was elected to the Pennsylvania House of Representatives in 1935 and in 1940 was elected a US congressman until his resignation in 1946. He stood up to the ranting, anti-Semitic congressman John Rankin in the House of Representatives. He later became a judge.

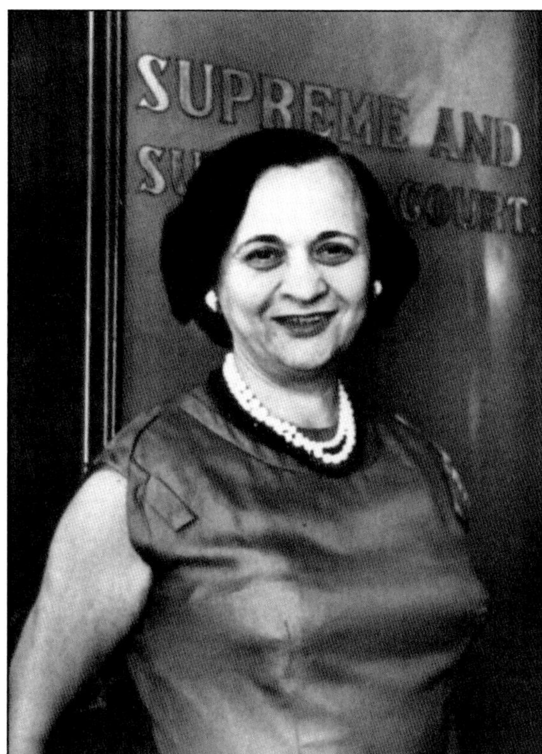

Anne X. Alpern, born in Russia in 1903, graduated from the University of Pittsburgh Law School in 1927. She was the first woman in a major city to become city solicitor. In 1954, she was elected to the Court of Common Pleas, another first. In 1959, she was the first woman in the country to become state attorney general, and in 1961, she became the first woman on the state supreme court.

Sadie Adler (left) and Florence Reizenstein (right) were Silberstein sisters totally dedicated to social justice causes. Adler was president of the Urban League, and Reizenstein was in the forefront of multiple civil rights issues, serving on the city and state Human Rights Commission and as a founder of the Negro Educational Emergency Drive. Reizenstein was also chosen a Distinguished Daughter of Pennsylvania and had a public school (since demolished) named in her honor.

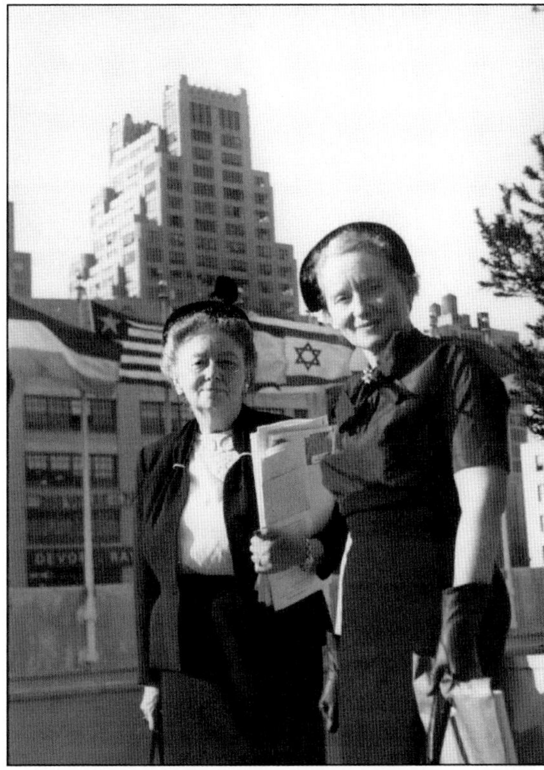

In 1956, the Louis Caplan Award was established by the Pittsburgh chapter of the American Jewish Committee. The picture is of the committee in the mid-1970s. Seated in the first row, fourth from left, is attorney Louis Caplan. The award has been given annually to an outstanding high school junior or senior in Allegheny County who has worked to build bridges between diverse groups in his or her school or community.

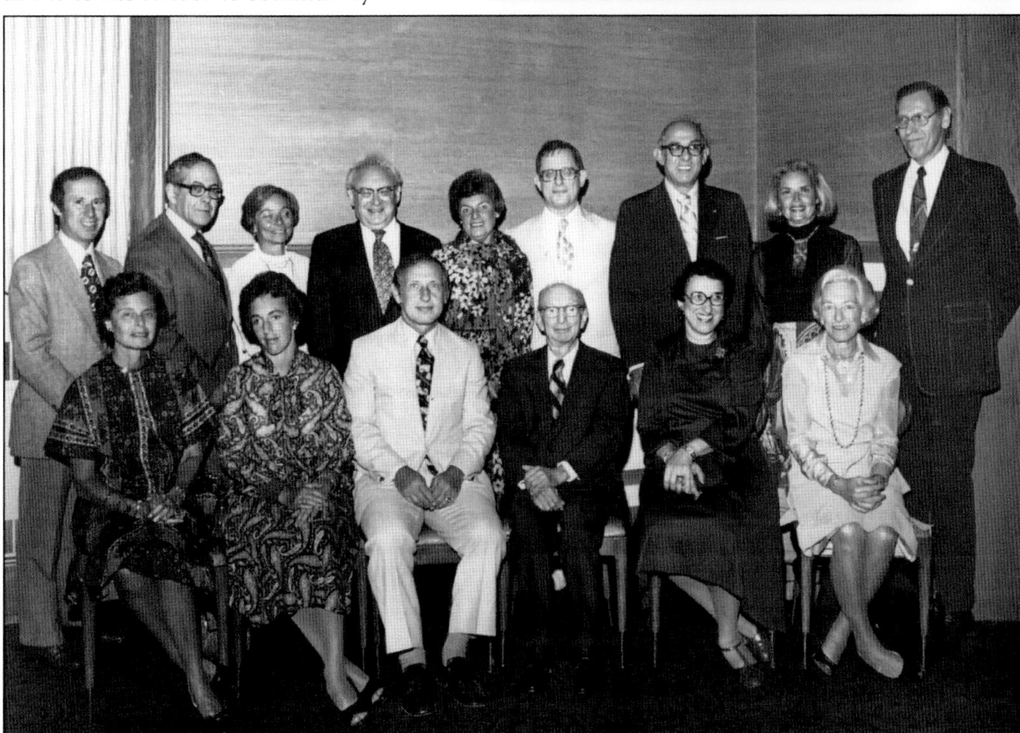

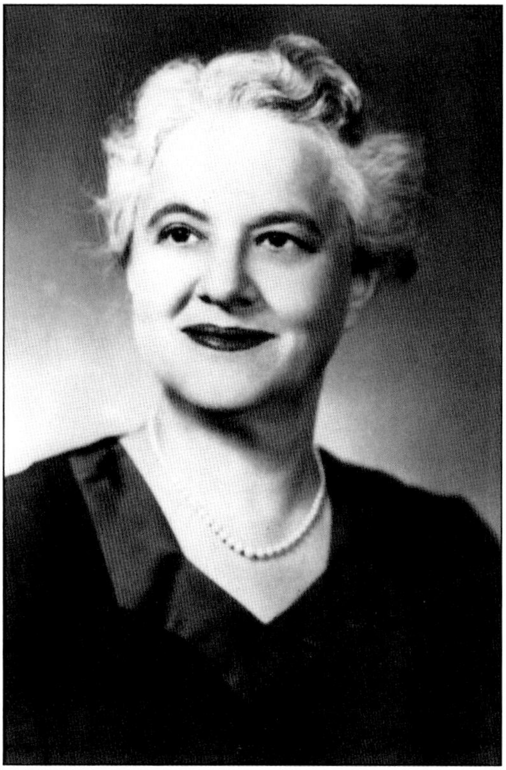

Lillian Friedberg was a pioneer when she took over as director of the United Jewish Federation's Community Relations Council in 1942 during World War II. She served until 1965. Like her compatriot Florence Reizenstein, she was a force for social justice and multicultural understanding. She also was named a Distinguished Daughter of Pennsylvania. As with many other Jews, Jewish ideals helped shape her commitment.

In this 1966 photograph, Frieda Shapira (standing, third from left) is with Pittsburgh mayor Joseph Barr. Frieda, the daughter of Joe Goldstein of Giant Eagle fame, married her college sweetheart, Saul Shapira, in 1933. Together they worked on a variety of social causes over the years. Frieda, a trained social worker and Distinguished Daughter of Pennsylvania, sat on many cultural and civil rights boards until her death in 2003.

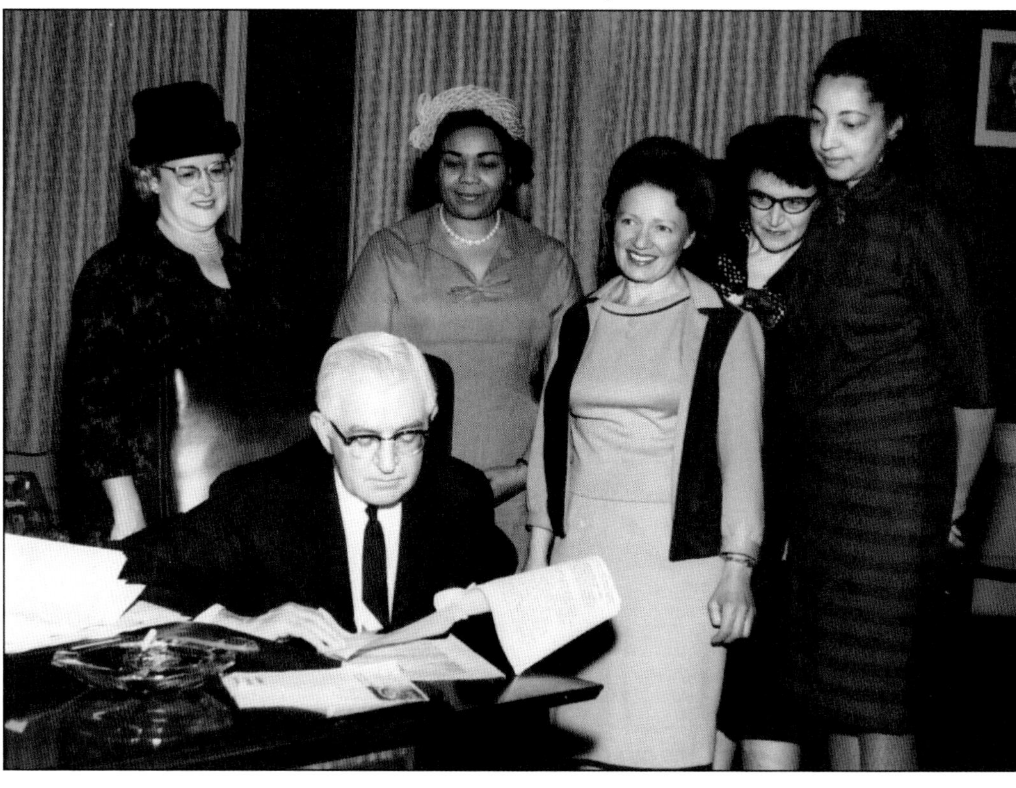

Maxine Aaron, the daughter-in-law of Marcus Aaron, was appointed to the Pittsburgh City School Board in 1948, one year after her father-in-law retired. She was a vocal supporter of school desegregation during a turbulent time and served until 1975, including three years as board president. She also was named a Distinguished Daughter of Pennsylvania. Her daughter Elinor Langer was among the first elected school board members.

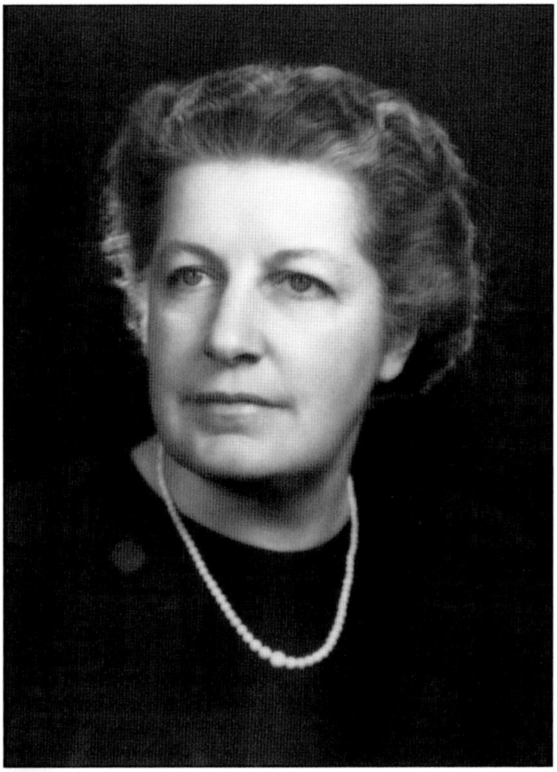

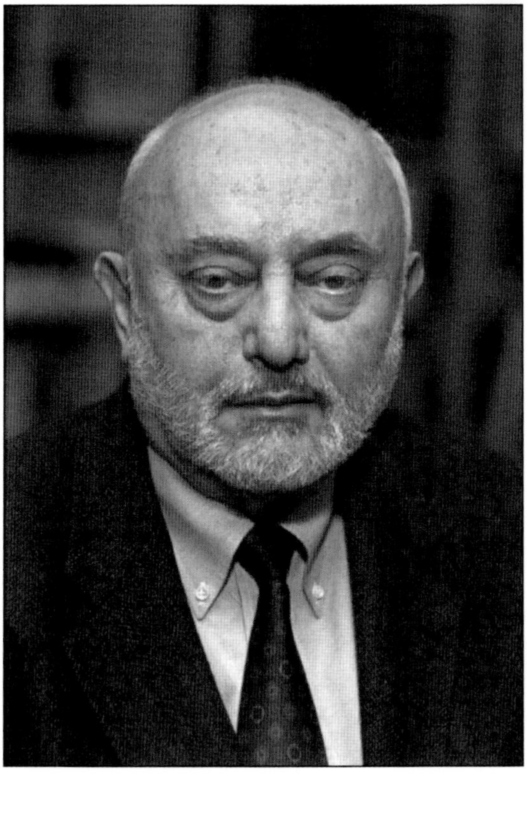

Philip Chotsky grew up in a poor family on the Hill during the Depression. He graduated as an electrical engineer from Carnegie Tech thanks to the GI Bill of Rights. Ultimately, he founded three highly respected trade schools: the Rosedale Technical Institute and the Electronic Institutes in Pittsburgh and Harrisburg. He established a charitable foundation that has given nearly $10 million to cultural arts and educational programs around Pittsburgh.

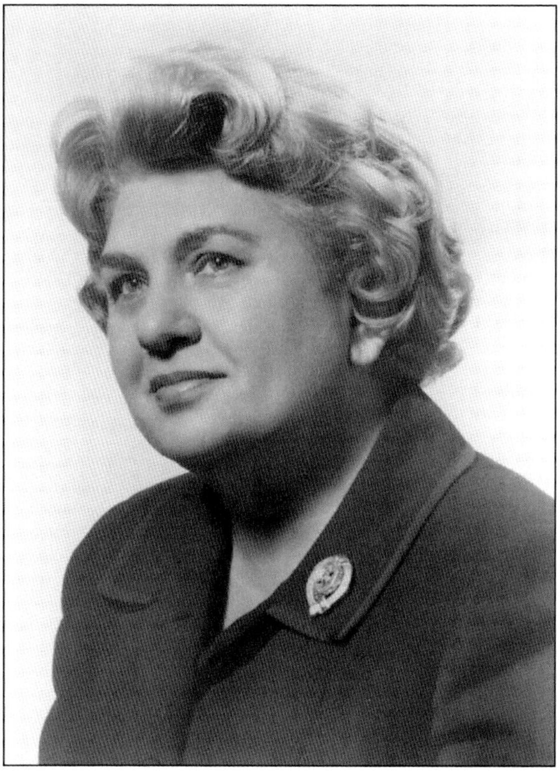

Dr. Dorothy Finkelhor and her husband, Dr. L. Herbert Finkelhor, founded the Business Training College in downtown Pittsburgh in 1933. This school trained students in business careers. In 1960, the State of Pennsylvania chartered the institution as Point Park Junior College, which became Point Park University in 2003. Dorothy Finkelhor served as the first president of the college from 1960 to 1967.

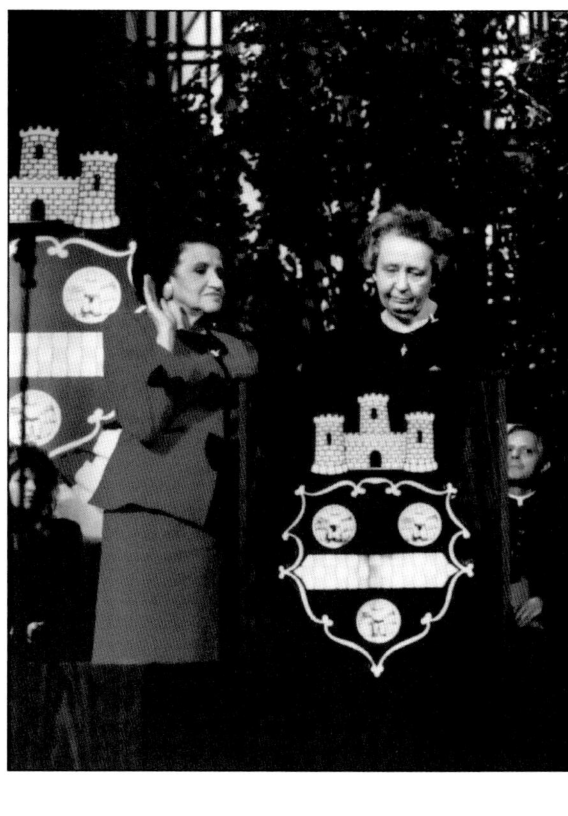

Sophie Masloff, the daughter of illiterate Romanian immigrants, got into politics and rose from city council president to become the first woman and the first Jew elected mayor of the City of Pittsburgh. When Mayor Richard Caliguiri died in office, the 70-year-old Sophie not only completed his term, but also won an election herself in 1990. She was beloved by many and called "Pittsburgh's favorite grandmother." She died in 2014.

Six

Jews in America's Wars

Ever since the Civil War, when members of the tiny Jewish community in Pittsburgh signed up to fight for the Union cause, Jews have participated in America's wars. Jacob Brunn was the first soldier from Allegheny County to fall in the Civil War. According to war records, about 100,000 Jews served in World War I, constituting four to five percent of the total military personnel at a time when Jews made up only three percent of the population. In World War II, 550,000 Jews served. As one historian has written, "The participation of eleven percent of the Jewish population in the service or fifty percent of the men age eighteen to forty-four ensured that few Jewish families would not have a close relative in uniform." Pittsburgh Jews fought in all the theaters of the war—Europe, the Pacific, and North Africa—and served in all branches of the military. Like other GIs, they were shocked to see the concentration camps that they liberated. Marvin Josephs of Pittsburgh could never extinguish the memory of what he had seen. Eugene Cohen was at the Maidanek concentration camp and took testimony from captured Germans that was used in the Nuremberg trials after the war. Norman Waldman was a 17-year-old private in the 82nd Airborne Division who parachuted out over the beaches of Normandy on D-Day. "The scary part wasn't jumping; it was getting shot at when there was nothing you could do about it." Leroy Bloom, a 1936 Taylor Allderdice High School graduate, was awarded the Distinguished Flying Cross for flying more than 30 missions, mostly over Germany. These men were not alone in their exemplary service and sacrifice. Most returned after the war. Some did not. 2nd Lt. Arthur Buchman, the son of the second president of Temple Sinai, Harry Buchman, was killed in action December 15, 1944, after being taken prisoner when the Japanese conquered the Philippines. Buchman was posthumously awarded the Purple Heart, a Presidential Accolade, and a Silver Star for his bravery. These men were all part of "the greatest generation."

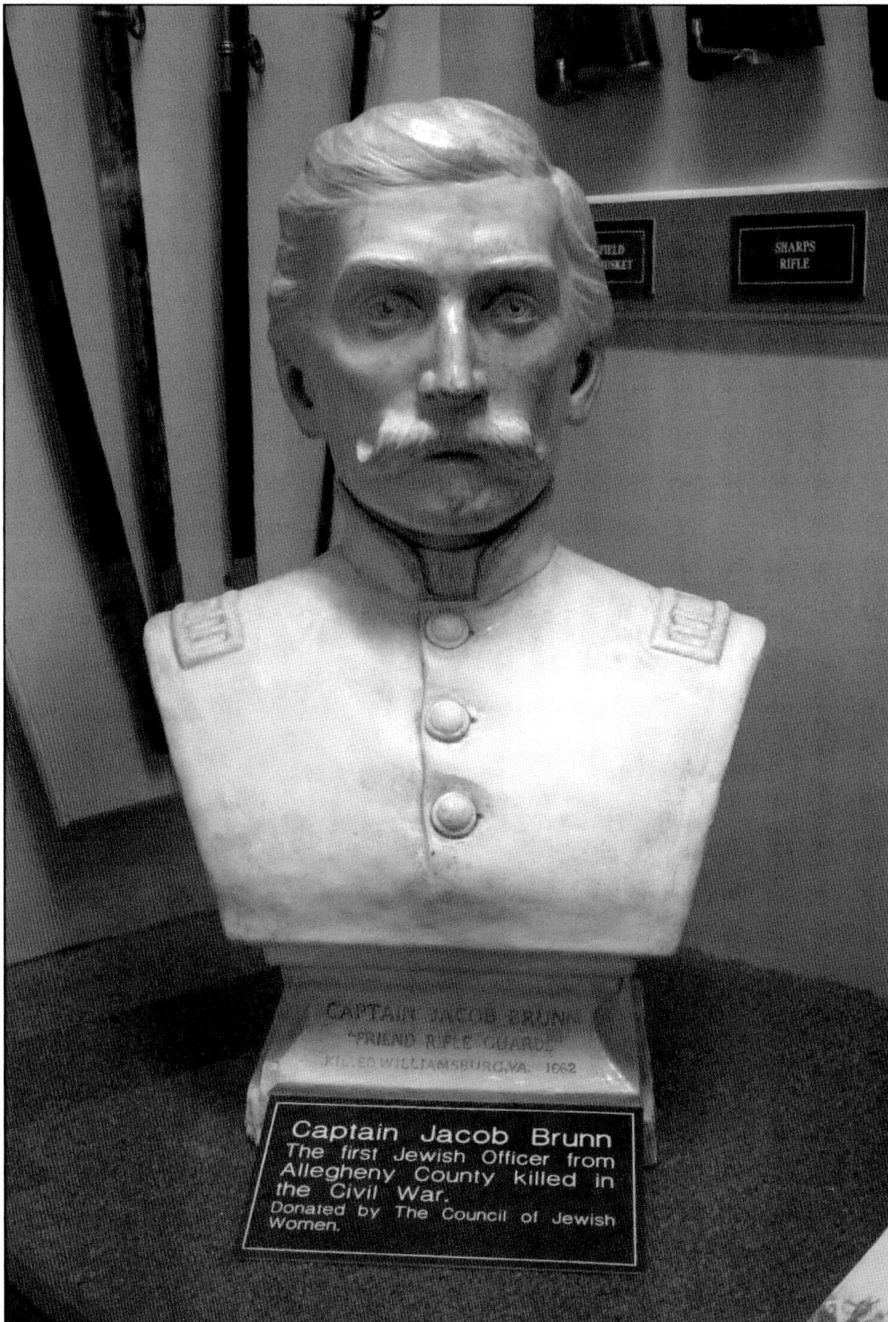

Capt. Jacob Brunn, a German immigrant, was one of the 10 young men from the tiny Pittsburgh Jewish community of several hundred in 1861 who signed up for the Union cause. He obtained the highest rank among the Pittsburgh Jews, becoming captain of a New York infantry company. He was killed in action in 1862 and was buried at the cemetery on Troy Hill, with all expenses paid by the Morganstern brothers, his employers. Pittsburgh Jews overwhelmingly supported the Union cause and greatly admired Pres. Abraham Lincoln. (Soldiers & Sailors Memorial Hall & Museum Trust, Inc.)

Eugene B. Strassburger was one of the four sons of Samuel and Julia Morganstern Strassburger. A graduate of Harvard College and Law School, he served in World War I. After the war, he returned to Pittsburgh, became a Duquesne University law professor, and ultimately served as a principal in what became the law firm of Strassburger and McKenna.

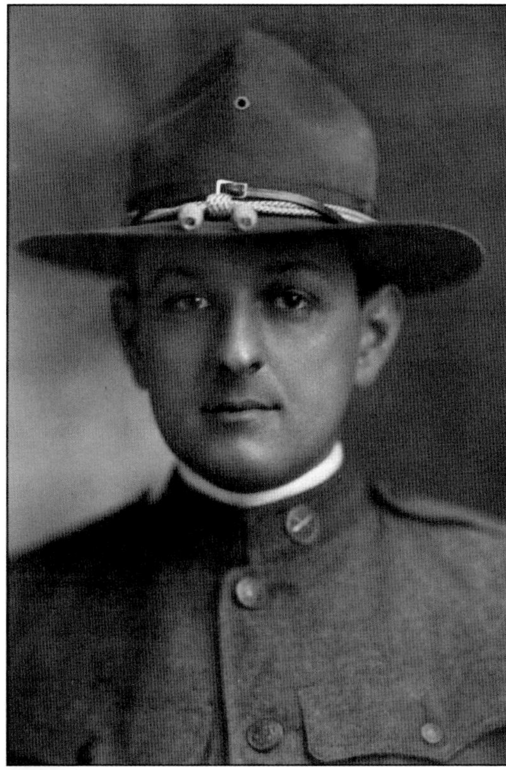

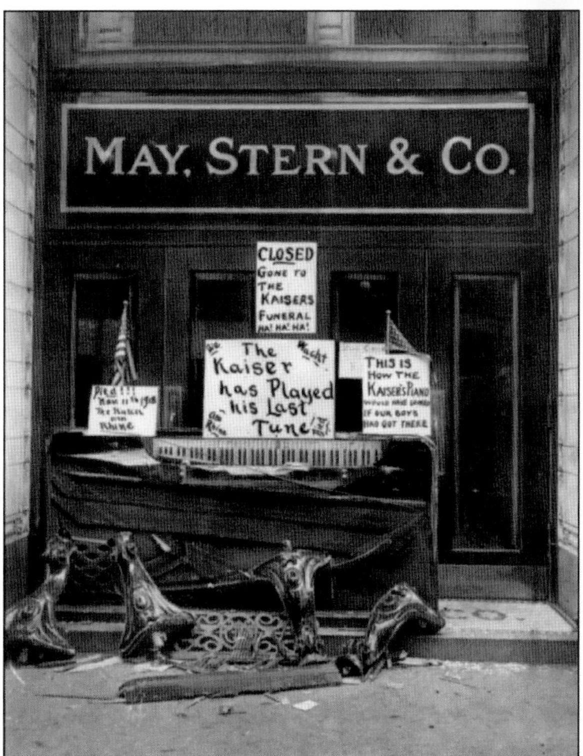

This sign in the window of the May, Stern & Co. furniture store after World War I expresses the sentiment of the victorious Americans. Leo Lehman, who rose from stock boy to president, was active in the Red Cross during World War I. In his will, he bequeathed monies "to promote tolerance and good will."

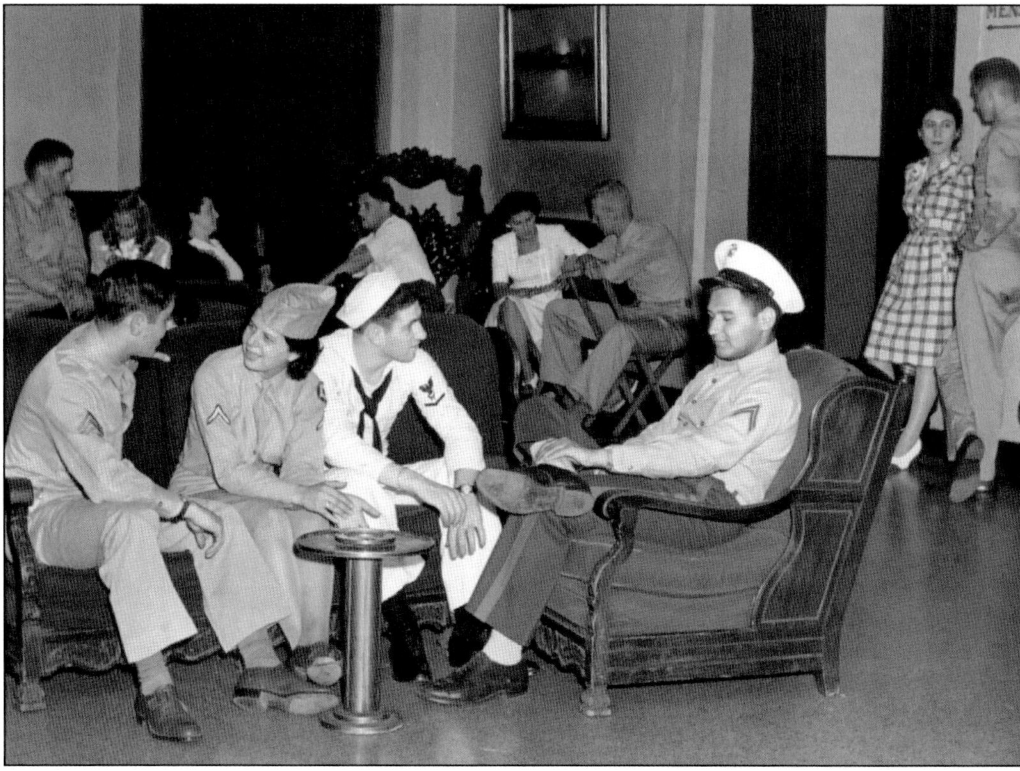

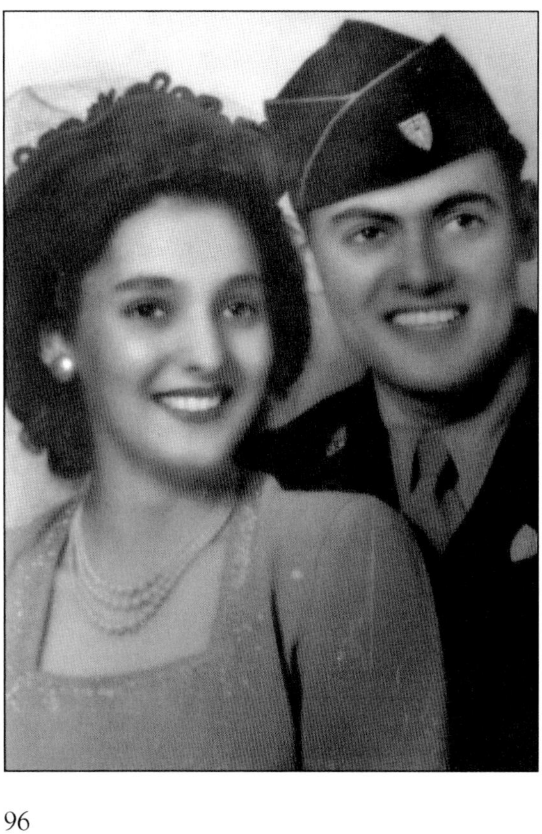

This picture is of young servicemen relaxing at the Y Canteen before being shipped to the front in 1943. There are no exact figures on the numbers of servicemen from Pittsburgh, let alone Pittsburgh Jews, who served in World War II, but the Jewish War Vets in 1948 numbered among its four posts at least 5,000 veterans, including those from the Spanish-American War and the two world wars.

Harry Melnick and his three brothers were all in World War II. Ben was in the Army in Africa and Europe, Pershing, in the Air Force in Hawaii, and Milton, with the Navy in the Pacific. Harry was in the Battle of the Bulge, and his 26th Infantry Division liberated the Gusen concentration camp. They were first-generation Americans. Harry married Mollie Spokane in 1943. (Rene Abrams.)

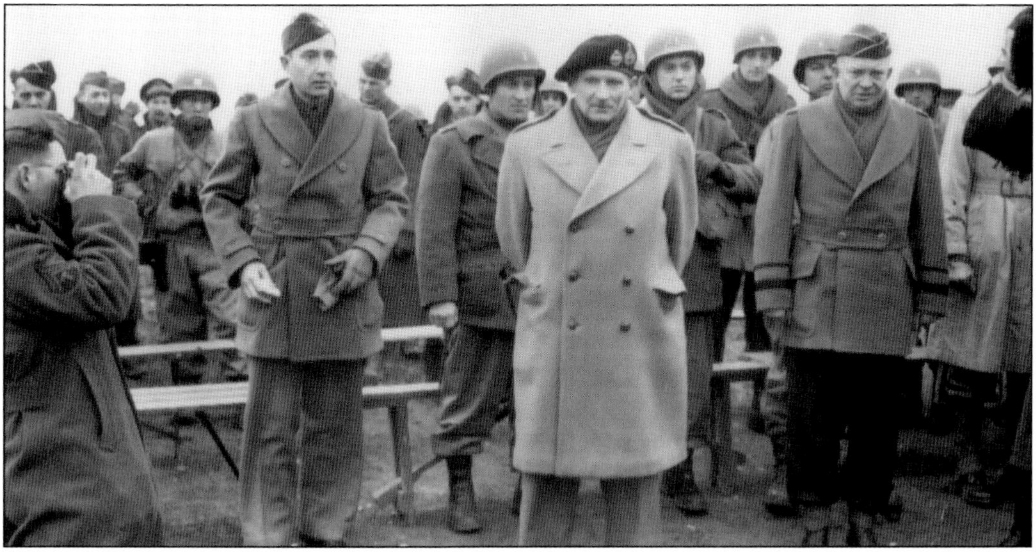

Col. Irving J. Newman (left) was head of all photography and filming for the Supreme Headquarters Allied Expeditionary Force in Europe. In this picture taken on D-day, he is standing next to British field marshal Montgomery (center) and General Eisenhower (right). He was the brother of Nancy Newman Frank, a respected professional social worker with what now is called the Jewish Family and Children's Service.

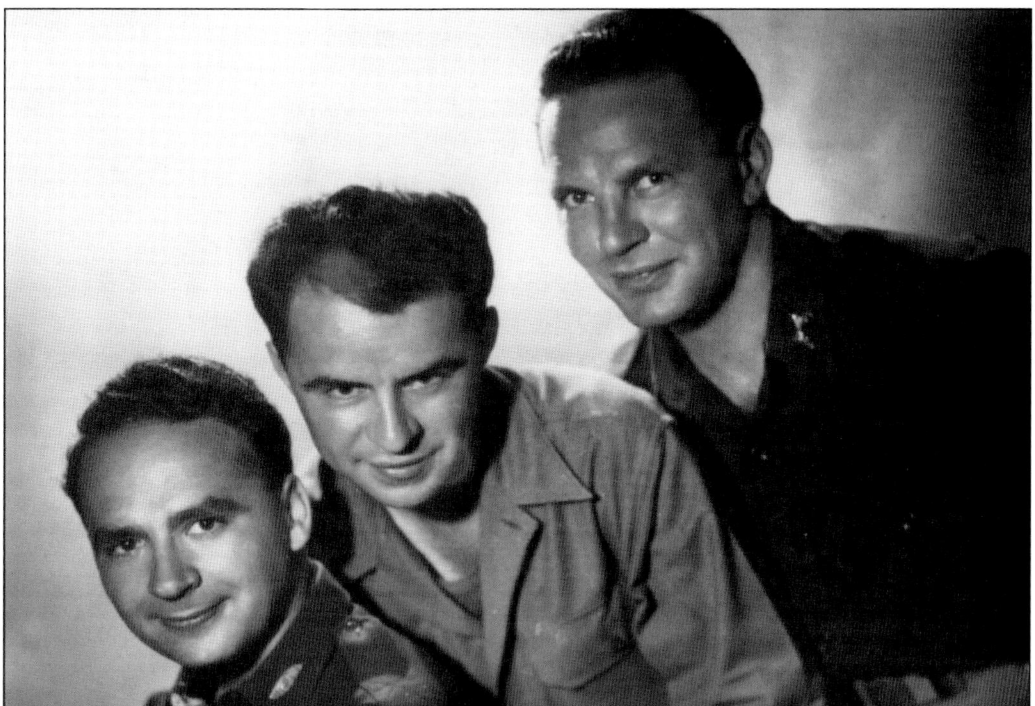

From left to right, Jack, Sam, and Gerald Ziskind were three of the five children of Polish Jewish immigrant parents who ran a grocery store in the Strip District. They all served simultaneously. Jack became a colonel in the Army Reserve Intelligence Unit. Sam stayed with the Army for the rest of his career, working in public relations. Gerald fought in the Battle of the Bulge.

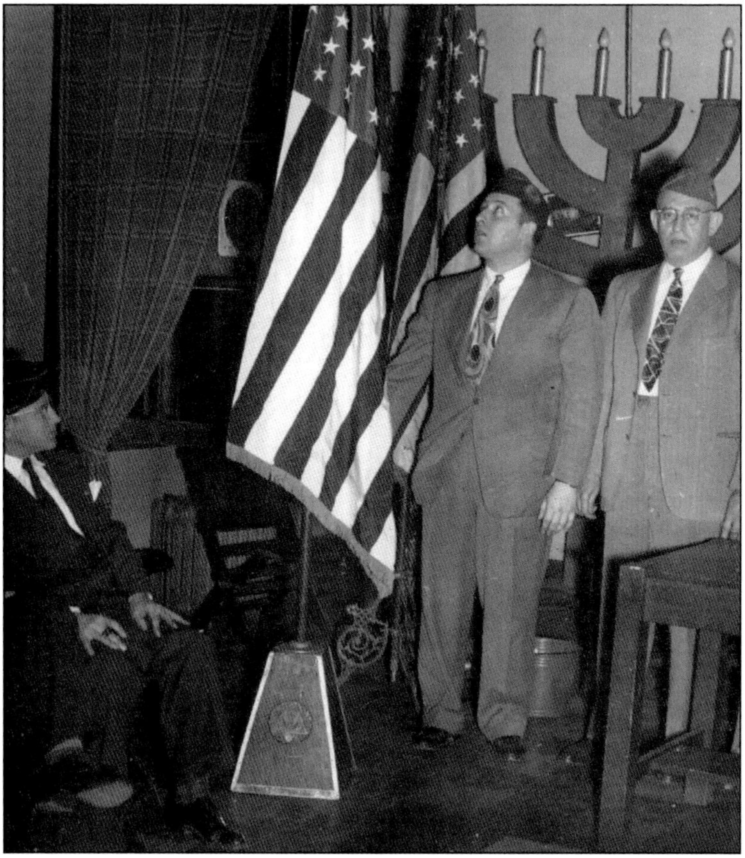

This is Harvey Deaktor raising an American flag at a Jewish War Veterans Post No. 49 event on May 13, 1948. The Deaktor family ran Star Markets, a popular grocery chain in Pittsburgh. (Clarence "Code" Gomberg.)

Clarence (Code) Gomberg (left) was commander of the Jewish War Veterans in Pittsburgh and a World War II veteran. He was with the 343rd Medical Battalion in Europe. Harry Schaeffer (right) of Pittsburgh rose to become national commander of the Jewish War Vets and pushed for a boycott of the 1936 Olympic Games in Berlin. (Clarence "Code" Gomberg.)

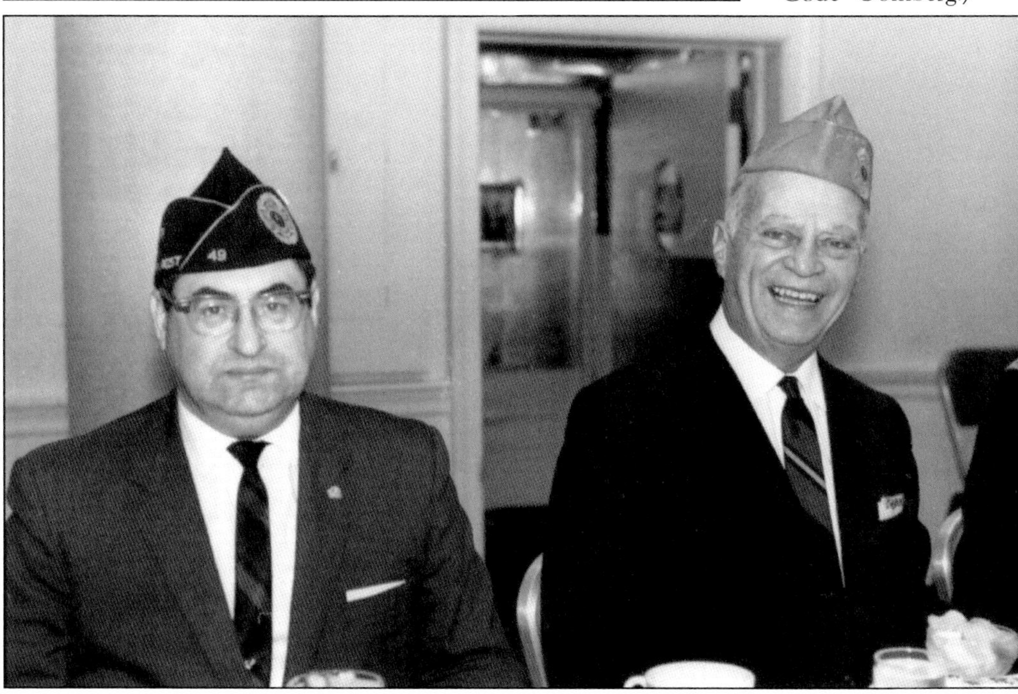

Seven

THE STRUGGLE FOR ISRAEL

The Zionist movement, the movement to found a Jewish homeland in Palestine, began in the latter decades of the 19th century. Pittsburgh was one of the earliest and most enthusiastic bastions of Zionist support in America. It was a cause embraced by many Eastern European Jews, young and old, who had experienced the ravages of anti-Semitism in Europe and who were imbued with a Jewish nationalistic spirit. Among the early pioneers in Pittsburgh were Ralph Raphael, Maurice Avner, Henry Jackson, Morris Neaman, and others. When the Balfour Declaration was promulgated in 1917, seemingly pledging England's support for the establishment of a Jewish homeland in Palestine, Jews in Pittsburgh and around the world rejoiced. Sol Rosenbloom, a wealthy businessman, contributed to the founding of Hebrew University on Mount Scopus in Jerusalem and traveled there in 1922 to attend the university's opening. Monies were raised throughout the 1920s and 1930s to help develop the land and support the needs of the Jewish refugees who were able to get there. Those needs increased dramatically in the 1940s with the struggle to establish the state of Israel, declared by David Ben-Gurion in May 1948 after a vote by the United Nations to establish a Jewish and a Palestinian Arab state. The Arabs rejected the plan, and the fight was on. While Americans generally favored the creation of the state of Israel, a number of young Pittsburghers actually left Pittsburgh to help in the battle. David Lowenthal, an avid Zionist, joined the Haganah, the Jewish defense forces, and in 1947 was on the ship named *Exodus*. That ship was filled with more than 4,000 Holocaust survivors who were turned back to Europe by the British after a battle on the ship. Al Twersky became a jeep driver in a platoon in the Palmach's Negev Brigade of the Haganah. Nikki Reidbord and Ruth Levine were volunteer nurses during the war. Art Jaffe, who was trained as an intelligence officer in World War II, was involved in intelligence-gathering operations in Palestine. Jews at home made prodigious efforts to raise money and provide support for the fledging state. Pittsburgh Jews have continued to make important contributions to the welfare needs of Israeli citizens throughout the years.

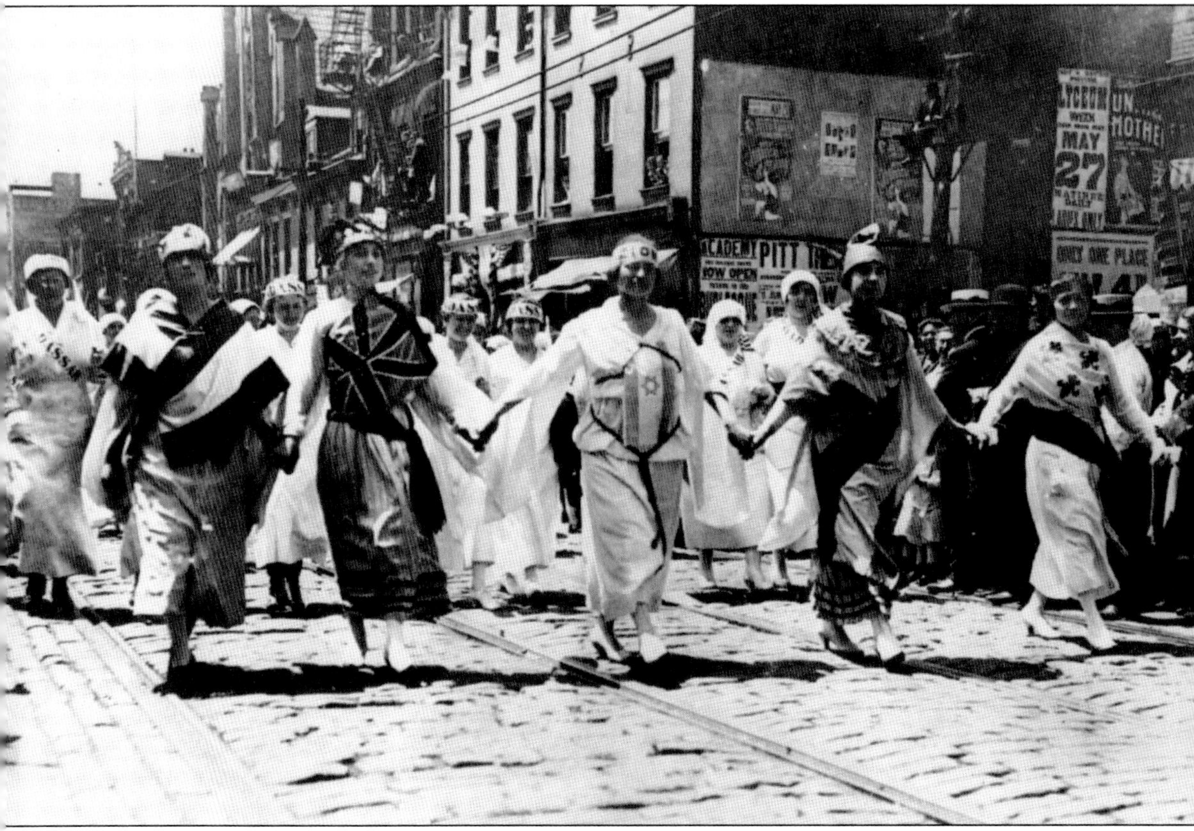

In 1918, the American Federation of Zionists held their national convention in Pittsburgh. Ten thousand men, women, and children marched in a parade. Among the marchers were several hundred "Mothers of Democracy," whose sons had been in World War I. One writer called the parade "the greatest Jewish spectacle yet to take place in Pittsburgh." There was great excitement in the city because of what the Jews saw as the promise of the Balfour Declaration and a sense that the dream of Theodore Herzl and the Zionists to reestablish their ancient homeland in Palestine was about to be fulfilled. Not only had the British promised to support a Jewish homeland, but the Ottoman Turks who had been in possession of the land were about to lose it as a result of their defeat in World War I. Those hopes, however, would soon be dashed when the British began to retreat on their promise in the 1920s and 1930s in the face of Arab violence.

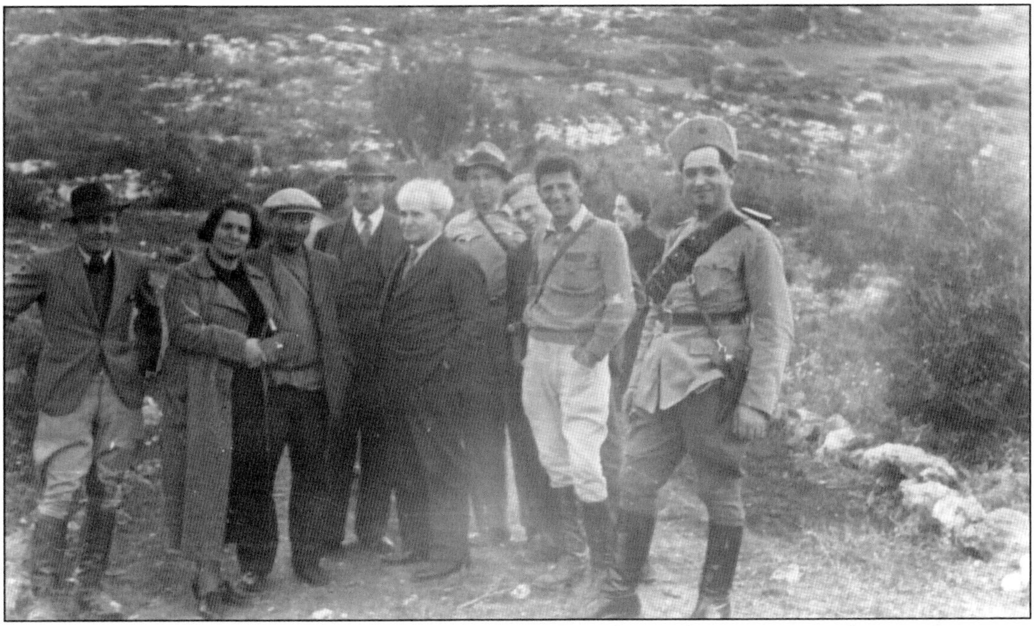

Ralph Atlas immigrated to Pittsburgh from Poland in the early 1930s to study engineering at Carnegie Tech. On the far left in this 1938 picture with David Ben-Gurion (center), Atlas went to Palestine, translated military manuals into Hebrew, helped train Haganah fighters (he was the boxing champion in college) and fought with the British Army against the Germans in North Africa during World War II.

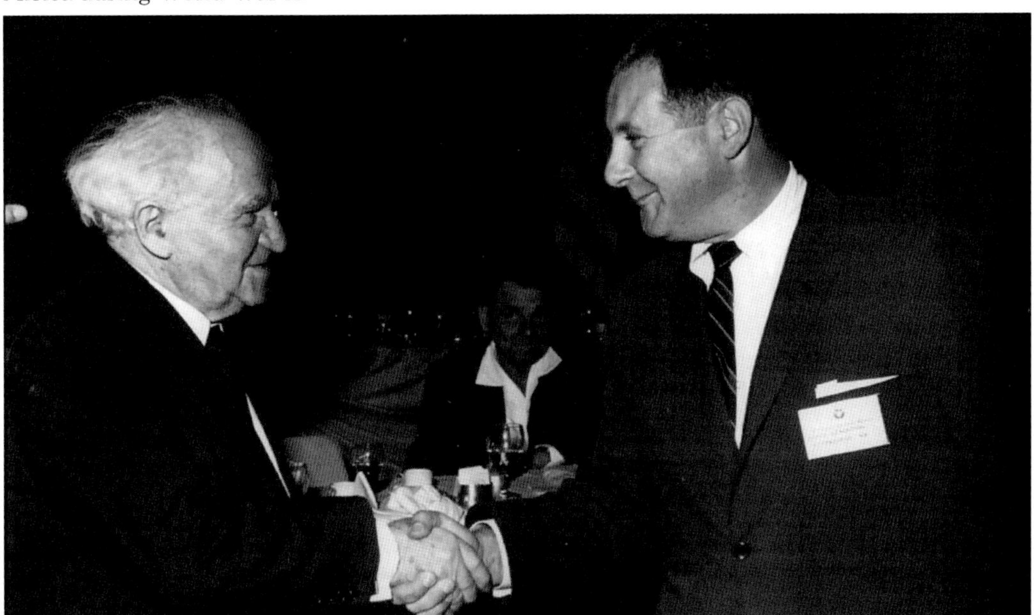

David Lowenthal (right) is pictured with Ben-Gurion, the prime minister of Israel. Lowenthal left Pittsburgh in 1947 to join the Haganah, as they struggled first against the British and then against the Arabs for independence. He was on the *Exodus*, as well as the *Pan York*, trying to avoid the British blockade and land refugees on the shores of Palestine. He returned to Pittsburgh and led the Zionist movement in the city for many years.

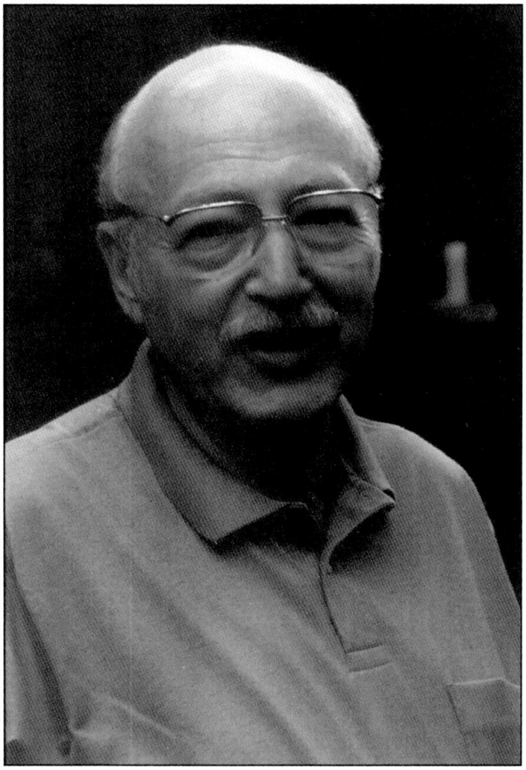

Al Twersky served with the US Merchant Marine Naval Reserve in the Pacific during World War II. A few years later, as an avid, young Zionist, he joined the fight for the state of Israel. He was driving a jeep in the Negev Desert to protect isolated kibbutzim when an Egyptian mine blew up under him. Twersky was hospitalized for a year before heading home minus a leg.

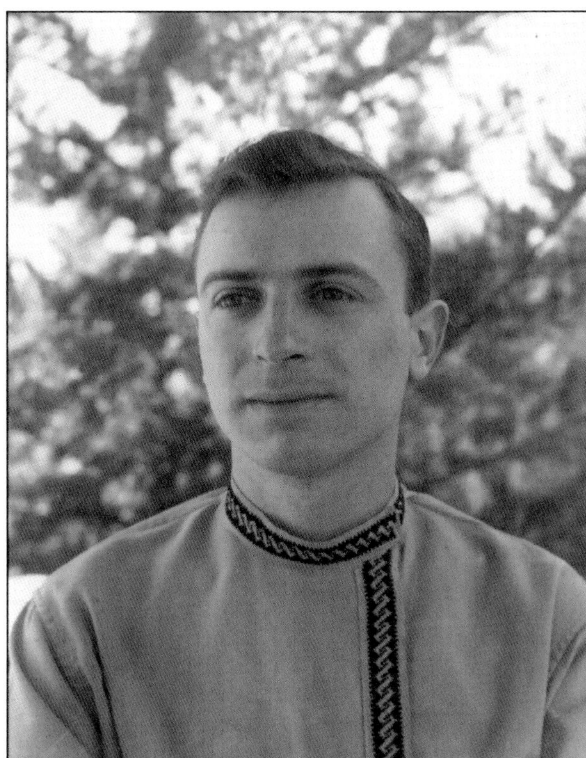

After training as an officer at Penn State, Arthur Jaffe served in a US Army Combat-Intelligence Unit, landing on Omaha Beach on D-Day, June 6, 1944. He went to the Hebrew University on the GI Bill of Rights and continued his intelligence work, this time for the future state of Israel. Later on, Jaffe worked for the Carnegie Museum of Art and then the United Jewish Federation of Pittsburgh.

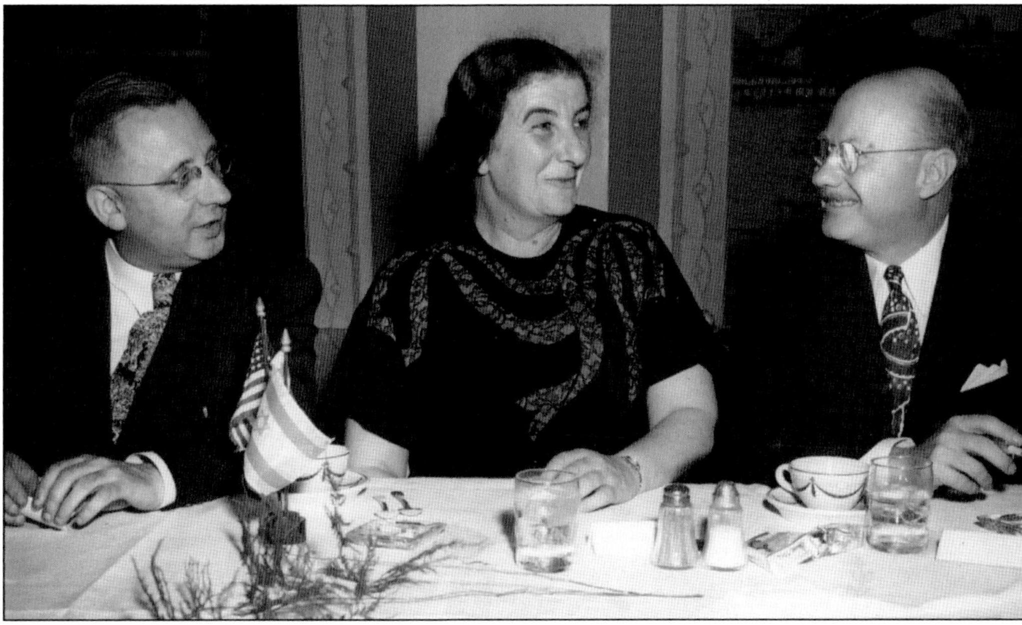

The Pittsburgh Jewish community, like Jewish communities around the world, launched fundraising campaigns to help support the new state of Israel in 1948. In this picture are, from left to right, Emanuel Spector, a Fifth Avenue clothing merchant who chaired the campaign; Golda Meir, a future prime minister; and Charles Rosenbloom, an active Zionist and heavy contributor to Jewish causes. A remarkable $2.9 million was raised locally.

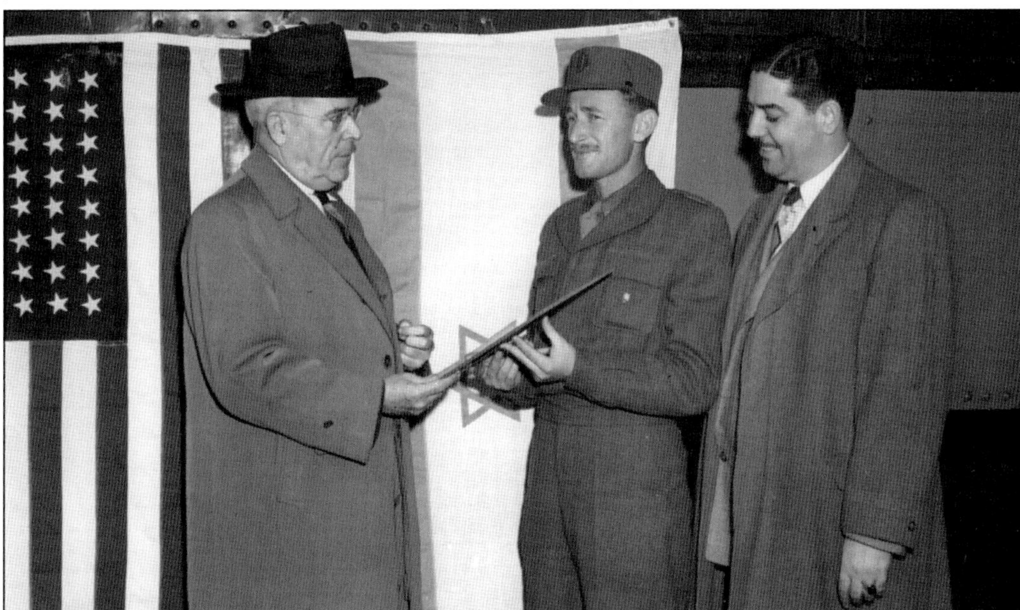

Pittsburgh mayor David L. Lawrence (left), a staunch friend of Israel, and Herman Fineberg (right) are greeting an Israeli soldier who arrived in Pittsburgh on the United Jewish Appeal's "Caravan of Hope" railway tour in 1949. Herman Fineberg, owner of Iron City Uniform and Towel Service, was a lifelong Zionist, local leader of B'nai Brith, and a Federation volunteer. A forest in Israel was established in honor of David Lawrence.

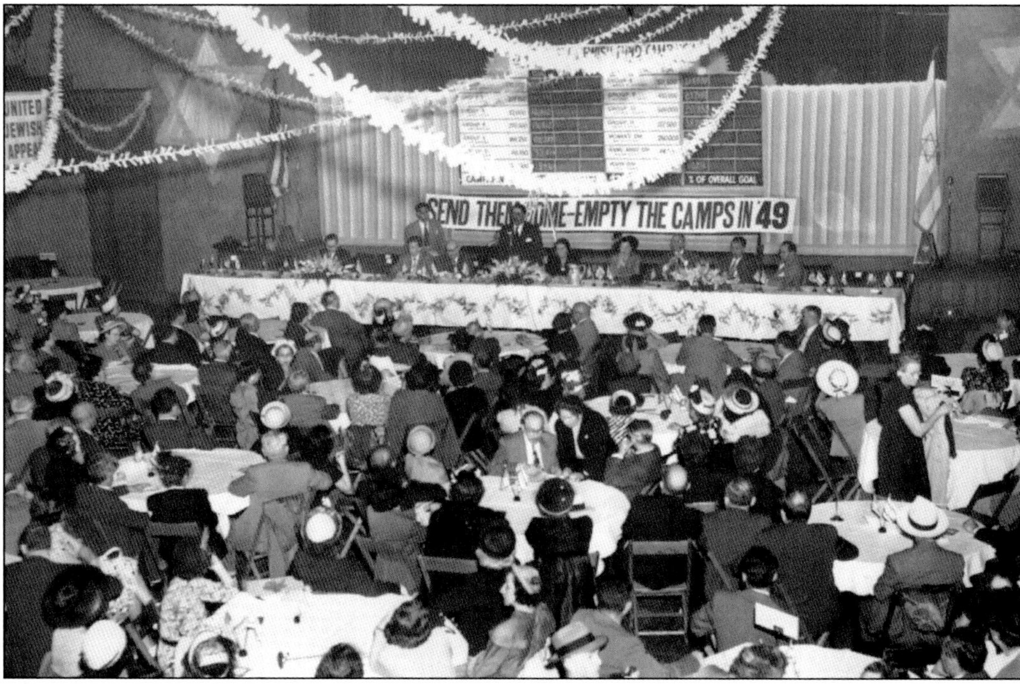

This 1949 "Empty the Camps" dinner was part of the campaign to empty the displaced persons camps in Europe where Holocaust survivors were languishing after the war. The hope was to get those survivors resettled in the United States despite discriminatory and restrictive immigration laws or in the new state of Israel.

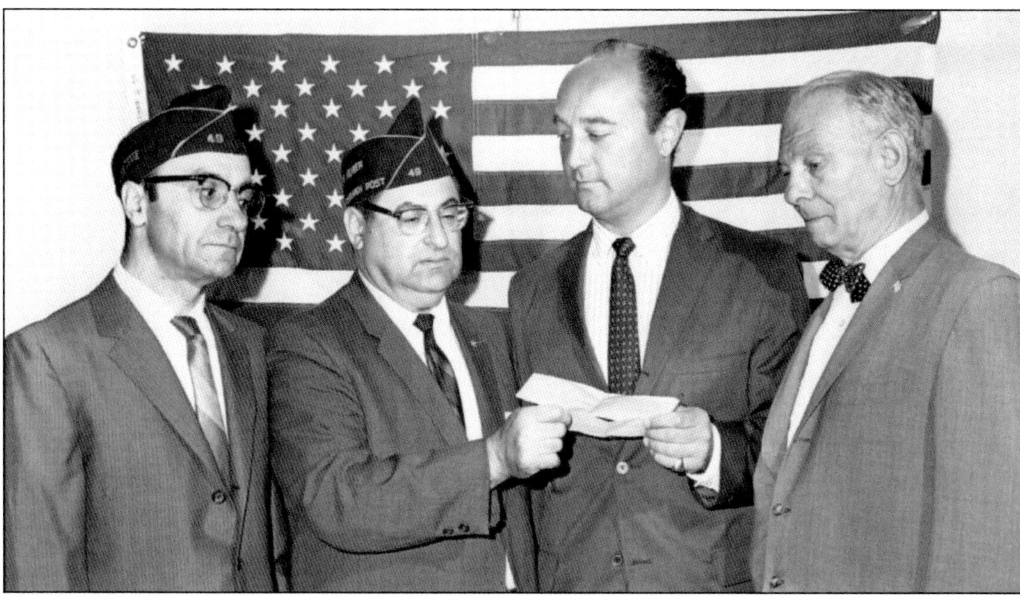

Clarence (Code) Gomberg, commander of Jewish War Veterans Post No. 49, is giving Alvin Rogal, United Jewish Federation president, a check for $1,000 in 1967. In the months leading up to the Six-Day War in June 1967, American Jews were fearful of Israel being destroyed as the neighboring Arab states, led by Pres. Gamal Abdel Nasser of Egypt, threatened to "throw Israel into the sea." Money was raised to help support Israel. (Clarence "Code" Gomberg.)

Eight

Jews in the Arts, Medicine, and Sports

The famous Jewish comedian Sam Levinson, in talking about his immigrant mother, once remarked that, as far as she was concerned, one violin lesson equaled four ice-cream cones, so she cancelled the ice-cream cones, and he took the violin lessons. Music was important in Jewish life, and music classes were a staple at both the Y and the Irene Kaufmann Settlement. The Pittsburgh Symphony owed its revival to attorney Edward Spector, who gave up his law career to provide management and raise money, often from willing Jewish donors. But music was not the only cultural interest of Pittsburgh Jews. Aaron Gorson was a professional painter, glamorizing Pittsburgh's smoke-filled landscapes. Samuel Rosenberg spent his entire career in Pittsburgh, teaching many local artists and producing many prize-winning pictures. Henry Koerner, Jane Haskell, Aaronel Gruber, and now Burton Morris are just four of the renowned Pittsburgh Jewish artists. Arthur Carl Lehman, owner of Blaw-Knox Company, was a major philanthropist and art patron, as was Charles Rosenbloom. In architecture, as in the art world, prominent Jews were important patrons to world-famous architects. Edgar Kaufmann employed Frank Lloyd Wright; the Franks used Walter Gropius and designer Marcel Breuer. Pittsburgh spawned its own architects, including James Speyer and Alexander Sharove. The Rauh family, with Helen Wayne Rauh as a famous actress of her day, established the Pittsburgh Playhouse. Councilman Abe Wolk and Edgar Kaufman founded the Civic Light Opera. Joan Apt was instrumental in the establishment of the Pittsburgh Public Theater. Richard Karp directed the Pittsburgh Opera, and Loti Falk was key in launching the Pittsburgh Ballet. These are only some of the people who contributed their talents to Pittsburgh, and this does not include the people who left the city to launch their careers and contribute nationally.

The field of medicine has attracted many Jews, and a number have made breakthrough contributions to their profession and to the city. And in sports, several Pittsburgh Jews have proved notable through their action and, perhaps more importantly, through their vision. No one has been more beloved in the sports world than the creator of the Steelers' Terrible Towel. Myron Cope is gone, but his towel lives on.

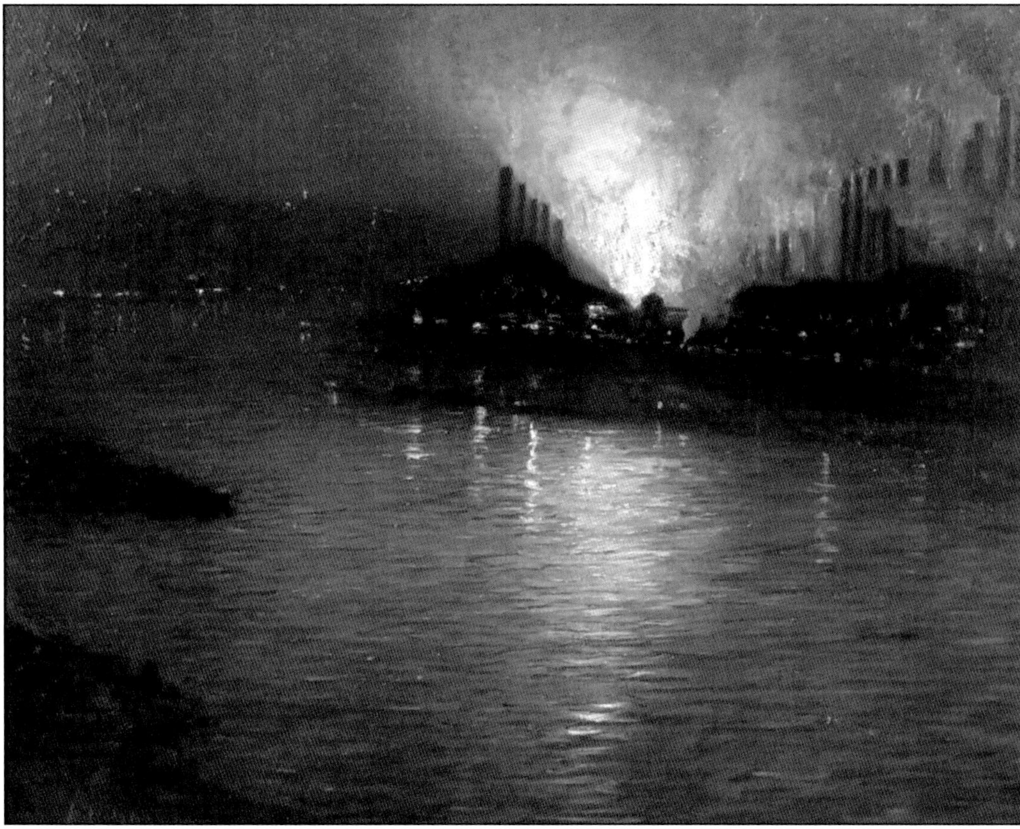

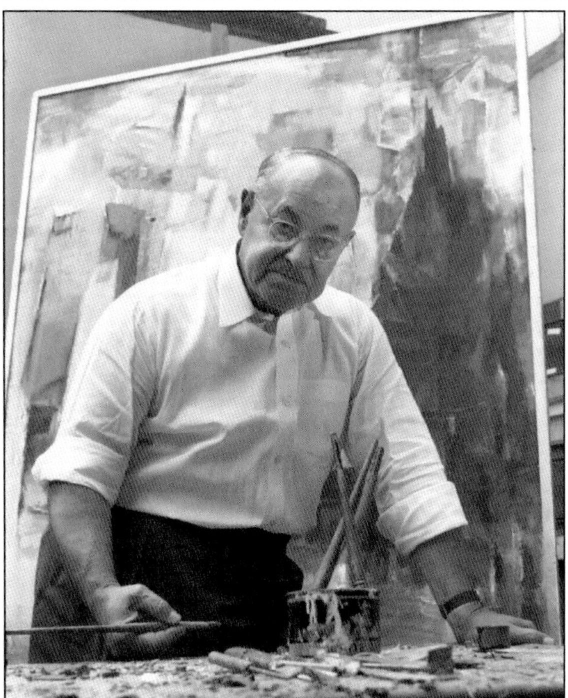

Steelmaking at Night on the Mon is by Aaron Gorson, a struggling artist of the early 20th century. Gorson loved the smoke-filled, darkened air of the city. To him, Pittsburgh at the turn of the century was beautiful, which was a very different view from the prevailing notion! Today, seven of Gorson's paintings, including a self-portrait, hang in the Duquesne Club downtown.

Samuel Rosenberg was a beloved teacher in Pittsburgh who started teaching at the Irene Kaufmann Settlement as a young man. He taught at the Y and at Carnegie Tech, where his pupils included Philip Pearlstein and Andrew Warhola (better known as Andy Warhol). He had 21 one-man exhibitions and won many prizes, and his art today is in collections around the country. He died in 1972.

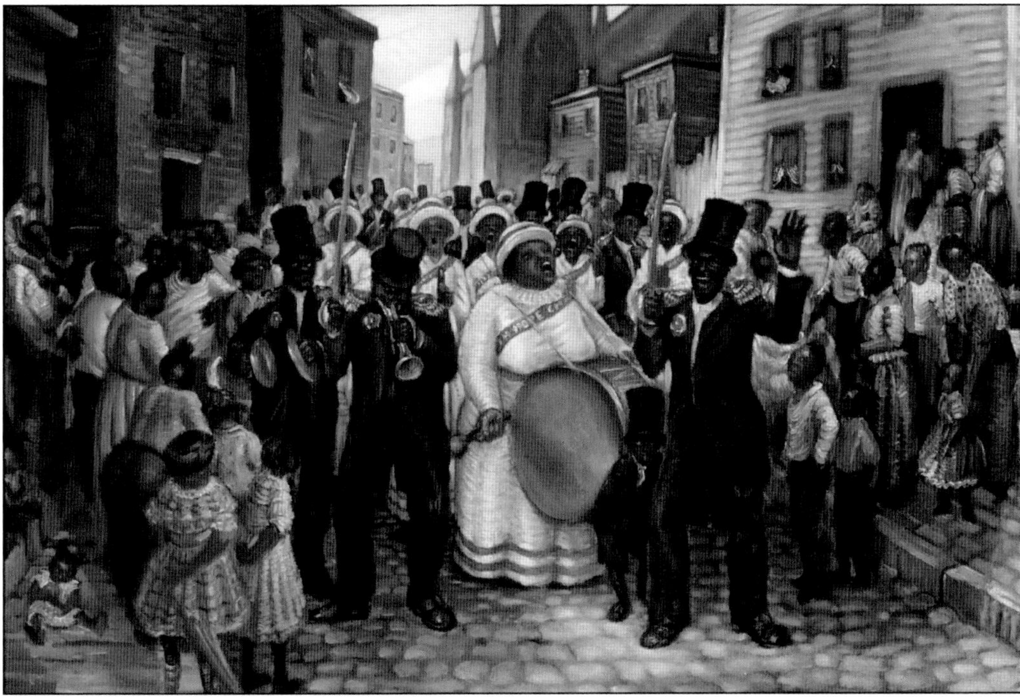

God's Chillin by Samuel Rosenberg in 1934 is a sympathetic portrayal of poor blacks living on the Hill during the Depression. While this painting is upbeat, many of Rosenberg's other works, like *Eviction* one year later, are poignant pictures depicting the plight of African Americans at this time. Rosenberg himself had lived on the Hill a decade earlier.

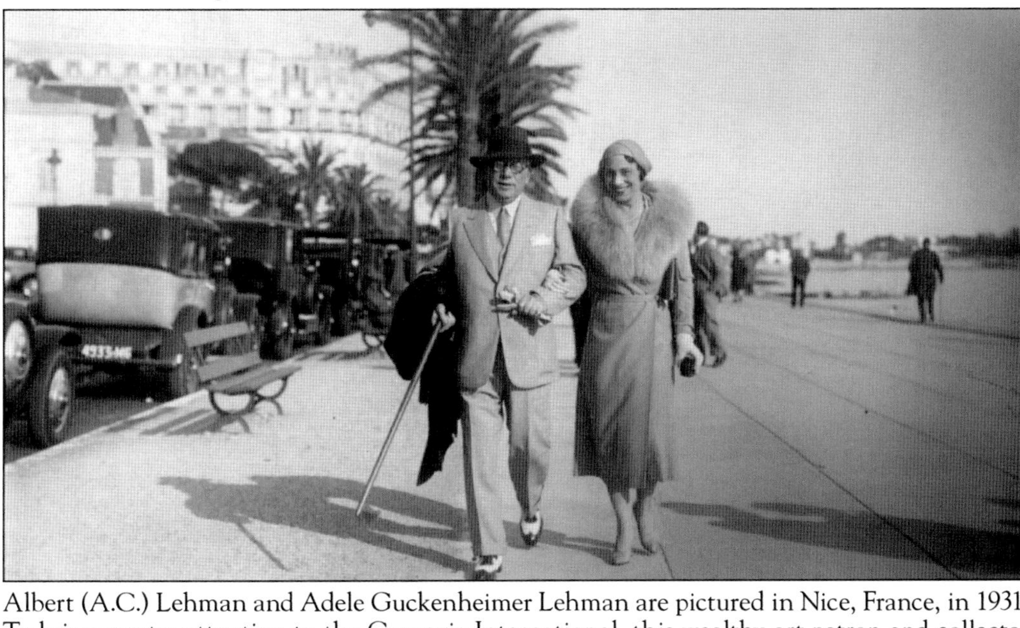

Albert (A.C.) Lehman and Adele Guckenheimer Lehman are pictured in Nice, France, in 1931. To bring greater attention to the Carnegie International, this wealthy art patron and collector offered prize money for the first-place painting and an offer to buy that painting for up to $10,000. Lehman was appointed to the board of the Carnegie Institute in 1930, considered then "the last, most visible bastion of WASP leadership in Pittsburgh."

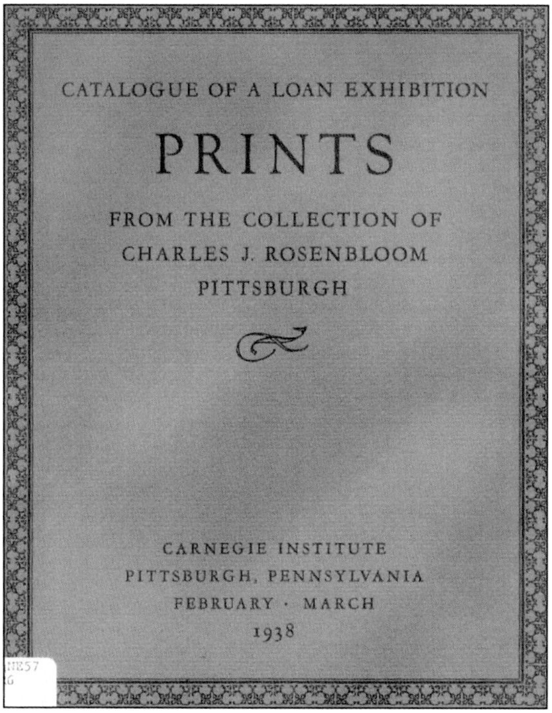

CATALOGUE OF A LOAN EXHIBITION

PRINTS

FROM THE COLLECTION OF
CHARLES J. ROSENBLOOM
PITTSBURGH

CARNEGIE INSTITUTE
PITTSBURGH, PENNSYLVANIA
FEBRUARY · MARCH
1938

Charles Rosenbloom was another major art collector. When he died in 1973, he bequeathed his entire art collection to the Carnegie Museum of Art. His print collection totaled some 300 prints and encompassed every period of printmaking. Along with his paintings, sculpture, and graphic art, it represented one of the most significant gifts to the museum since its founding. Rosenbloom, the son of Sol Rosenbloom, had an investment firm.

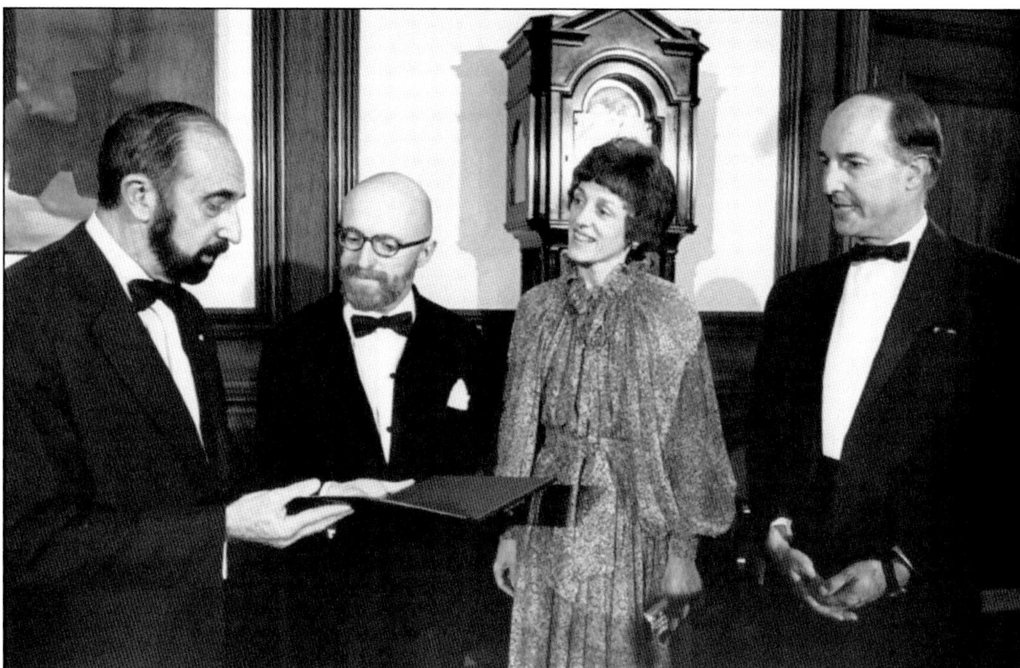

In 1968, Leon Arkus (left) was named director of the Carnegie Museum of Art. He guided the development of the museum's Sarah Mellon Scaife Galleries and increased the size of the museum's permanent collection by 50 percent. He is presenting an award to Pierre Alechinsky, with Joan Mondale and Bill Walton, president of the museum, looking on. Arkus married Jane Callomon, a prominent Pittsburgh advertising executive. (Arkus family.)

Aaronel DeRoy Gruber had an artistic career lasting 61 years until her death in 2011. She studied under Samuel Rosenberg and explored painting, sculpture, photography, and video. She wanted to create her own forms. "I don't want to recreate," she once famously said. A prize-winning artist, many of her works today are in permanent museum collections. She was married to Irving Gruber for 71 years.

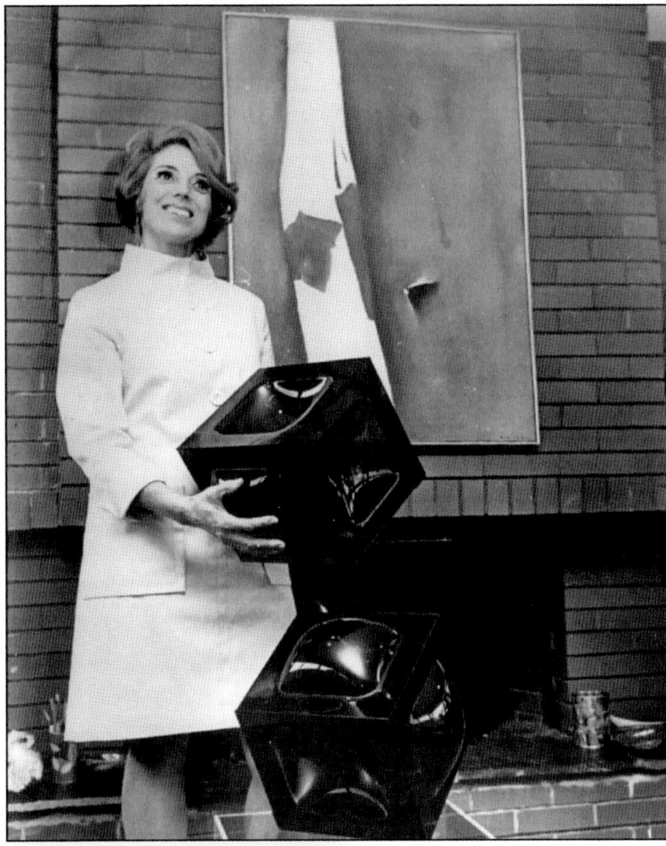

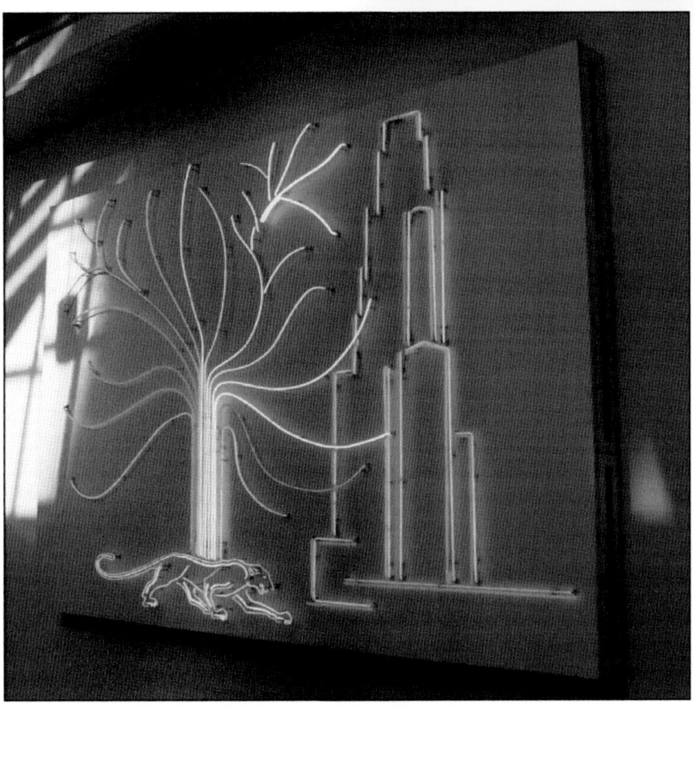

Jane Haskell came to Pittsburgh in 1949, studied under Sam Rosenberg like so many others, and became a teacher and studio artist herself. She was a painter and sculptor until 1979, when she turned to neon, intrigued with the play of light. She established the Haskell Family Acquisition Fund at the Carnegie Museum.

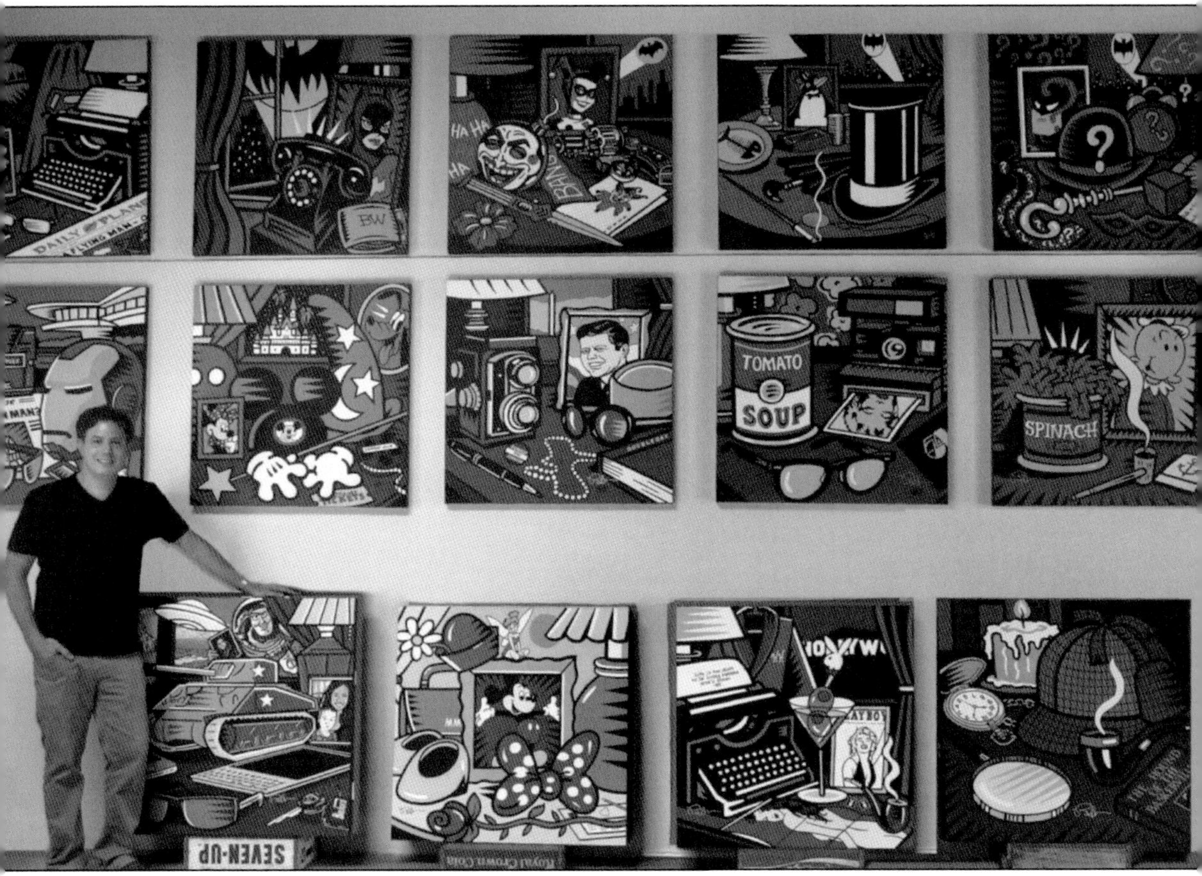

Burton Morris, born in Pittsburgh in 1964, graduated from Carnegie Mellon University. His pop art featuring bold, graphic depictions first appeared on the set of the television series *Friends* in the early 1990s. Since then, Morris has had his artwork selected for the 76th Academy Awards, the 2004 Summer Olympic Games, and the 2006 Major League Baseball All-Star Game, among other major events. He has raised millions for charity. (Morris family.)

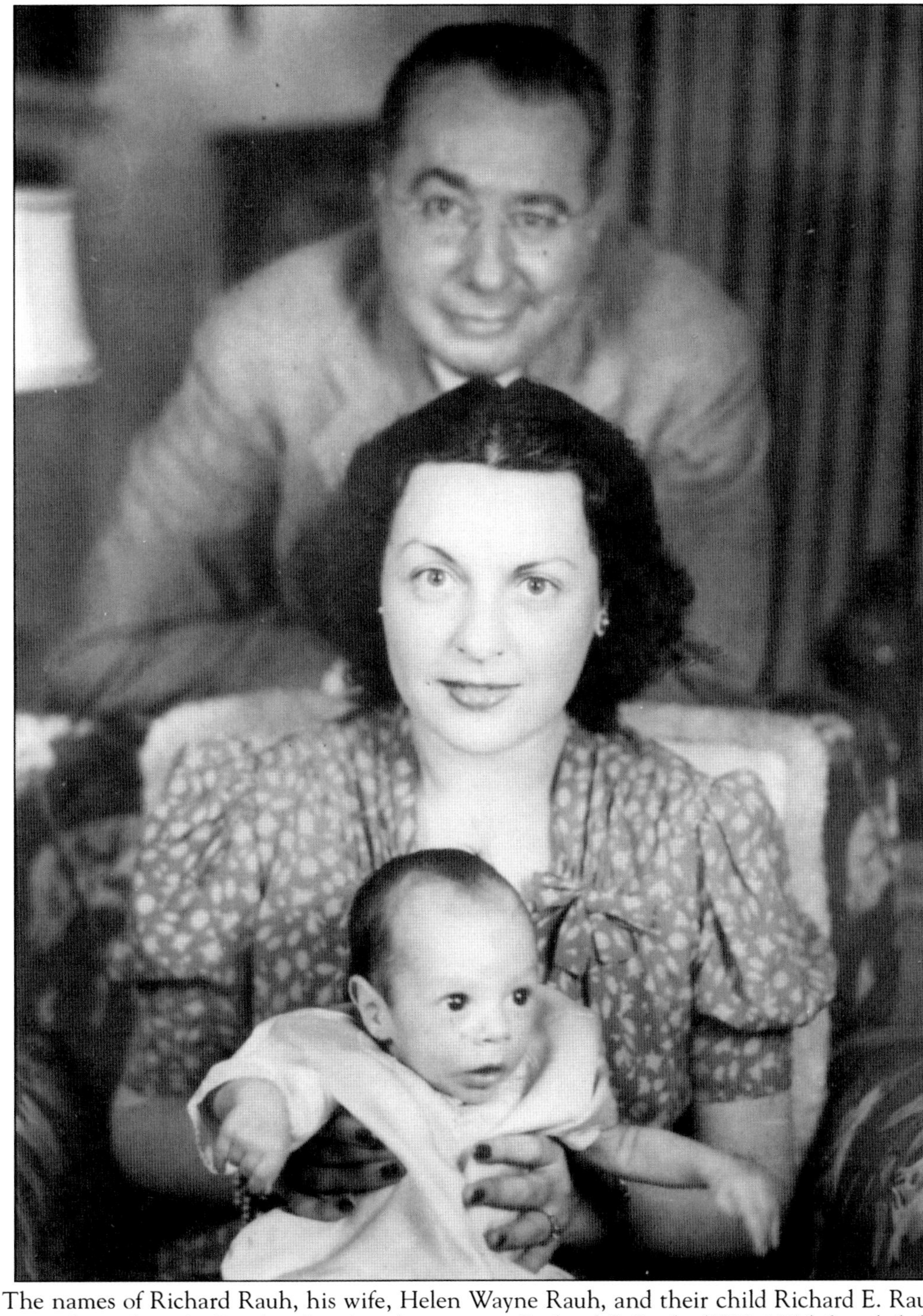

The names of Richard Rauh, his wife, Helen Wayne Rauh, and their child Richard E. Rauh are enshrined on the Pittsburgh cultural arts scene. Richard S. Rauh, (1893–1954) founded the Pittsburgh Playhouse and was a major supporter of the symphony; his wife, Helen (1922–1993), was a famed Pittsburgh actress. Their son Richard E. Rauh (born in 1941) has been an actor, teacher, and major philanthropist to arts programs throughout the city.

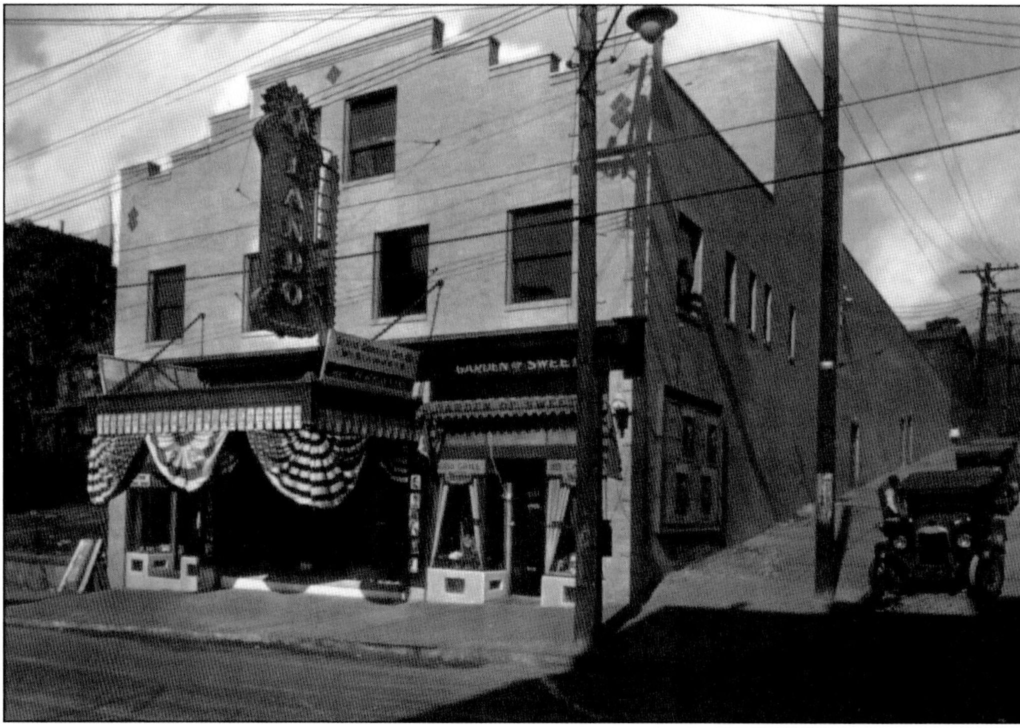

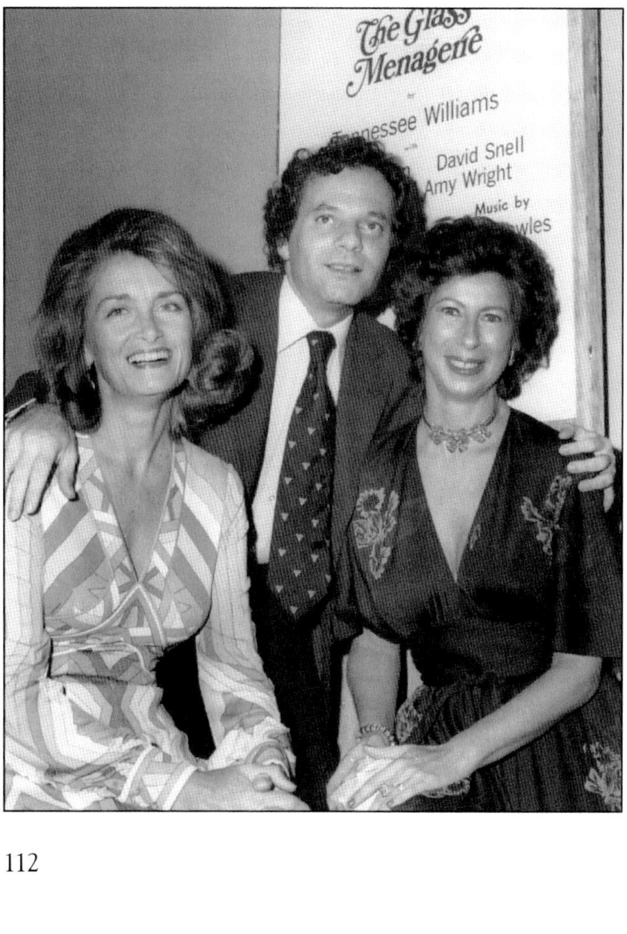

The Lando Theater opened in 1924 on the site of the former Zionist Institute at Centre and Green Streets on the Hill. Founded by William Lando, it was the home of the Yiddish theater in Pittsburgh. However, by 1935, with the passing of the Eastern European immigrant generation, there was no longer the audience to keep the Yiddish theater alive.

In 1974, Joan Apt (right), along with Margaret Rieck (left) and Ben Shaktman (center), founded the Pittsburgh Public Theater. Joan, a child of Cecilia and Robert Frank, loved theater and music. In addition to her lifelong commitment to the public theater, she has been active with the Pittsburgh Symphony and has sat on many cultural boards. In 1997, she was named a Distinguished Daughter of Pennsylvania. (Apt family.)

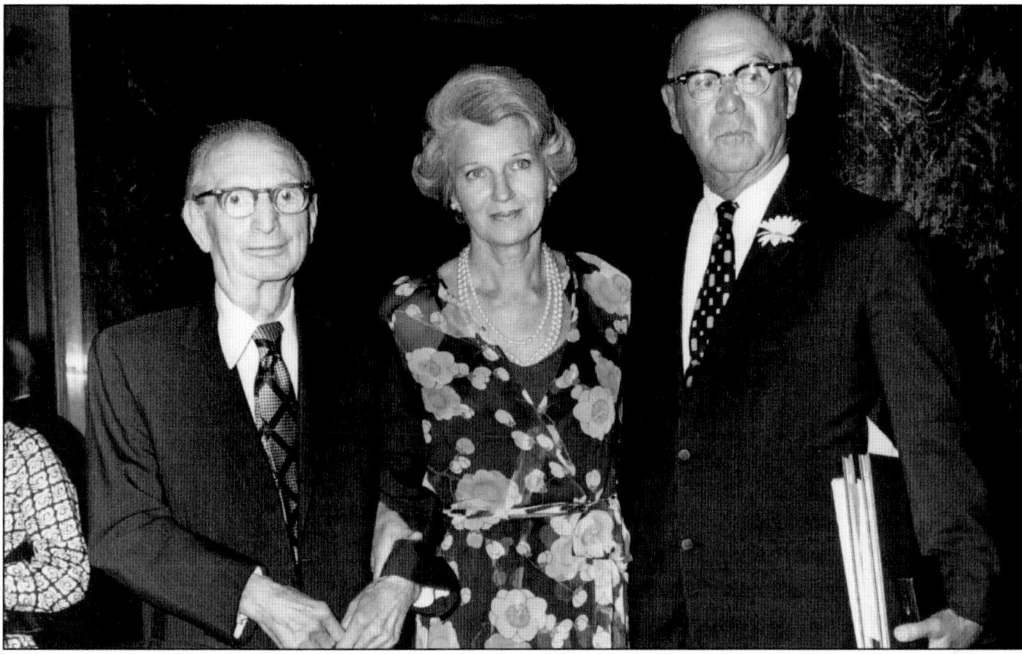

Loti Falk—flanked in this photograph by attorney Louis Caplan (left) and her husband, Leon Falk Jr. (right)—was the force behind the founding of the Pittsburgh Ballet. While raising money to sustain the Pittsburgh Playhouse in 1966, she became aware of the need for a professional ballet company. She provided funding and direction until 1987, when she retired to take care of her ailing husband. Loti later married Frank Gaffney.

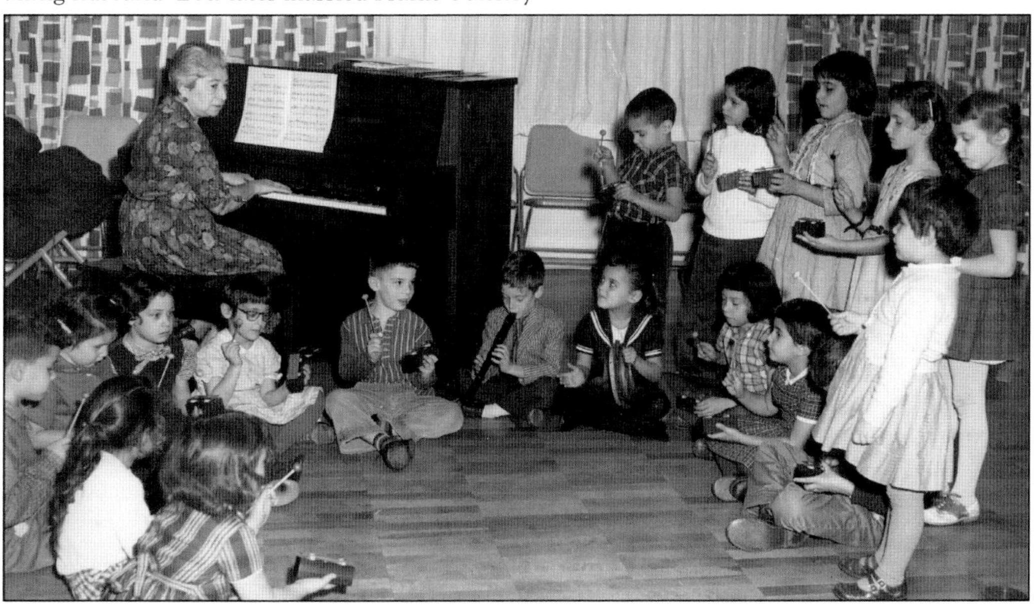

Music education was a major part of the programming at the Irene Kaufmann Settlement. Anna Perlow, an accomplished pianist, founded the music school at the IKS in 1923. She held that position for nearly 40 years until her retirement in 1965. She and her husband, Benjamin Perlow, established a fund that today is worth well over $1 million and benefits the successor to the IKS, the Jewish Community Center.

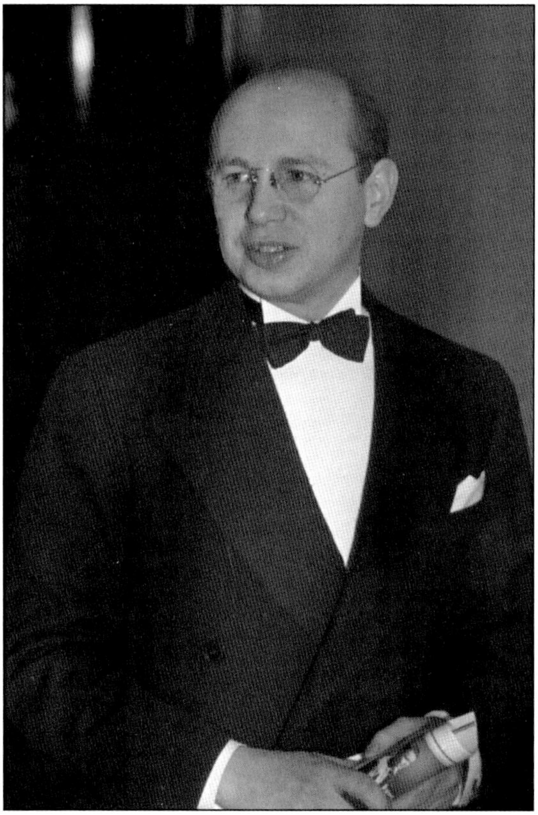

Edward Specter, a young musician who grew up on the Hill, put himself through University of Pittsburgh Law School. He determined to help the struggling Pittsburgh Symphony raise money to sustain itself, tapping Richard S. Rauh among others. By 1936, he resigned from the law firm of Weil, Christy & Weil to work full time for the orchestra until his retirement in 1952. His devotion is credited with saving the Pittsburgh Symphony.

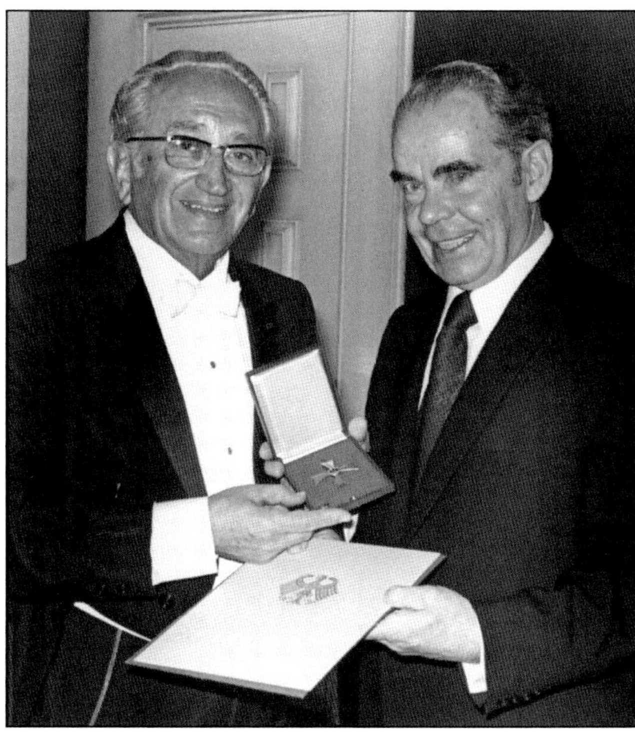

Richard Karp (at left, receiving an award) was born in Vienna, fled the Nazis, and came to Pittsburgh to play viola with Fritz Reiner and the Pittsburgh Symphony. He left the symphony to join the fledgling Pittsburgh Opera Society and soon became its musical director, a position he held until his death in 1977. His wife, Ilse, taught piano and clarinet at the IKS. (Photograph by Elton Schnellbacher.)

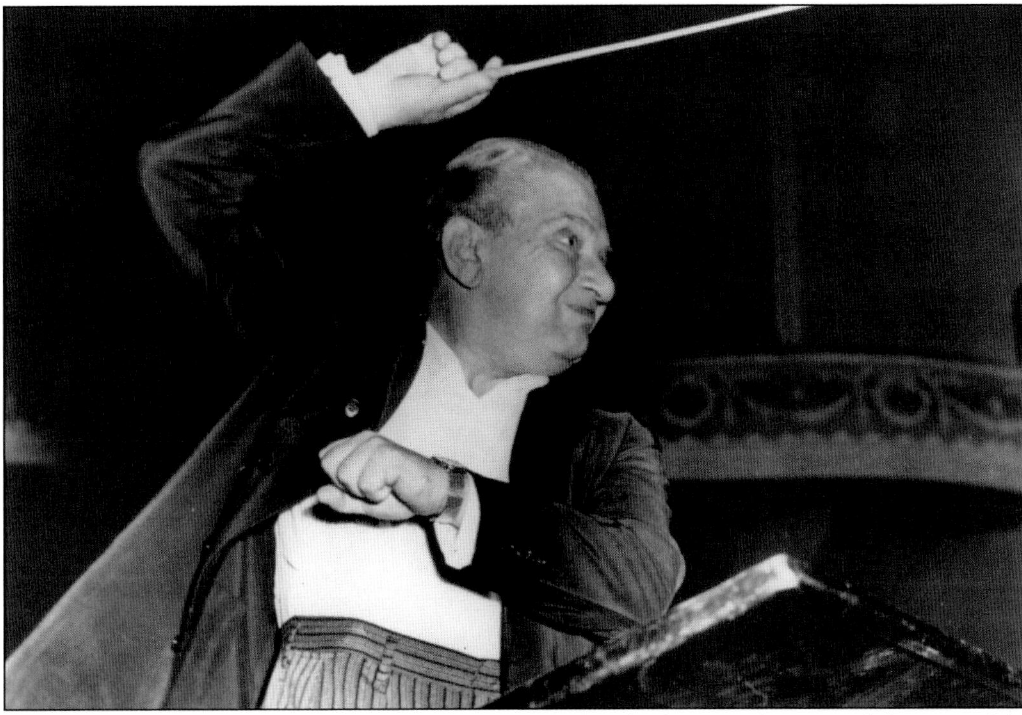

Fritz Reiner, born in Hungary, was already a legend when he became the musical director of the Pittsburgh Symphony in 1938. Under him, the symphony for 10 years garnered national and international fame. He was known as a very tough taskmaster who inspired fear among his players, 20 to 40 of whom he fired every year. (Pittsburgh Symphony Orchestra.)

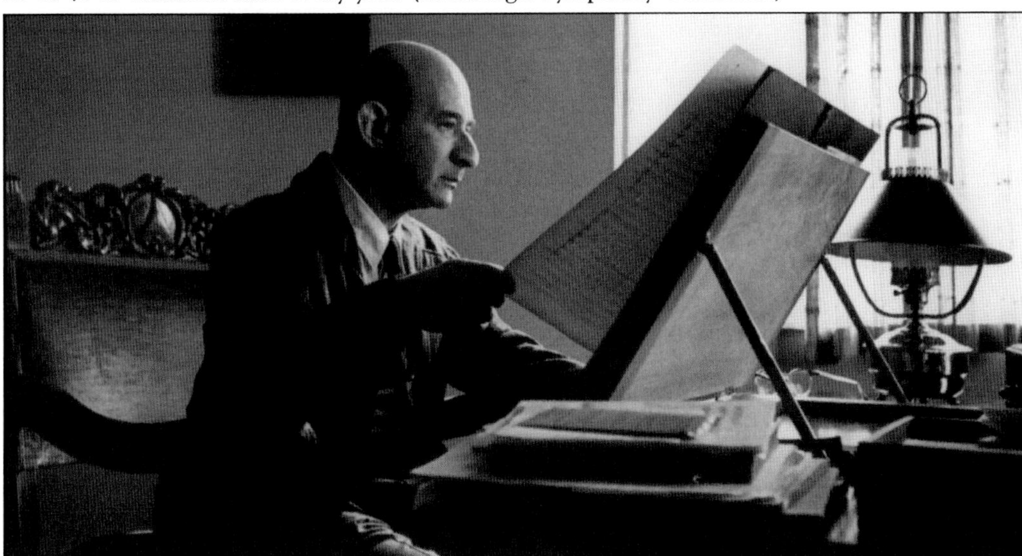

William Steinberg, relieved of his position as music director of the Frankfort Opera when Nazi storm troopers literally stormed into a rehearsal, soon left for Palestine, where he helped develop what became the Israeli Philharmonic Orchestra. He immigrated to the United States in 1938 and became the acclaimed music director of the Pittsburgh Symphony from 1952 until 1976. (Pittsburgh Symphony Orchestra.)

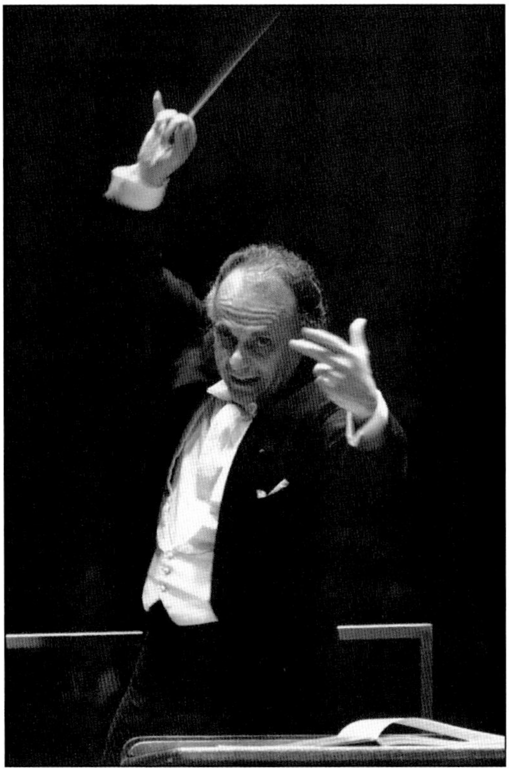

A child prodigy, Lorin Maazel studied conducting under Vladimir Bakaleinikoff of the Pittsburgh Symphony and went to the University of Pittsburgh. While still a student, he was a violinist and served as apprentice symphony conductor in the 1949–1950 season. Years later, Maazel returned to Pittsburgh as symphony conductor from 1988 to 1996. His mother, Marie Maazel, helped revive the Pittsburgh Youth Orchestra. (Photograph by Jim Steere; Pittsburgh Symphony Orchestra.)

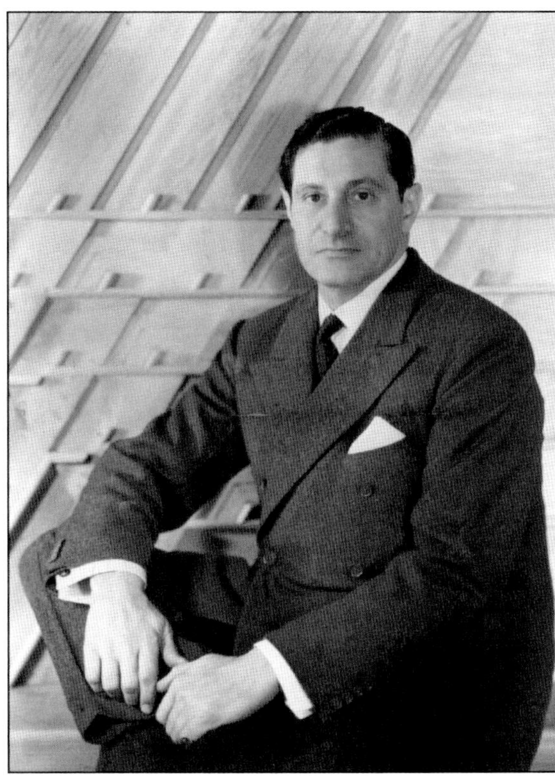

Edgar J. Kaufmann was a trendsetting businessman and art patron. His office was designed by the renowned architect Frank Lloyd Wright. The office on the 10th floor of Kaufmann's Department Store was finished in 1937. After Kaufmann's death in 1955, his son Edgar Kaufmann Jr., had the office dismantled and shipped to the Victoria and Albert Museum in London.

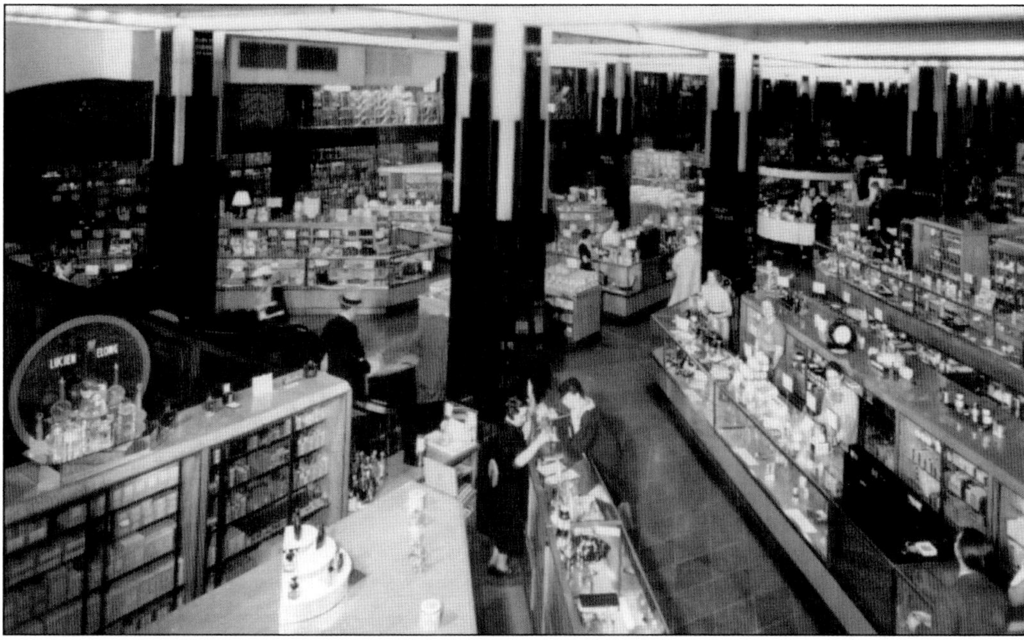

In 1930, when Edgar Kaufmann redid the first floor of his department store, *Harper's Magazine* wrote that it was "perhaps the most beautiful department store in the United States, if not in the world." With black Carrara glass columns, new decorative lights, and a black and brown terrazzo floor, the effect was dramatic. In addition, American artist Boardman Robinson produced 10 monumental murals illustrating the history of commerce for the store.

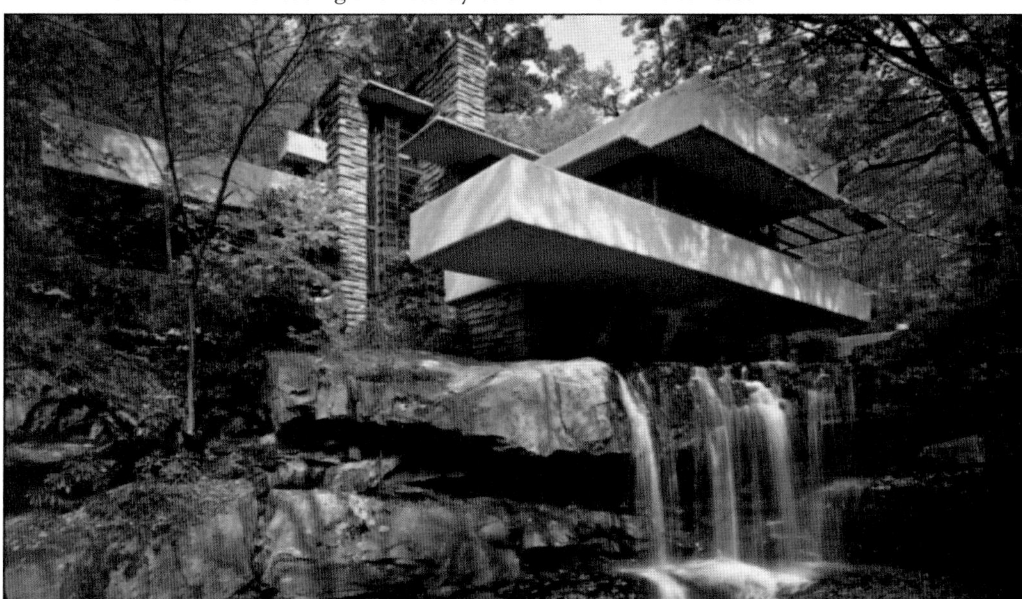

Of all Kaufmann's efforts to promote the arts, none was more famous or bold than Fallingwater, his summer retreat in the nearby Laurel Mountains. Built by Frank Lloyd Wright at the same time that Kaufmann's office was being built, Fallingwater today is recognized as a modern masterpiece. It has been chosen by the American Institute of Architects as "the best all-time work of American architecture."

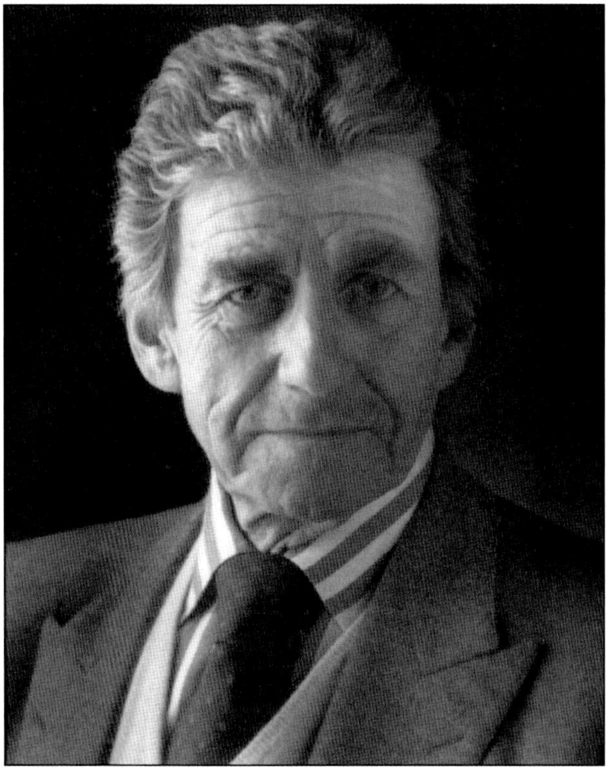

The Speyer family was friends with the Kaufmanns and frequent guests at Fallingwater. James Speyer, the son of Alexander and Tillie Speyer (an artist in her own right), studied architecture at Carnegie Tech. He designed the award-winning Apt and Speyer houses in Pittsburgh and went on to become the longtime curator of painting and sculpture at the Art Institute of Chicago. (Carnegie Museum of Art.)

Alexander Sharove was an important architect in the firm of Sharove & Friedman. This is a drawing that was done by him for the future Beth Shalom Congregation in Squirrel Hill, which was built in 1922. Sharove contributed to the design of B'nai Israel on Negley Avenue, a building that was widely admired. Today, that building is the home of the Urban League Charter School.

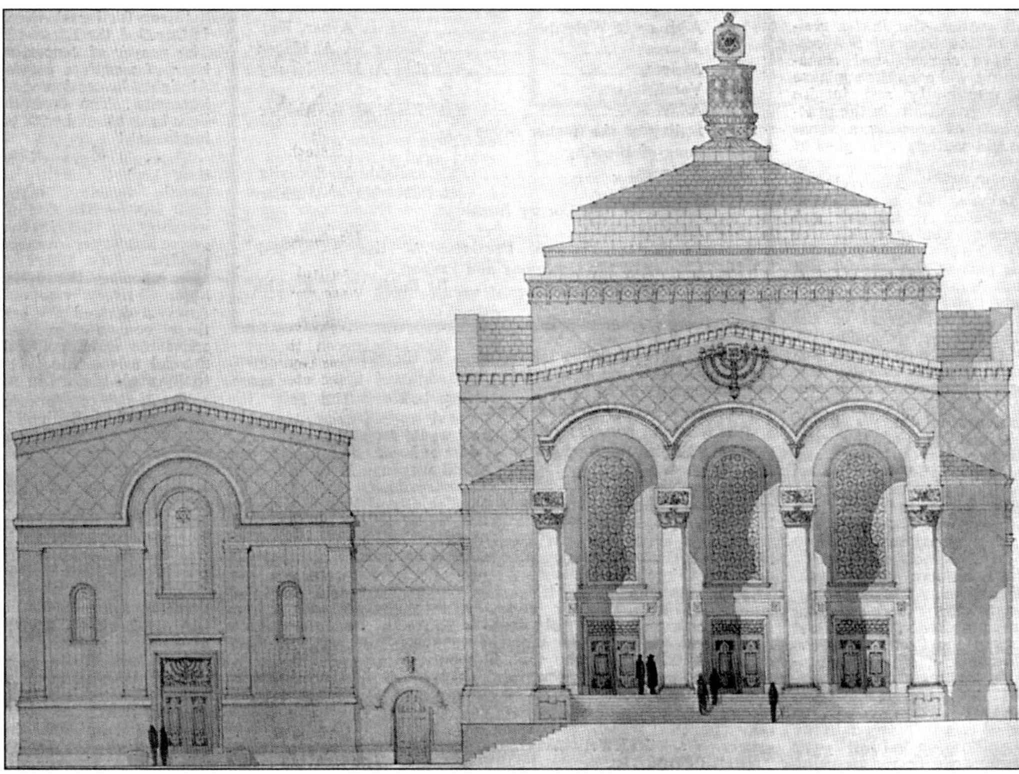

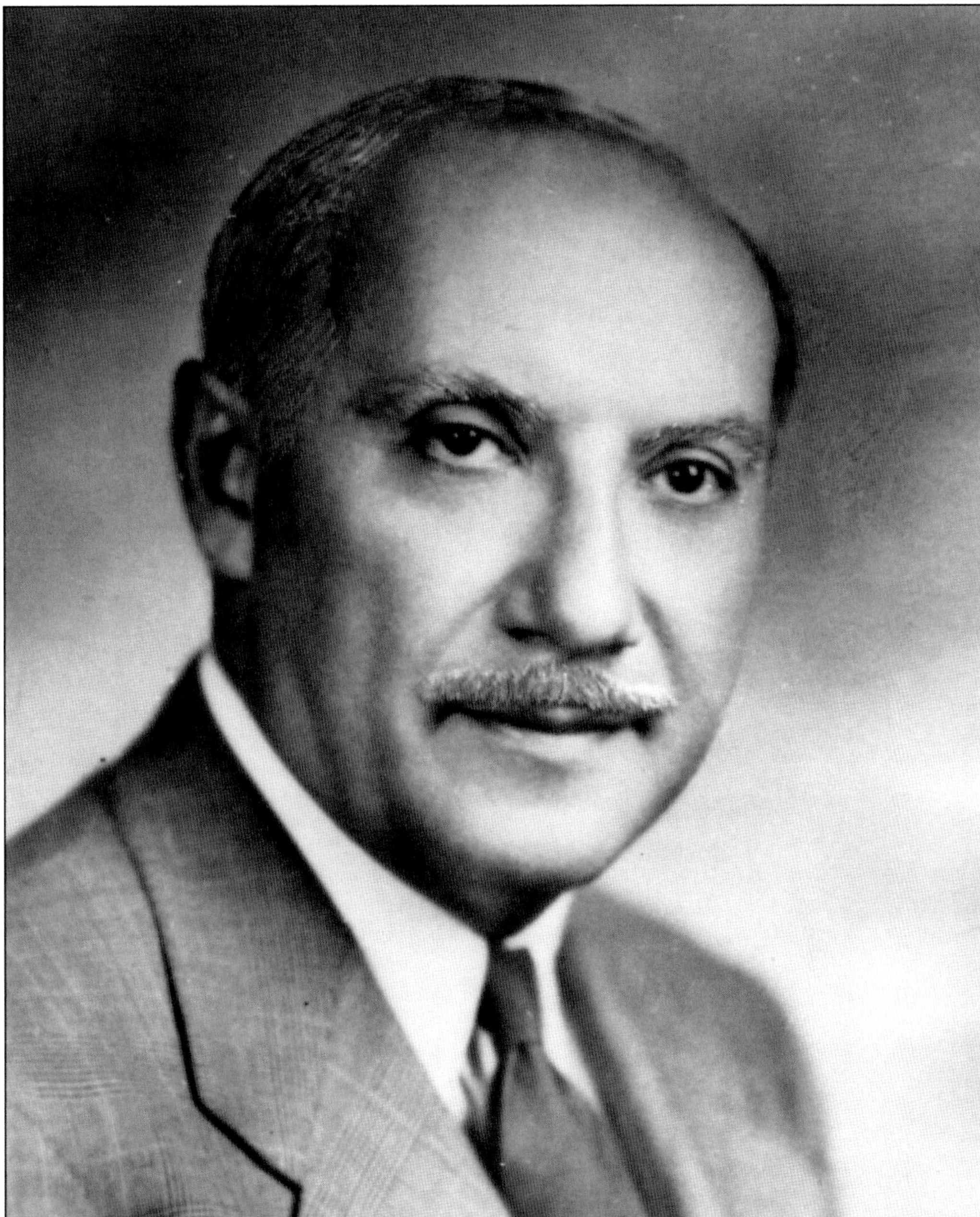

Dr. Harvey Thorpe, an immigrant from the Baltic province of Kurland, came to Pittsburgh at age 11. A product of Pittsburgh schools, he developed several devices that were used to treat eye diseases. Despite his worldwide reputation, he was for years not invited to join the Pittsburgh Ophthalmological Society because he was Jewish. He was ophthalmologist in chief at Montefiore Hospital from 1928 to 1965.

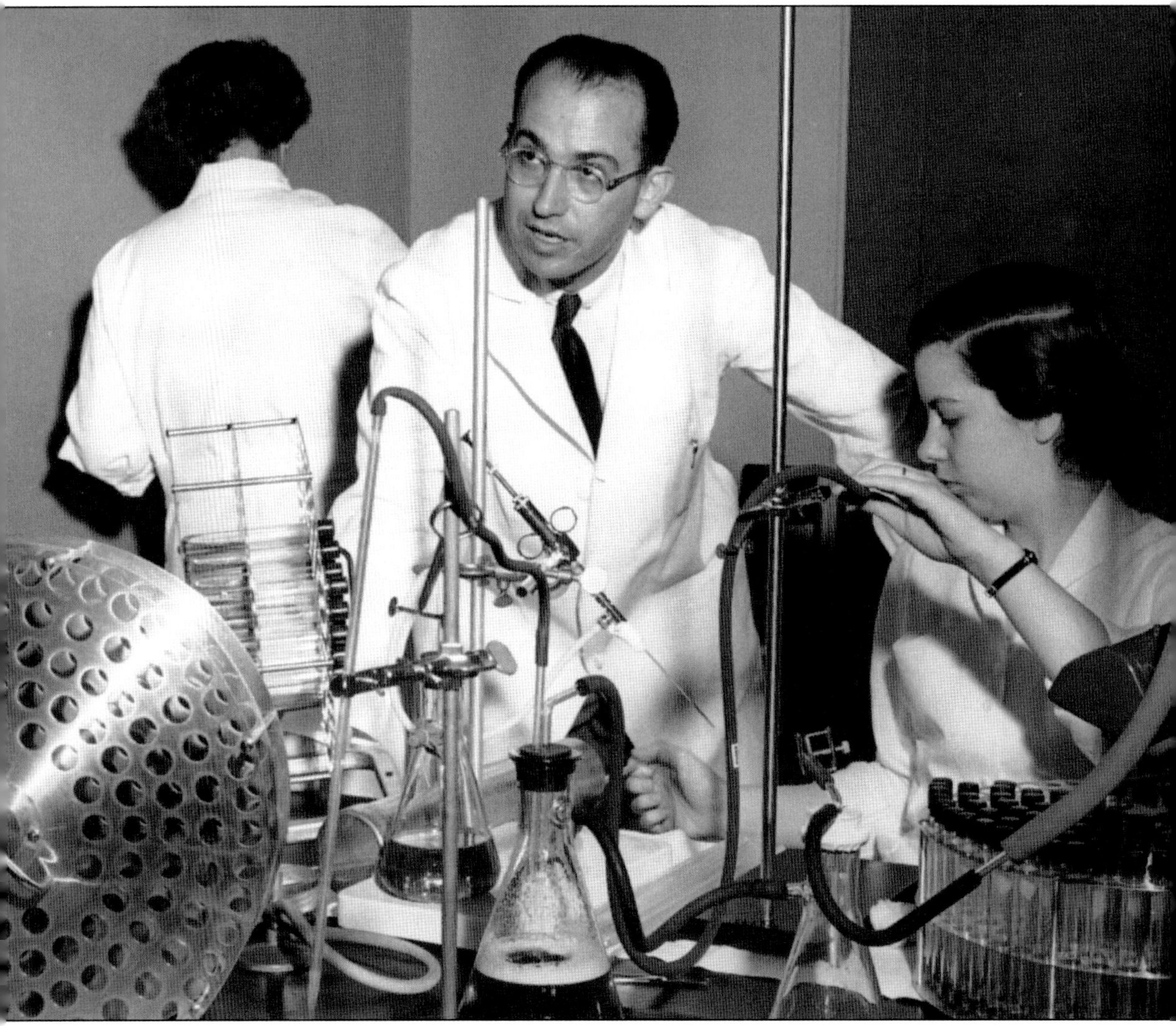

In 1947, Dr. Jonas Salk came to the University of Pittsburgh, where he began research on polio, also known as infantile paralysis. He developed a vaccine using polio viruses that had been grown in a laboratory and then destroyed. After several years of clinical trials, the vaccine was approved for general use. Salk became a national hero; polio cases in 10 years dropped from 57,000 to fewer than 1,000. (Heinz History Center.)

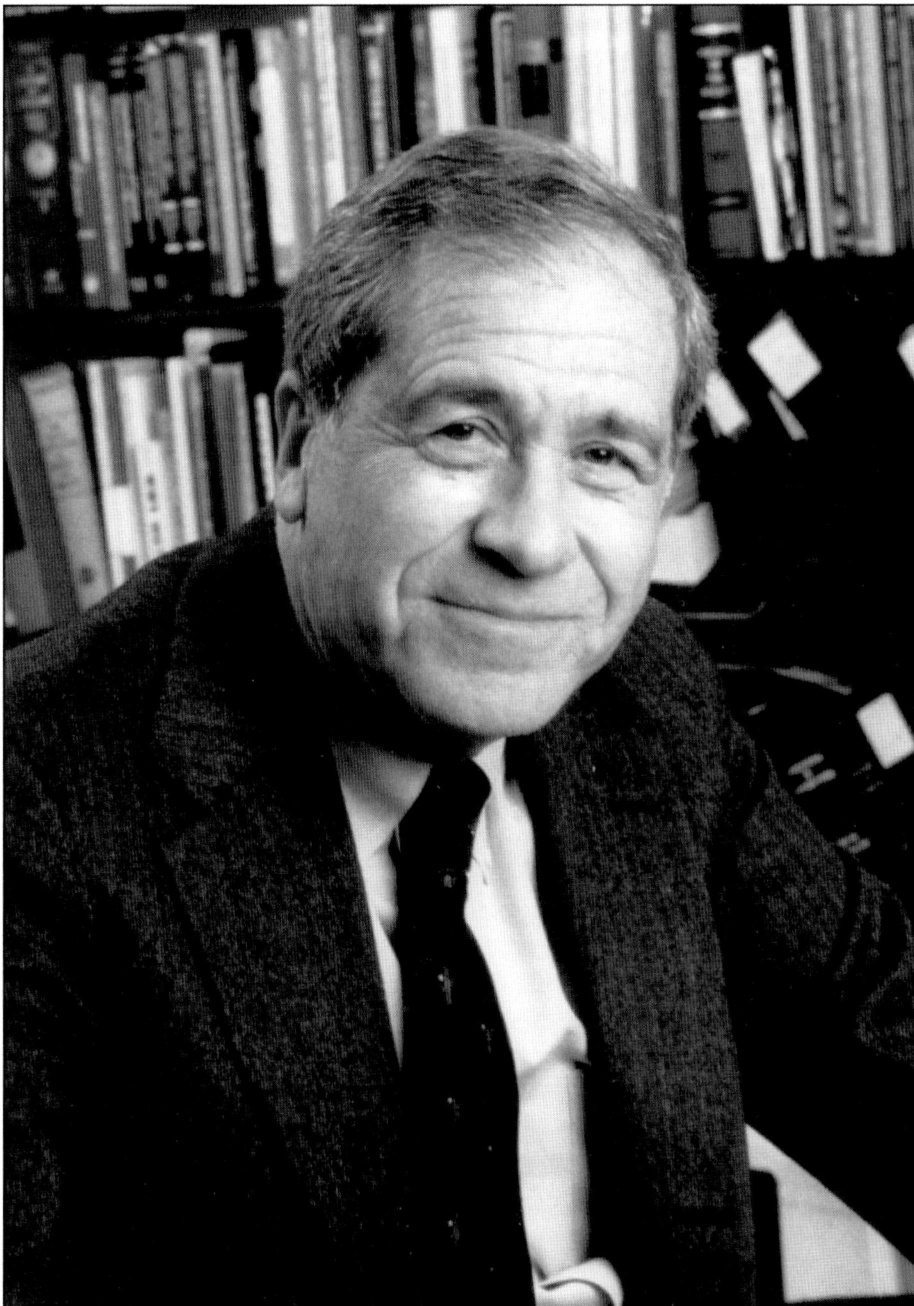

Dr. Bernard Fisher is internationally recognized today for his groundbreaking research in breast cancer, which resulted in changing the way women were treated. Rather than performing a radical mastectomy, he defied critics and showed a lumpectomy was just as effective in cancer treatment. He also showed that the drug tamoxifen decreased the incidence of breast cancer by nearly 50 percent. He was one of the doctors featured in the Ken Burns documentary *Cancer: The Emperor of Maladies*. He was a graduate of the University of Pittsburgh School of Medicine in 1943 and today is a Distinguished Service Professor at the university.

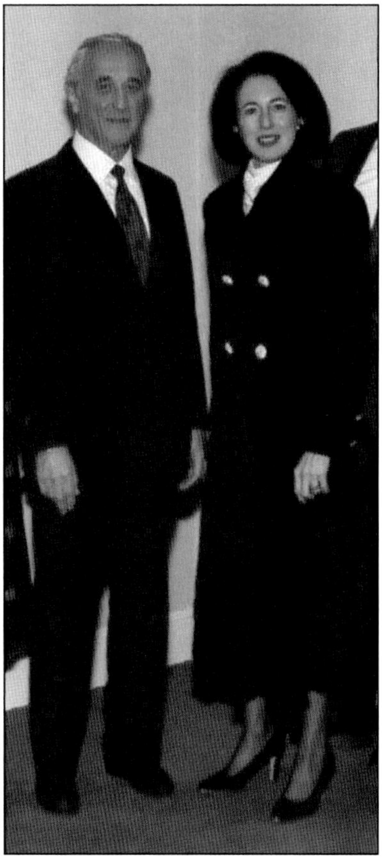

The Jewish Healthcare Foundation was established in 1990 with the proceeds from the sale of Montefiore Hospital to the University of Pittsburgh. Businessman Stanley Gumberg was the last chair of the board. Pictured are Alvin Rogal, the first chair of the foundation board, and Dr. Karen Feinstein, its longtime executive director. The foundation has been on the cutting edge of medical research and health care education and services, particularly to vulnerable populations.

Drs. Katherine and Thomas Detre were two internationally known leaders in their respective fields, she in epidemiology and he in psychiatry. They were both Holocaust survivors from Hungary who lost their entire families. They arrived in Pittsburgh in 1973. She came to the School of Public Health, and he ultimately served as senior vice president of Health Sciences at the University of Pittsburgh Medical Center. The Western Psychiatry building was renamed in his honor.

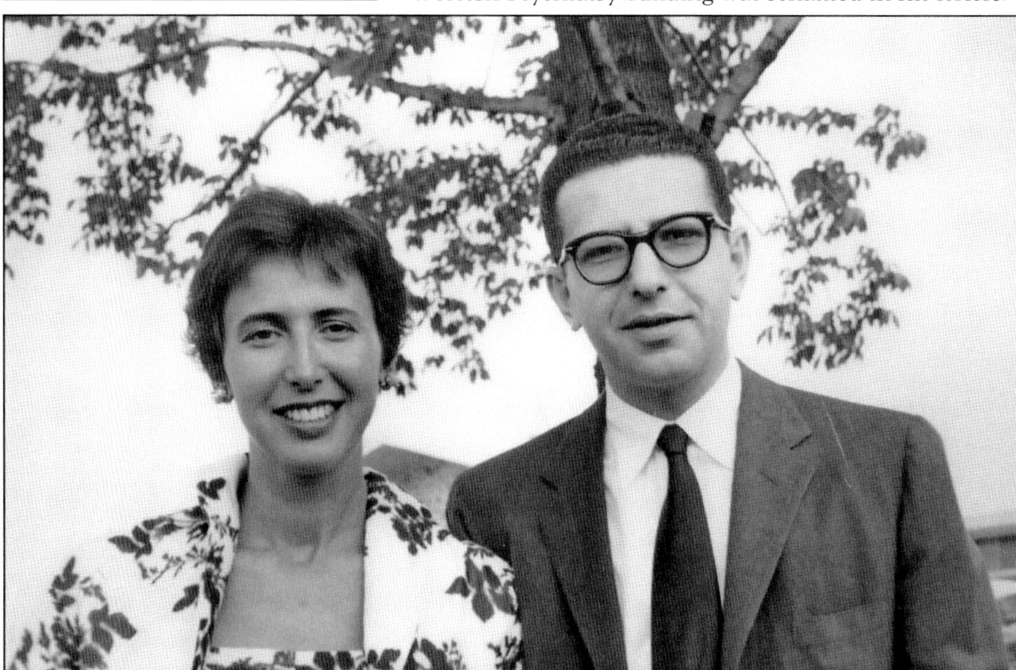

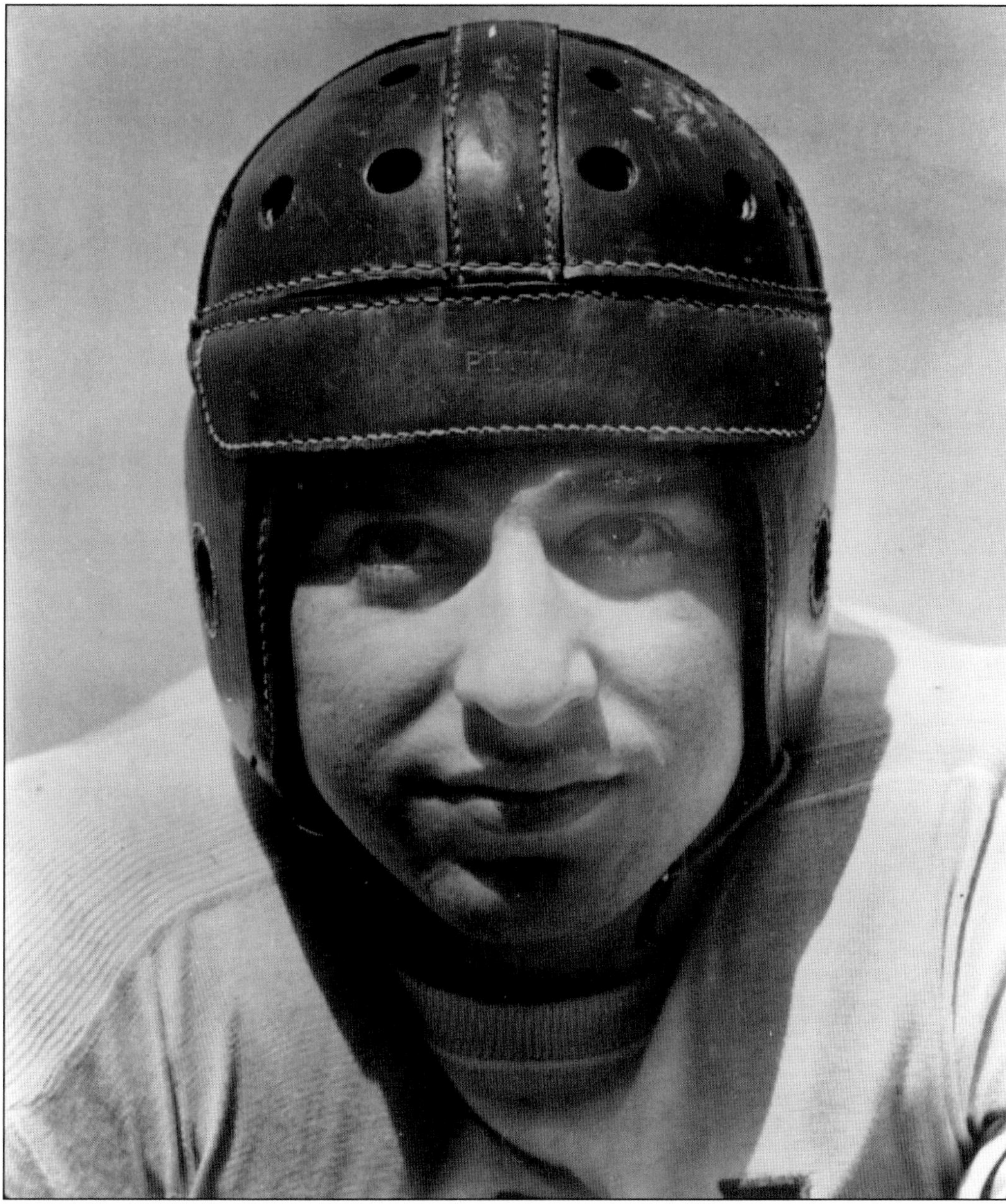

Marshall Goldberg led the Pitt Panthers to two national football championships in 1936 and 1937. He finished third in the Heisman Trophy voting in 1937 and was runner-up in 1938. He was an All-American for two years. After his death in 2006, his family established the Marshall Goldberg Traumatic Brain Injury Fund to investigate the effects of brain concussions, which Goldberg's family felt affected Goldberg in his later years.

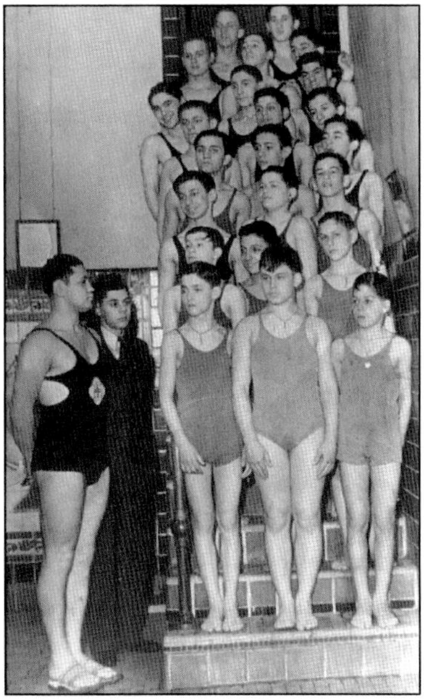

Nathan "Natie" Kaufman was the assistant athletic coach under Ziggy Kahn at the Irene Kaufmann Settlement. He started the swimming programs in the 1930s and developed a neighborhood team that quickly produced champions—including Hy Richman, who considered Kaufman "an excellent mentor, a taskmaster, who brought out the very, very best in us." Most became scholarship swimmers on Pitt's swim team.

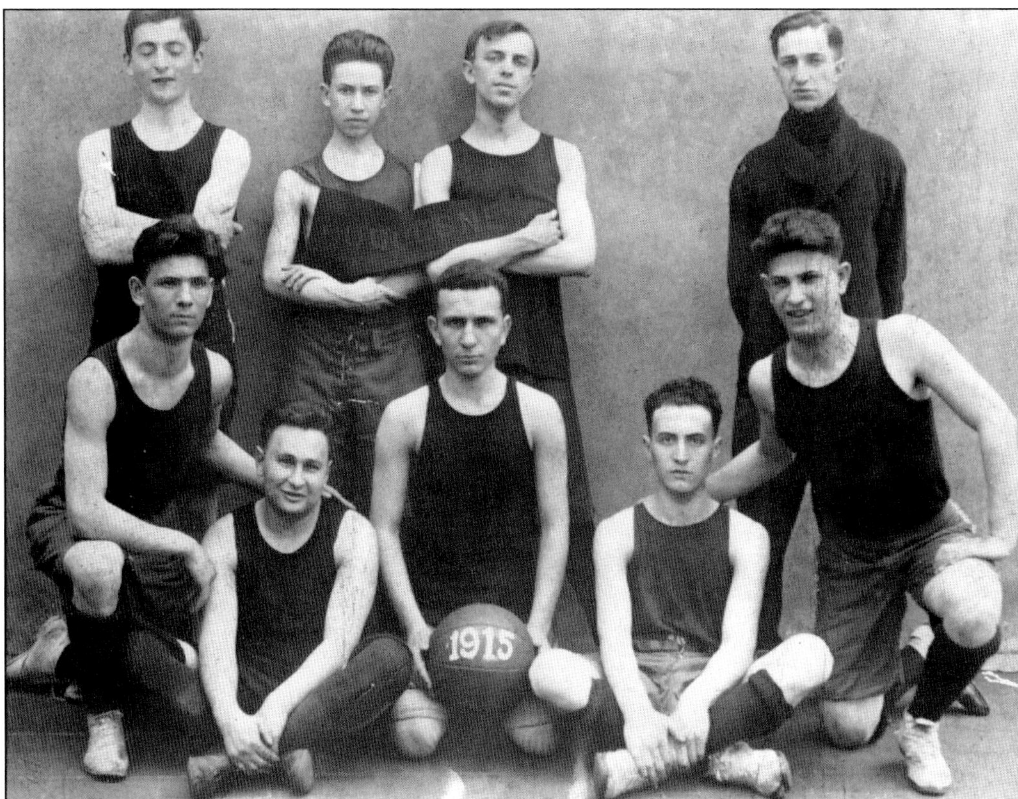

The Duquesne College (now University) basketball team in the 1930s and in later years was the home team of notable Jewish players. Moe Becker was a star in the 1930s; Sid Dambrot and Mickey Winograd were stars in the 1950s. Many Jews got scholarships to Duquesne, a Catholic college, where there was no discrimination against Jews.

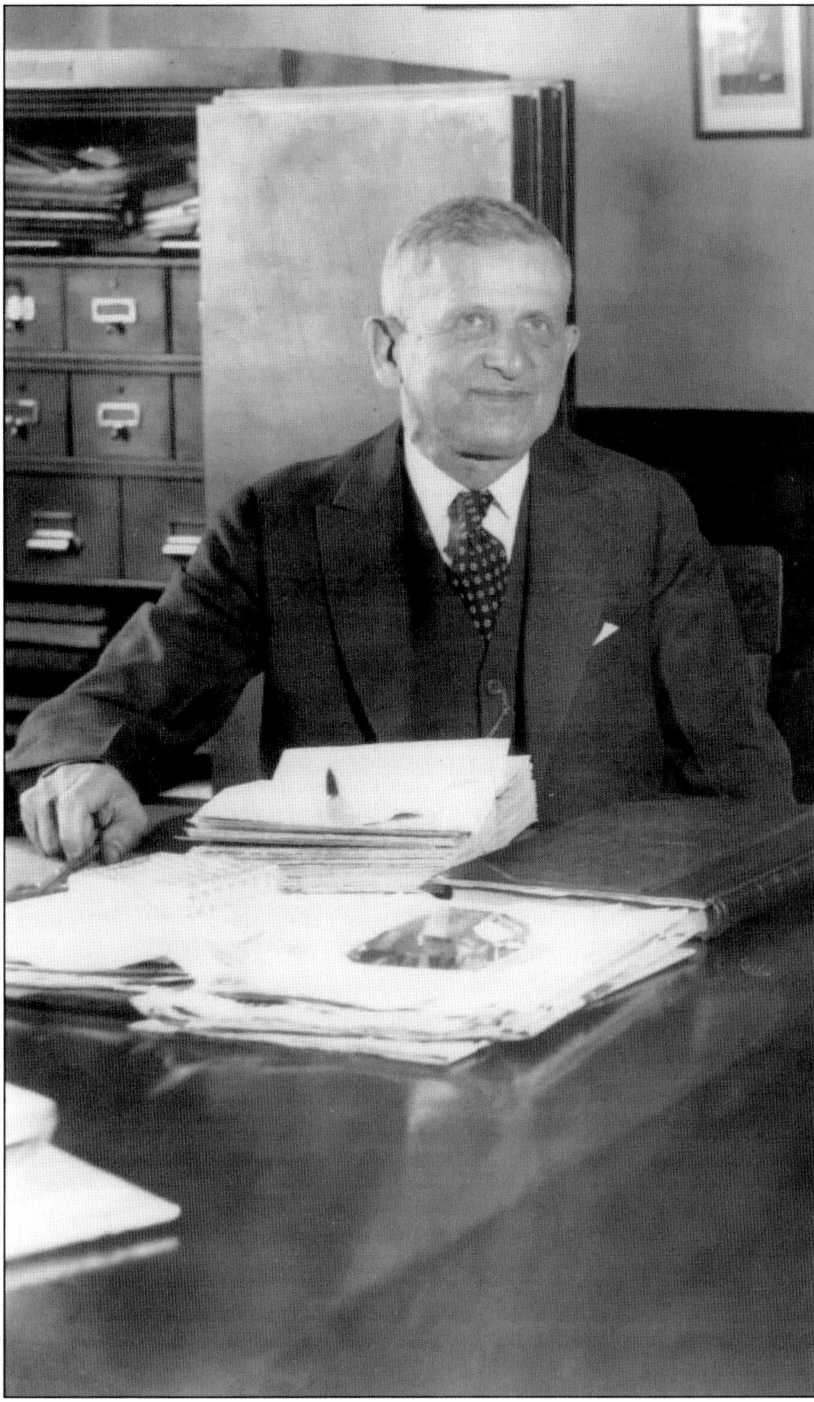

Barney Dreyfuss, the owner of the Pittsburgh Pirates, brought the team from Louisville to Pittsburgh in 1900 with the likes of Honus Wagner. The team went on to win national league pennants in 1901, 1902, and 1903. In 1903, Dreyfuss started what became the World Series, which Pittsburgh won in 1909 and 1925. He built Forbes Field and remained the Pirates owner until his death in 1932.

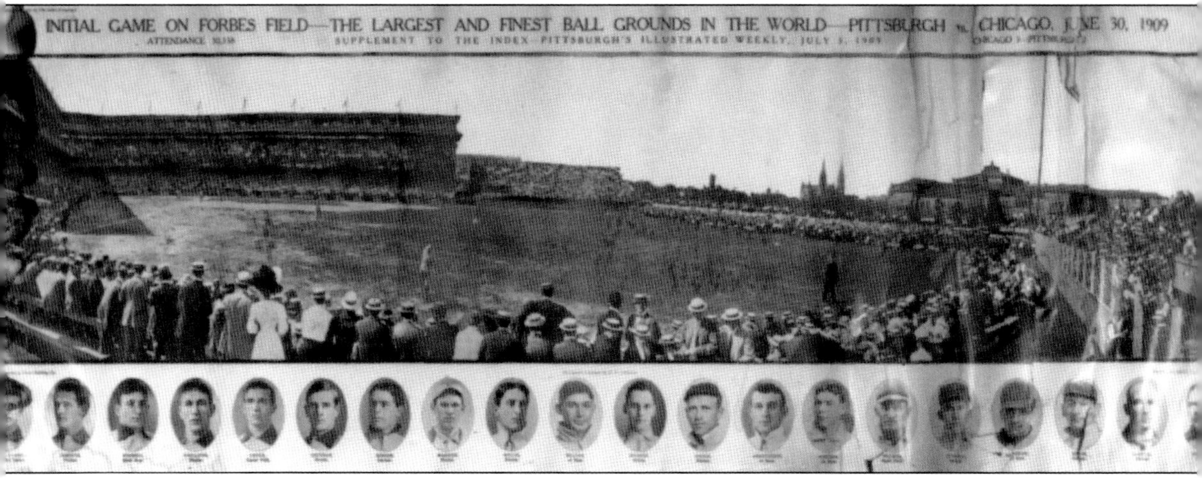

Forbes Field, built in 1909, was the first baseball stadium built of steel and concrete. Initially, it was called "Dreyfuss's Folly" because of its expense and location in Oakland, an exclusive part of the city near the Carnegie Museums. Dreyfuss proved his critics wrong, however, when the 25,000-seat stadium became immensely popular. The stadium was ultimately torn down and replaced by Three Rivers Stadium in 1970. Where it once stood is now part of the University of Pittsburgh campus. Dreyfuss was voted into the Baseball Hall of Fame in 2007.

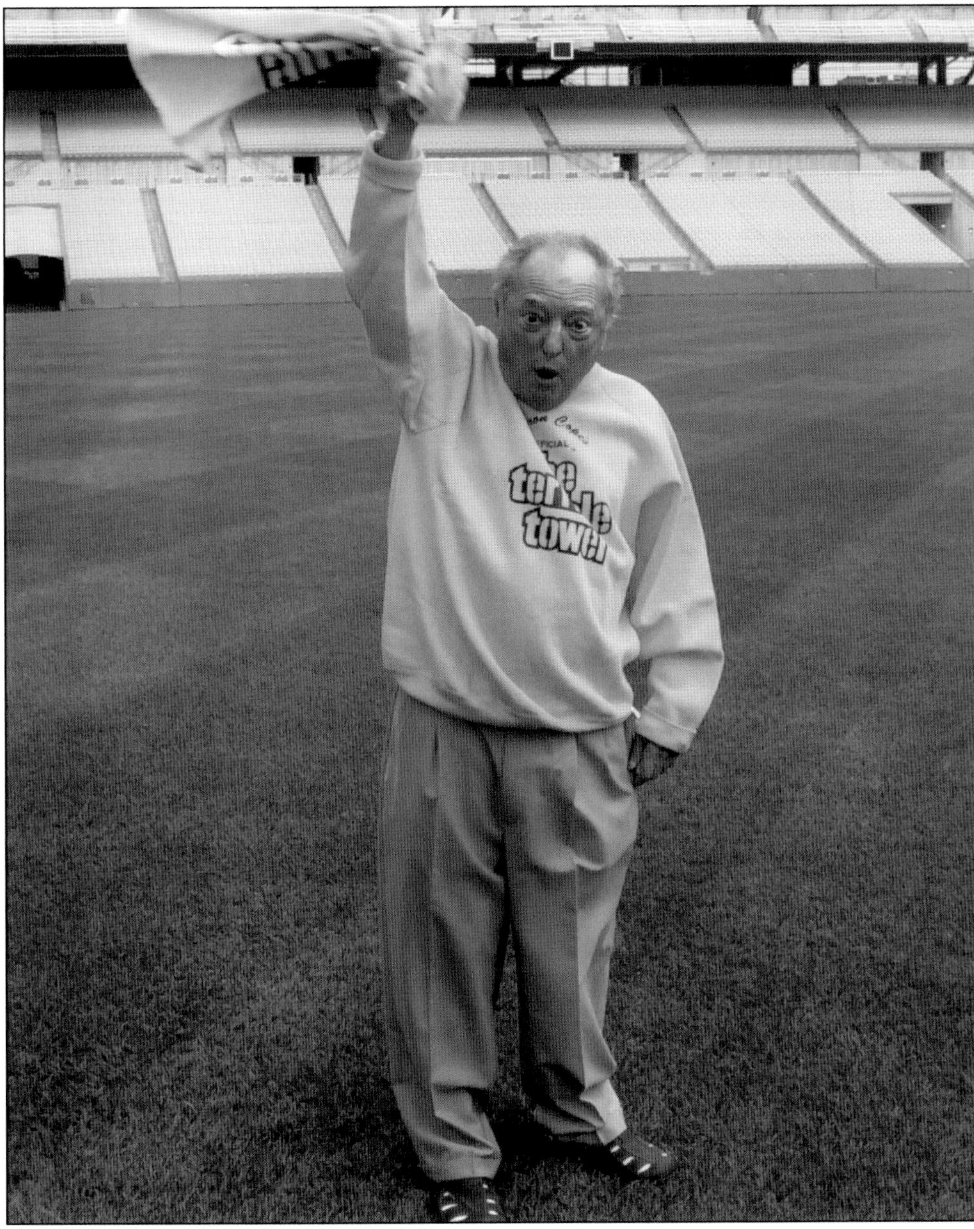

Born Myron Sidney Kopelman, Myron Cope was the voice of the Pittsburgh Steelers. He was a color commentator for the Steelers' radio broadcast for 35 years. Known for his distinctive voice and his Pittsburgh accent, Cope entertained with his excitement in the broadcast booth, his peppered speech replete with Cope-isms, including "yoi" and, even worse, "double yoi." Cope was the first football announcer inducted into the National Radio Hall of Fame. He invented the Terrible Towel in 1975, and it has become a necessary accessory at any Steeler game. The Terrible Towel has even gone around the world, including to the peak of Mount Everest and to the international space station. Sales from the Terrible Towel have raised over $3 million for Allegheny Valley School, which cares for people with mental and physical disabilities. The towel has been so admired that it has been imitated in other sporting venues and with other football teams. The legendary journalist and radio personality died at the age of 78 in 2008.

Discover Thousands of Local History Books Featuring Millions of Vintage Images

Arcadia Publishing, the leading local history publisher in the United States, is committed to making history accessible and meaningful through publishing books that celebrate and preserve the heritage of America's people and places.

Find more books like this at
www.arcadiapublishing.com

Search for your hometown history, your old stomping grounds, and even your favorite sports team.

Consistent with our mission to preserve history on a local level, this book was printed in South Carolina on American-made paper and manufactured entirely in the United States. Products carrying the accredited Forest Stewardship Council (FSC) label are printed on 100 percent FSC-certified paper.

MADE IN THE USA